Change in Chains

Change in Chains

Break Toxic Patterns By Decoding The Emotional Logic That Keeps Them Alive.

Mira Ellison

Mindful Pages

Published in 2025

ISBN: 9789371771603 (PB)
ISBN: 9789371772686 (eBook)

Published by

Mindful Pages
Imprint of Alpha Editions LLC
312 W. 2nd St #1834
Casper, WY 82601, USA

This book was developed using advanced writing tools to support the drafting and ideation process. All content has been thoughtfully curated, refined, and reviewed to ensure quality and relevance.

Content

Introduction
Beneath the Behaviour

We like to believe we are rational, in control, capable of steering our own lives. We make plans, set intentions, reassure ourselves that tomorrow will be different. Yet, in the quiet hours—when no one else is watching—we often revert to the very habits that undermine us. We overeat, procrastinate, snap at those we love, isolate ourselves, overwork, numb out, or tumble back into cycles we thought we had left behind. And each time, we wonder, with quiet frustration: why am I doing this again?

The familiar answers—"I'm lazy," "I lack discipline," "there must be something wrong with me"—are not just incorrect; they are actively harmful. They place the blame on character rather than context, prompting us to treat symptoms while ignoring the structures beneath. In doing so, they trap us within the loops we are trying to escape.

This book begins from a different premise: destructive behaviours are not signs of weakness, but evidence of intelligence. They are not accidents of a flawed mind, but strategies—emotional strategies—that once protected us. Each so-called "toxic" habit, every act of avoidance, excess, or withdrawal, emerged as a solution. Perhaps imperfect, perhaps unsustainable, but a solution nonetheless. To dismiss these behaviours as failures is to overlook their deeper function.

Change in Chains invites a reframing of the conversation around change. It asks us to stop blaming ourselves and start decoding ourselves. Instead of asking, "what's wrong with me?" we begin to ask, "what need was I trying to meet when I learned to do this?" In answering that question with curiosity and precision, we can begin to dismantle patterns at their roots—without shame, without self-betrayal, and without the exhausting tug-of-war between intention and impulse.

Much of modern habit-change advice skims the surface: what you do, how often you do it, and how to stop. It focuses on hacking routines, enforcing discipline, substituting one behaviour for another—treating the human psyche as if it were software that can be reprogrammed. But behaviour is not code. It is biology woven through biography. Behind every repeated action lies a chain of emotional events—some remembered, many not—that gave that behaviour its urgency and logic. Until we understand why a pattern exists and what it fears will happen if it disappears, we are not truly changing. We are merely layering new masks atop old ones, swapping one socially acceptable version for another.

The question, then, is not merely how to change, but how to stop waging war on ourselves in the process.

When you repeat a destructive pattern, you are not weak—you are in conflict. Two parts of you are working at cross purposes: one that desires growth, healing, freedom, and another that insists the habit keeps you safe. One is rational, the other emotional. One perceives long-term cost, the other seeks immediate relief. Most of us attempt to resolve this by overpowering the emotional side with willpower, resolutions, or punishment. Force alone never suffices. The emotional logic must be heard, understood, and renegotiated. If it is not, the emotional part will prevail—not because it is stronger, but because it is immediate, familiar, and charged with feeling.

The chapters ahead are not quick fixes. They do not celebrate streaks, apps, or superficial behavioural substitution. Instead, this book maps the emotional terrain beneath the surface: fear, shame, attachment, identity, and the quiet logic of protection that animates them. It draws on decades of psychology, cognitive neuroscience, emotional development, and trauma research—not as abstract theory, but as practical illumination. This is a book for those who have tried and failed—not because they didn't care, but because they did not yet understand the full architecture of their patterns.

Understanding, not discipline, is the foundation of transformation.

To comprehend a toxic pattern, we must abandon the idea that it is senseless. Even the most seemingly irrational actions—pushing away someone you love, procrastinating on important work, returning to harmful relationships—serve an internal purpose. They may shield you from vulnerability, protect against being truly seen, or preserve a familiar identity in a world that demands constant reinvention. The goal is not to excuse behaviour, but to trace its origin and emotional logic. Only then can it be replaced with something that serves the same need—without the same cost.

Change in Chains is structured around this principle. We begin by dismantling the myth of self-sabotage, showing how even self-defeating behaviours often have self-preserving roots. We examine how early emotional experiences become encoded into habits—not as conscious choices, but as embodied memories of what once kept us soothed, safe, or significant. We explore the hidden rewards these behaviours continue to provide, even when their external consequences are harmful.

We then address the forces that maintain these patterns: shame, culture, attachment, inner conflict, and emotional repression. Each is not merely an obstacle, but a clue. Shame, for example, does more than punish—it protects more vulnerable emotions beneath, such as grief, envy, or longing. Cultural narratives of discipline, positivity, or relentless productivity often reinforce toxic patterns under the guise of virtue. Attachment wounds from childhood resurface in adult coping mechanisms, shaping how we relate to others—and to ourselves.

You will learn to work with, rather than against, the parts of yourself you have labelled "bad," "lazy," or "addictive." Drawing on frameworks inspired by Internal Family Systems, we introduce "parts work"—a compassionate, structured approach to inner conflict that treats each impulse as a voice worth hearing. Instead of dominating unwanted behaviours, you will dialogue with them, uncover their fears, and help them relinquish roles they no longer need to play.

This book also challenges conventional notions of emotional control. Emotion is not a nuisance; it is intelligence. Feelings are signals, rich with information about unmet needs, unhealed wounds, and unconscious expectations. Tracking the emotional chain that leads to a relapse—a thought, a bodily sensation, a belief—creates a space between feeling and reaction. And in that space, change becomes possible.

One of the most overlooked barriers is identity. Who are you if you stop being the person who binge eats, lashes out, overworks, or stays small? Real change often requires grieving not just a behaviour, but the version of self that relied on it. That grief must be honoured. The safety of the familiar self acknowledged. Otherwise, we risk abandoning parts of ourselves we do not yet understand, repeating the internal exile that drove the behaviour in the first place.

True change is frightening because it is not merely action—it is transformation. It is becoming someone who no longer needs the old strategy. It requires tools, insights, and emotional scaffolding: environments, relationships, and rituals that support the nervous system in the absence of the old pattern. Shame cannot create this change. Speed cannot. But gradual, steady, wise building can.

Throughout, you will find not only explanations but invitations: ways to reflect, reframe, and experiment—not to achieve perfection, but to cultivate alignment. Microshifts ripple inward before they manifest outward. Sometimes, progress is invisible, felt as a new inner stance—curiosity instead of judgment, compassion instead of condemnation, choice instead of compulsion.

If you have ever felt at war with yourself, this book is a ceasefire. If you have tried to heal by force, it is a reorientation. If you have doubted your capacity to change, it is a quiet reminder: you are not broken. You are bound—but not beyond release.

The chains that once protected you can now be understood, redesigned, and—when chosen wisely—laid down.

Welcome to *Change in Chains*. Let us begin beneath the behaviour.

Chapter 1
The Myth of Self-Sabotage

The phrase "self-sabotage" has become something of a shorthand—a convenient label for everything from procrastination and emotional outbursts to unhealthy relationships and late-night binges. It appears everywhere: in therapy sessions, self-help books, corporate workshops, and even Instagram captions. We mutter, "I keep sabotaging myself," or "I'm my own worst enemy," as if some rogue version of ourselves were bent on undermining everything we value. But what does this label actually explain? And more crucially, what does it obscure?

At first glance, self-sabotage suggests intent: a part of you actively working against your own wellbeing. It frames the struggle as a battle between desire and destruction. Yet, if you examine these behaviours closely—without moralising—you begin to see something far more nuanced. These actions are not mindless destruction; they are strategies, responses to unseen emotional pressures: internal tensions, long-learned associations between risk and safety, or subtle rules embedded in memory. To call them sabotage is to overlook their deeper function.

Consider the professional who consistently delays submitting major work, knowing it may damage their career. On the surface, it seems like procrastination, laziness, or avoidance. Look closer, and you may uncover an unspoken rule: "If I do well, more will be expected of me, and I'll inevitably fail under pressure." Or perhaps: "If I succeed, I'll outshine someone I care about, and they'll withdraw." What seems like sabotage is actually a sophisticated form of emotional logic—a protective measure against overwhelm, guilt, exposure, or loss.

This is not unusual. It is human.

The central argument here is that most destructive behaviours are adaptive rather than oppositional. They are not failures of willpower, but expressions of internal conflict. You are not sabotaging yourself;

you are protecting yourself, often in the only way your emotional system knows how. Until we interpret these behaviours through that lens, we remain trapped in cycles of shame and confusion, mistaking instinct for betrayal.

To grasp this fully, we must reconsider the assumptions embedded in the notion of self. Popular psychology often treats the self as singular and coherent. In lived experience, it is anything but. You can intend to wake early and hit snooze repeatedly. You can crave intimacy and withdraw when someone approaches. You can aspire to speak confidently in public, yet freeze when the moment arrives. These contradictions are not weaknesses; they are evidence of multiplicity.

Human consciousness resembles a coalition rather than a monarchy: different inner voices, each with its own agenda, fears, and logic, jostling for influence. Some are rational and forward-looking; others are emotionally reactive and memory-bound. This internal dissonance is not pathological—it is a feature of how we operate. Acceptance of this reality is the first step toward working with, rather than against, ourselves.

A core tension underpinning many of these patterns is the clash between logic and emotion. Dual-process theory from cognitive science offers a helpful framework. System 1 is fast, automatic, emotional, and intuitive. It keeps you safe on instinct, jerks your hand from a hot stove, or triggers anxiety before a difficult conversation. System 2 is slower, deliberate, logical, and effortful. It plans, strategises, and delays gratification for long-term goals.

Normally, these systems cooperate. When they clash—when logic sets an intention that emotion perceives as threatening—behaviour tends to default to the emotional system. Not because it is wiser, but because it is more immediate. Emotional systems evolved to prioritise short-term survival over long-term gain. When that survival is perceived to be at risk—through vulnerability, shame, or perceived inadequacy—your nervous system acts to protect you. Even if that means cancelling a date, sabotaging a prepared interview, or repeating a pattern you have intellectually outgrown.

Here lies the dilemma: knowledge rarely alters emotional conditioning. You may understand why something occurs, yet remain unable to stop it. This is not lack of discipline; it is biology. Emotional instincts are altered not by logic, but through new emotional experiences. Hence, purely cognitive strategies—mantras, affirmations, rational arguments—often fail, because they address the wrong system. They debate with fear, which is not listening.

This brings us to one of the most overprescribed, yet least effective tools for personal change: willpower.

Willpower is the ability to override impulses in favour of long-term goals, often framed as a finite resource. Research consistently shows that it is profoundly limited when the behaviours in question are emotionally charged. You can force yourself to exercise, meditate, or abstain from a vice—for a time. But if the underlying behaviour serves emotional survival, willpower will eventually collapse. It cannot outlast the emotional logic that sees the habit as essential.

And when willpower fails—as it inevitably does—shame fills the void. You internalise the failure as evidence of your character: weak, undisciplined, unworthy. The cycle tightens. The more you push, the more resistance builds. The more you fail, the more you believe something is inherently wrong with you. The notion of being at war with yourself becomes self-fulfilling.

But what if you are not at war? What if you are simply divided?

Internal Family Systems (IFS), developed by Richard Schwartz, offers a transformative framework for understanding this division. Its insight is simple: the mind consists of distinct parts, each with a voice, role, and worldview. These parts are not symptoms to be eliminated, but protectors to be understood.

Take, for example, the part that avoids confrontation. It may frustrate you, even provoke resentment. Yet approached with curiosity, it may reveal a memory of humiliation, rejection, or loss. Its avoidance is not cowardice—it is protection. Or consider the part that binges late at night. It may seem reckless, yet its motive is temporary relief from loneliness, pressure, or emptiness. What once seemed self-sabotage now reads as earnest, if inelegant, self-care.

When you recognise these internal parts—not as enemies, but as protectors—you gain choice. You are no longer bound to a single dominant impulse. You can create space between urge and action. You can listen without obeying, question without condemning. Roles can be reassigned: the part that lashes out need not lead; the part that numbs can be thanked and relieved. Healing, in this view, is less about conquering the self and more about integrating it.

This chapter unfolds these ideas with care. It examines real scenarios, offers practical tools, and challenges prevailing narratives about self-sabotage. You are invited to reflect not as a passive observer, but as an active participant in the logic of your behaviour. The goal is not to excuse harm, but to trace the emotional lineage: to understand what the behaviour once achieved, and what it still protects.

If your habits sometimes seem to have a life of their own, they are not foreign invaders. They are parts of you—young, scared, overburdened—doing their best with the resources available. They do not need to be silenced. They need to be heard, understood, and eventually relieved of duty.

The myth of self-sabotage persists because it offers a tidy explanation for human inconsistency. Yet tidy explanations rarely serve the truth. Behaviour, particularly destructive behaviour, is patterned and purposeful. Until we discern that purpose, change remains elusive.

This chapter is the start of that deeper understanding. What follows is not a manual, but a reorientation: a way to perceive yourself not as an adversary, but as a system of parts capable of reorganisation through care, clarity, and dialogue. True transformation begins not with punishment, but with insight. And insight begins when we stop asking, "Why do I keep ruining everything?" and start asking, "What is this behaviour trying to protect me from?" The answers may surprise you—but they will also set you free.

Sabotage or Strategy?

It is a peculiar contradiction of the human mind that we often resist the very things we say we want. We sabotage opportunities, delay our goals, undercut relationships, and cling to habits that actively harm us. From the outside, such behaviour appears irrational. To the untrained eye, it looks like laziness, fear of success, lack of discipline, or low self-worth. But labelling these acts as *self-sabotage*—a term now deeply embedded in popular psychology—doesn't bring us any closer to understanding why they occur. In fact, it may push us further from the truth.

The phrase *self-sabotage* suggests malice turned inward, as if part of the psyche has gone rogue, determined to upend progress out of spite or dysfunction. It frames the behaviour as a problem of weakness or self-opposition, not one of strategy or adaptation. But this framework overlooks something vital: these so-called sabotaging behaviours are often the result of finely-tuned emotional strategies developed in response to earlier circumstances. They may no longer be helpful in the present, but they once served a function—protection, avoidance, control, connection, or escape. What looks like sabotage is, more often than not, an unconscious effort to maintain safety.

To understand this distinction, consider the employee who repeatedly misses deadlines, despite valuing their career and fearing consequences. From the surface, it reads as resistance or incompetence. But look closer, and it may reveal a pattern established in adolescence, where perfection was expected and failure was punished. Procrastination in this case functions as a delay mechanism—buffering the self from the full exposure of being seen and judged. It's not that the person doesn't care. It's that the emotional logic behind the delay associates performance with pain. Avoidance becomes a form of self-defence.

Another example: someone in therapy commits to setting firmer boundaries in relationships, only to find themselves, once again, saying "yes" to requests they resent. While this might appear as weakness or people-pleasing, the behaviour may stem from a much older template—the belief that love is conditional on self-sacrifice.

Boundaries, then, don't just risk minor discomfort; they threaten the very mechanism by which the person has historically secured belonging. The resistance isn't illogical; it's deeply coherent within the emotional landscape in which it formed.

Emotional coherence is key to decoding behaviour that appears self-defeating. The cognitive dissonance we feel—*Why would I do something that hurts me?*—can only be resolved when we stop assuming the behaviour is about logic in the first place. Emotional logic is not the same as rationality, but it is no less consistent. The psyche is built to protect, even at the cost of growth. It chooses safety over success, familiarity over fulfilment, and predictability over freedom when it senses danger—even symbolic or imagined danger. To break this cycle, we must first understand what the behaviour is protecting us from, not just what it is costing us.

That protection often centres around emotional threats: rejection, failure, vulnerability, or abandonment. If someone grew up in an environment where expressing needs led to ridicule or neglect, they may learn to suppress those needs entirely. In adulthood, this can manifest as overfunctioning in relationships, denying their limits, or emotionally disappearing when intimacy deepens. It looks like sabotage, but it is better understood as a loyal pattern trying to shield the self from historical pain.

This raises a critical question: when does a survival strategy become a self-sabotaging habit? The line is blurred. A coping mechanism that was once adaptive can become maladaptive when the context changes—but the body and brain don't automatically update to new conditions. Habits form not just through repetition, but through emotional significance. If a behaviour once secured comfort or protection, it gains power—not because it's logical, but because it worked. It created relief, connection, or escape at a time when those were not otherwise available. The repetition of the behaviour becomes the repetition of the solution, regardless of its cost in the present.

The process of unlearning such patterns is not a matter of discipline, but of understanding. You cannot shame a protective part of the psyche into compliance. You can only build new associations that make safety available through healthier means. That begins with compassion—not indulgence, but precise, discerning compassion that sees the logic behind the loop.

This is particularly important in the case of perfectionism, a trait often mistaken for ambition or drive. At first glance, perfectionists appear to be striving for excellence, yet many are paralysed by the fear of inadequacy. Perfectionism isn't a strategy for success; it's a strategy for protection. It says, *If I do this flawlessly, I won't be criticised, rejected, or exposed.* But the cost is high: procrastination, burnout, disconnection from creativity, and a chronic sense of failure. Once again, what appears to be sabotage—missing deadlines, abandoning projects, resisting visibility—is, at its core, a way of minimising risk.

Understanding the emotional function of behaviour invites a radically different response. Instead of asking *How do I stop this?*, we begin asking *What is this protecting me from?* and *What need is this trying to meet?* These are not therapeutic questions alone; they are deeply strategic. They allow us to replace a rigid, costly behaviour with a more flexible and sustainable one—without triggering the internal alarms that sabotage attempts at change.

This framework also helps explain why many well-intentioned attempts at change fail. Behavioural science often promotes the use of willpower, habit stacking, accountability systems, and environmental design. These are not without merit. But when emotional safety is at stake, cognitive strategies alone fall short. You cannot habit-track your way out of a fear response. You cannot gratitude-journal your way out of a nervous system that perceives a boundary as a threat to attachment. The emotional logic must be addressed—not just the behaviour it produces.

This is where many change frameworks falter: they treat the behaviour as isolated from the emotional system that sustains it. But if a behaviour is being used to regulate fear, soothe shame, or assert control in a chaotic environment, removing it without replacing its function creates internal panic. The system rebels. The behaviour returns. Not because the person lacks willpower, but because they lack an emotionally safe alternative. The strategy was never about the action itself; it was about the *emotional resolution* that followed it.

In organisational settings, these dynamics play out in subtle but significant ways. A manager avoids giving feedback, not because they're conflict-averse, but because confrontation was historically punished or modelled as unsafe. A high-achiever undermines a promotion opportunity, not because they lack ambition, but because success triggers fears of isolation or visibility. The workplace becomes a theatre for unconscious strategies—patterns that are misinterpreted as professional shortcomings, when in fact they are emotional reflexes in disguise.

The same principle applies to addiction. While the substance or behaviour may appear as the problem, it often functions as a solution to an unmet need—connection, relief, regulation. Removing the substance without addressing the underlying emotional architecture leads to relapse, not recovery. This is why sustainable change requires a deeper inquiry: *What is this behaviour doing for me?* rather than *Why am I so broken that I keep doing this?*

It is tempting to pathologise these patterns, especially in a culture that prizes autonomy and productivity. But pathology implies something is inherently wrong. Strategy implies something was working—at least once. Reframing so-called sabotage as strategy restores dignity to the person. It shifts the narrative from *I'm broken* to *I adapted intelligently to a difficult context.* That context may no longer be relevant, but the adaptation remains, waiting to be understood and updated.

Of course, not all maladaptive behaviours have easily traceable origins. Some are composites—formed gradually, subtly, through dozens of emotional moments rather than singular traumas. But the principle holds: the more disruptive a behaviour appears, the more likely it is serving a function that feels non-negotiable to the emotional brain. Until that function is understood and honoured, the behaviour will persist—no matter how much logic, punishment, or strategy is applied.

This understanding also forces a rethink of how we approach motivation. We tend to assume that people are motivated by progress, achievement, and reward. But often, they are more powerfully motivated by *avoiding emotional discomfort.* The drive to stay safe can outweigh the drive to grow. Especially if safety has been historically fragile. In this light, motivation itself becomes emotionally coded—it is not just about desire, but about the absence of internal threat.

So what replaces the idea of self-sabotage? Not a simple binary, but a new lens. A recognition that beneath every behaviour lies a question: *What am I protecting? What am I avoiding? What does this action prevent me from feeling?* And once those answers begin to surface, we can begin to design new strategies—ones that honour the original emotional need while expanding the behavioural repertoire available to meet it.

This is not about condoning destructive behaviour. It is about decoding it. Only through that decoding does change become not only possible, but durable. Because when a behaviour is no longer the sole available strategy to soothe or protect, the system can finally let it go—not through force, but through trust.

The truth is, most of us are not sabotaging our lives. We are negotiating with ghosts. And until those ghosts are named, listened to, and released, the pattern will persist—strategic, loyal, and devastatingly misunderstood.

When Logic and Emotion Clash

A person can spend hours crafting a plan, rehearsing new habits, and committing, with complete sincerity, to a better future—only to unravel in the presence of a familiar trigger. One harsh word, a flicker of doubt, a subtle feeling of exposure, and the whole structure collapses. The morning routine is skipped, the healthy boundary abandoned, the old behaviour resumed as if none of the prior resolve had ever existed. This is not a failure of logic. It is the activation of emotion. And the two are not equals when they collide.

The notion that humans are primarily rational beings has been challenged for decades, yet it remains embedded in how we judge our own behaviour. When we do something that contradicts what we know to be best for us, we assume we've failed to apply our rational mind—failed to be sensible, disciplined, or mature. But this interpretation misunderstands the architecture of the human psyche. Rationality is not the operating system of the mind; it is one process among many. And when in conflict with emotional instincts—particularly those charged with memory or survival—rationality frequently takes a back seat.

This is not a character flaw. It is the outcome of a divided system, evolved for speed and safety rather than coherence.

Dual-process theory, a cornerstone of modern cognitive psychology, helps explain this division. It describes two fundamental modes of thinking: *System 1*—fast, automatic, emotional, and unconscious—and *System 2*—slow, effortful, logical, and conscious. System 1 operates beneath awareness, scanning for threats, rewards, and patterns. It makes snap judgments, creates associations, and governs much of our moment-to-moment behaviour. System 2, by contrast, is the reflective part of the mind that can plan, inhibit, and analyse. It is what allows us to set goals, imagine future outcomes, and delay gratification.

While we like to believe System 2 is always in control, the reality is that System 1 often dominates, particularly under stress or when emotions run high. This is not a design flaw—it is an evolutionary adaptation. Our ancestors did not survive by calculating risks with spreadsheets. They survived by reacting swiftly to danger. The brain is still wired for speed, not subtlety. Emotionally loaded stimuli—like shame, rejection, or perceived failure—activate System 1's protective instincts far more quickly than System 2 can intervene. And when the two systems are in conflict, the more emotionally urgent signal tends to win.

This internal dissonance explains why a person can deeply *want* to change yet still find themselves sabotaging that change the moment discomfort arises. The rational mind may see the benefits of setting boundaries, saying no, or walking away from toxic relationships. But if the emotional system associates those actions with rejection, abandonment, or loss of identity, it will resist—powerfully and persistently. It is not irrational in the strict sense. It is simply prioritising emotional safety over logical outcomes.

Consider a high-functioning adult who struggles with public speaking. They may understand intellectually that their fears are exaggerated, even unfounded. But when they stand before a room of people, their body responds as if they are under threat—sweating, trembling, blanking out. System 2 knows the audience is benign. But System 1 has a different memory: a moment in childhood when being seen meant being ridiculed. That imprint governs the present. Logic has no access to override it in real time.

These clashes are not limited to dramatic moments. They occur in quiet, habitual ways every day. You intend to wake early, but hit snooze. You plan to eat clean, but reach for the sugar. You want to speak honestly, but soften your truth. In each case, there is a part of you acting in opposition to your declared goal. Not out of sabotage, but because it feels threatened by what the goal implies. It may fear being judged, deprived, abandoned, or exhausted. And the emotional brain is exquisitely sensitive to those threats, even when they are not consciously registered.

The mistake most people make is treating this internal conflict as a failure of willpower. They believe that if they were just more committed, more focused, more disciplined, they could overcome their inconsistencies. But this view ignores the emotional cost of certain actions. System 2 can hold a value—like success, health, or authenticity—but if that value triggers unresolved emotion, System 1 will intervene to protect. It doesn't matter that your adult self wants to change; your emotional self may still be carrying the protective mandate of your younger, more vulnerable self.

That younger self often encoded beliefs based on incomplete information: *If I'm too visible, I'll be punished. If I assert my needs, I'll be abandoned. If I rest, I'll fall behind.* These beliefs become the scaffolding of emotional logic—guiding behaviours that feel self-defeating on the surface, but are internally consistent with the aim of emotional survival. The rational brain may challenge them, but without emotional resolution, the protective reflex remains in place.

What's more, the clash between logic and emotion is not simply a contest of strength—it's a conflict of *timing*. System 1 reacts in milliseconds. It prepares the body, floods it with signals, and sets the emotional tone of an interaction before the rational mind has even begun to interpret what is happening. By the time System 2 weighs in, the physiological cascade is already in motion. The voice shakes, the mind blanks, the heart races. The rational argument is drowned out by the emotional noise.

This understanding reshapes how we approach change. It is not enough to set logical goals or repeat affirmations. Change requires creating new emotional associations that feel *safe enough* to allow the rational plan to be enacted. Safety is the condition under which logic can operate. Without it, emotion will always prevail.

Internal conflict models, particularly those informed by trauma theory and parts psychology, deepen this insight. They suggest that the mind is not a unified agent, but a constellation of parts—each formed at different developmental stages, each with its own beliefs, strategies, and fears. Some parts are rational and future-focused; others are stuck in emotional time, operating from the imprint of past wounds. When we attempt to change without integrating these parts—without listening to their concerns or addressing their fears—we generate resistance. Not because the parts are malicious, but because they are loyal. They are trying to protect the psyche from the same pain it once could not tolerate.

This protective impulse can be profoundly intelligent. The part that resists intimacy may be shielding you from the chaos of a childhood where closeness meant volatility. The part that overspends may be trying to compensate for years of deprivation or shame. The part that procrastinates may be keeping you from exposure, fearing that success would demand more than you can bear. These parts are not flawed—they are under-resourced. They lack new information and emotional updating. Until they are engaged, change remains theoretical.

Engaging them does not mean indulging every impulse or being ruled by emotion. It means creating space within the self for dialogue—not a lecture from logic, but a conversation between internal stakeholders. It means recognising that emotion has its own intelligence: it tracks safety, signals unmet needs, and preserves coherence when change threatens to unravel a fragile identity.

This is why insight alone is often insufficient. A person can understand their patterns with precision and still be stuck. Because knowing *why* you do something is not the same as feeling *safe* enough to stop doing it. Safety is not an intellectual state—it is a nervous system condition. It must be cultivated relationally, somatically, and emotionally. Only then can the rational plan find a foothold in behaviour.

In practical terms, this means that effective change work must address both systems. It must honour the emotional logic while supporting the rational goal. It must create micro-experiences of success that feel safe—not just impressive. It must allow the emotional brain to learn, gradually and viscerally, that new behaviour does not result in the same old pain. This is not a matter of will, but of design.

Understanding the clash between logic and emotion reframes the work of change. It is not a heroic struggle of discipline versus temptation. It is a careful orchestration of trust-building between parts of the self—some of which are scared, others of which are striving. Both are valid. Both deserve respect. And both must be brought into conversation if lasting change is to occur.

When that conversation is avoided—when logic tries to dominate emotion—the result is often inner warfare: cycles of repression, rebellion, and collapse. But when that conversation is cultivated—when each system is given its due—change begins to feel not only possible, but coherent. You are no longer forcing yourself to behave. You are aligning yourself to evolve.

This alignment is not a static achievement. It is a living process. A negotiation between your aspirations and your anxieties, your future self and your former self, your reasoning and your reflexes. When those elements are in conflict, it is not a sign of brokenness. It is a sign that something is trying to be protected. Your task is not to eliminate that protection, but to update it—to bring all parts of your mind into the present, where safety can be redefined and your goals can finally be acted on, not in opposition to yourself, but in partnership with all that you are.

Why Willpower Doesn't Work

The prevailing belief that change is a matter of willpower has become one of the most enduring myths in modern self-improvement culture. It flatters our sense of agency, placing us at the helm of our behaviour. If we simply *try hard enough*, the logic goes, we can overcome cravings, silence distractions, and stick to our goals with grit and determination. The problem with this view is not that it's completely wrong, but that it is chronically incomplete. Willpower is real, but its power is both narrow and fragile. When invoked as the primary tool for transformation—particularly in emotionally complex behaviours—it consistently fails, not because the individual is weak-willed, but because the strategy is structurally flawed.

At the heart of this failure is a misunderstanding of what willpower actually is. Commonly mistaken for a trait, like confidence or patience, willpower is more accurately described as a *state-dependent cognitive function*. It is a temporary resource governed by a set of neurobiological mechanisms primarily located in the prefrontal cortex—the area of the brain responsible for executive function, decision-making, and impulse control. Like a mental muscle, willpower can be exerted—but it fatigues. It is sensitive to stress, depleted by overuse, and diminished by factors as simple as sleep loss, low blood sugar, or emotional overload.

Numerous studies in behavioural science have illustrated this point with startling clarity. One of the most well-known is the "radish and cookie" experiment conducted by psychologist Roy Baumeister and colleagues, in which participants who resisted eating freshly baked cookies were less persistent on subsequent tasks than those who were not required to exert self-control. The conclusion was straightforward: *self-control is a limited resource.* If you expend it resisting temptation, you have less to spend on following through. This model—popularised as "ego depletion"—has faced scrutiny in its replicability, but the broader principle has held: self-control draws on finite cognitive and emotional bandwidth, and that bandwidth narrows under stress, fatigue, or pressure.

This has significant implications for how we understand behaviour change. A person may have every intention of exercising daily, avoiding alcohol, or speaking kindly to their partner. But when their cognitive load increases—whether from a demanding job, financial stress, or emotional distress—their capacity to act on those intentions diminishes. It's not that they no longer care. It's that the neural systems responsible for goal-directed action have been overridden by older, more primitive systems geared toward relief and regulation.

This override is not accidental. The brain is constantly balancing two competing demands: *long-term goals* versus *short-term emotional relief.* Willpower belongs to the former—it delays gratification in service of future benefit. But when the emotional brain detects threat—real or symbolic—it initiates a shift toward short-term safety. This is not weakness; it is evolutionary design. Our ancestors did not survive by prioritising six-month goals over immediate protection. They survived by responding quickly to cues of danger, uncertainty, or loss. That survival bias still governs behaviour today.

Emotional states, therefore, are not just background noise; they are the conditions under which or against which willpower operates. Chronic shame, anxiety, grief, or loneliness can render willpower nearly useless, not because the person is unmotivated, but because their system is preoccupied with managing internal distress. In such cases, what looks like a failure of self-control is more accurately a reallocation of energy from restraint to regulation. The person drinks not because they lack discipline, but because alcohol is the fastest route to soothing. They avoid tasks not out of laziness, but because those tasks trigger emotional overwhelm. They return to harmful relationships not out of ignorance, but because the absence of connection feels more unbearable than the presence of conflict. In each instance, the emotional logic trumps the cognitive intention.

Another often-misunderstood aspect of willpower is its dependency on identity coherence. People are far more likely to sustain a behaviour when it aligns with their self-concept. For example, someone who sees themselves as "a runner" will run more consistently than someone who is "trying to run more." This alignment between action and identity reduces cognitive friction—it eliminates the need for daily decision-making by embedding the behaviour into one's internal narrative. But when new behaviours conflict with a person's ingrained identity—especially one shaped by trauma, shame, or social conditioning—willpower alone cannot bridge the gap. The behaviour may be intellectually valued but emotionally alien. And what is alien is rarely sustainable.

This helps explain why even the most structured plans—diet regimens, productivity apps, digital detoxes—often fail. These tools are designed to optimise decision-making. But decision-making is not the primary problem. The problem is *emotional congruence.* If the behaviour does not feel safe, meaningful, or self-relevant, no amount of scheduling or accountability will make it stick. People don't simply act based on goals; they act based on *felt meaning.* And when there is no emotional architecture to support the new action, willpower becomes a brittle bridge suspended over a vast emotional chasm.

Compounding this is the fact that most willpower-centric approaches frame behaviour in moralistic terms. You are either good or bad, disciplined or lazy, winning or failing. This binary framing activates shame—an emotion well known to impair self-regulation. Shame not only creates emotional distress, which depletes cognitive resources, but also fragments the self, turning the act of behaviour change into an act of internal war. You are no longer shifting a habit; you are trying to prove your worth. That emotional burden is unsustainable, especially under the strain of everyday life.

The neuroscience confirms this. Studies using functional MRI have shown that when individuals experience shame or self-criticism, the brain's default response is not self-correction but threat management. Regions like the amygdala and periaqueductal grey become active, signalling stress and defensive readiness. In contrast, when people engage in self-compassion or emotionally safe reflection, the medial prefrontal cortex—associated with insight and perspective-taking—becomes more active. Simply put: shame shuts down the very capacities needed for sustained change. It erodes the foundation that willpower depends on.

The alternative to willpower is not indulgence. It is *emotional design.* It is building systems, environments, and relationships that make the desired behaviour not only accessible but desirable—*not just logical, but soothing.* This might mean creating rituals that signal safety, cultivating inner narratives that align with the new behaviour, or addressing the underlying emotion that the unwanted behaviour has been regulating. It means recognising that behaviour change is not an act of force, but an act of *integration*—one that honours the needs of the emotional system while engaging the aims of the cognitive mind.

Real-world applications of this can be seen in trauma-informed therapy, which emphasises *bottom-up* regulation—working with the nervous system to create safety—before attempting *top-down* cognitive restructuring. Similarly, addiction recovery programmes that focus on connection, ritual, and community coherence tend to outperform those that rely solely on abstinence and monitoring. In organisational behaviour, leaders who embed psychological safety and emotional congruence into workplace culture see more durable changes in team habits than those who rely on incentives or compliance metrics alone.

In each case, the principle is the same: willpower is a spark, not a furnace. It can ignite change, but it cannot sustain it. That requires emotional scaffolding—structures that make the behaviour feel familiar, supported, and coherent with the self. These structures vary, but they are always rooted in safety, meaning, and internal alignment. Without them, the behaviour will collapse under stress, no matter how well-intentioned or meticulously planned.

Understanding the limits of willpower liberates us from the tyranny of shame-based self-improvement. It allows us to stop asking *Why can't I just do this?* and start asking *What does this behaviour protect me from? What emotional function is it serving? What would make the alternative feel safer than the current habit?* These are the questions that lead to durable change—not through force, but through clarity.

Ultimately, willpower is not the enemy. It is simply overrated. It is a fragile ally in a world of complex emotional landscapes. When used wisely, it can be part of the process—but never the foundation. That foundation must be built not on pressure, but on understanding. Not on self-coercion, but on self-coherence. Only then does change become more than possible. It becomes inevitable.

Naming the Internal Divide

People often speak of themselves as if they are singular entities, wholly consistent in thought and behaviour. But this illusion collapses quickly under self-examination. One part of you wants to wake up early, the other reaches for the snooze button. One part longs for connection, the other pushes people away. One part is trying to heal, and another keeps dragging you back into familiar dysfunction. These contradictions are not evidence of immaturity or lack of will. They are signs of an internal system—complex, plural, and often in quiet conflict. To understand why we repeat destructive behaviours, we must learn to identify *which* part of us is making that choice, and *why*.

The discomfort people experience in moments of behavioural inconsistency—saying one thing, doing another—is not always a lack of self-control. More often, it's the surfacing of internal opposition. The rational adult self may genuinely want to make a change. But another part, often younger and emotionally unresolved, carries a competing agenda. This part is not the enemy. It is doing what it believes is necessary to keep the psyche safe. The problem is not that these internal parts exist, but that we remain unaware of them—blending their voice with our own, assuming their reflexes are reality.

This is where the concept of "parts work" becomes essential—not as pop psychology, but as a structural lens on how human consciousness operates. Internal Family Systems (IFS), developed by Dr Richard Schwartz, offers one of the most elegant frameworks for understanding this divide. At its core is a deceptively simple premise: the mind is not a monolith, but a system of subpersonalities or "parts," each with its own perspective, emotion, and function. These parts are not metaphors. They are experientially distinct: they think differently, feel differently, and often contradict each other. Learning to name and dialogue with them is not an abstraction. It is a tangible skill that brings clarity, coherence, and self-compassion to behavioural change.

Consider someone who constantly self-sabotages relationships. They may genuinely want intimacy, stability, and trust. Yet, in moments of vulnerability, they pull away, pick fights, or ghost the other person entirely. If you ask why, they might say, "I don't know—I just panicked." But dig deeper, and you may hear another voice entirely: *They're going to leave eventually, so better I leave first.* Or: *If they really knew me, they'd be disgusted.* These are not passing thoughts. They are the inner scripts of a protective part—often one that formed in response to betrayal, neglect, or shame. Its actions may be extreme, but its goal is survival.

This divide is not pathological. It is adaptive. Parts emerge in response to experience. They are shaped by moments of pain, disconnection, or fear—moments the psyche could not fully process at the time. Rather than integrating those emotions, the system creates a specialised part to manage them. Some parts are hyper-vigilant, scanning for threats. Others numb out sensation. Others attack pre-emptively. Over time, these roles become habitual. And when left unnamed, they run our lives without our consent.

Naming these parts is the first act of reclaiming agency. It allows you to distinguish *yourself* from the behaviour. It shifts the internal narrative from "Why am I like this?" to "Which part of me is doing this—and what does it need?" That question alone can interrupt cycles of shame. When you realise that the bingeing, the lashing out, the withdrawal, is not *you*, but a part of you operating under an outdated rule, it becomes possible to engage with it differently. Not with contempt, but with curiosity.

One of the most powerful examples of this shift can be seen in addiction recovery. A person may hate the part of them that drinks, use, or escapes. They might try to silence it through force or moralising. But the addictive behaviour often serves a specific function—relief from pain, regulation of anxiety, suppression of memory. When that part is recognised and named—not just as "the addict," but perhaps as "the overwhelmed one," "the abandoned one," or "the one who never got to cry"—the entire inner landscape begins to shift. The behaviour may still be present, but it is no longer invisible. It is no longer driving from the backseat.

Naming a part is not about giving it power. It's about seeing it clearly enough to negotiate with it. It might sound like: *I hear you're scared we'll be judged if we speak up at this meeting. You're trying to protect us from humiliation, and that makes sense. But I'm also here now, and I know we can handle discomfort.* This kind of internal dialogue may seem unnatural at first—too therapeutic, too contrived. But it is, in essence, emotional literacy. It is a way of bringing online the observing self—the part of you that can witness without blending, choose without coercing, respond without reacting.

The challenge, of course, is that these protective parts often resist exposure. They don't want to be named, let alone questioned. Many of them believe, often rightly, that they've kept the system afloat during years of chaos. They are loyal, even if miscalibrated. When you try to override them too quickly—through force, shame, or premature cognitive reframing—they dig in. Their logic is not open to persuasion until it feels seen. Which is why intellectual insight alone is never enough. The part must *feel* understood before it can release its grip.

This brings us to a crucial distinction: *protective parts* versus *exiled parts.* Protective parts are the ones we most often encounter—they manage, defend, distract, or numb. They are outward-facing, action-oriented. Exiled parts, on the other hand, are the vulnerable ones—the holders of grief, fear, worthlessness, or unmet need. These parts are usually buried deep, hidden by the protectors who fear their re-emergence. When a protective part sabotages change, it is often doing so to prevent the emotional flood of an exile breaking through. The pattern may look irrational, but it is deeply coherent. It is saying, *If we stop controlling, we'll have to feel all the things we've spent years avoiding.*

Effective change, then, is not about bypassing these dynamics. It is about building internal relationships—relationships between the self and its parts. This requires presence, not perfection. The goal is not to get rid of the part, but to help it retire from a role it no longer needs to play. Sometimes this happens through insight; more often, it happens through consistent inner dialogue and real-world evidence that things are different now—that connection is possible without sacrifice, that needs can be expressed without rejection, that rest does not equal danger.

This relational approach also dissolves the internal hierarchy that often underpins self-hatred. Many people divide themselves into "good" and "bad" parts—the disciplined self versus the lazy one, the spiritual self versus the selfish one. But these binaries are false. Every part, no matter how dysfunctional its behaviour, is trying to serve a need. That doesn't make the behaviour acceptable, but it makes it understandable. And once it is understood, it becomes open to change—not through compliance, but through integration.

To name the internal divide is to exit the myth of singular will. It is to recognise that the self is a system—capable of conflict, contradiction, and conversation. It is to stop fighting the symptom and start listening to the part behind it. And in doing so, we move from judgement to clarity, from compulsion to choice.

You cannot change what you cannot see. Naming your parts does not solve everything. But it gives you the language to begin. It turns the chaos of impulse into a structure that can be worked with. And from there, a different kind of change becomes possible—not because the part has been silenced, but because it has been heard.

Chapter 2
Roots Before Routines

A habit is seldom merely a habit. Beneath every entrenched behavioural pattern—especially those we label as destructive, compulsive, or dysfunctional—there lies not laziness, ignorance, or moral failing, but history. Emotional history. Habits that defy reason and resist alteration are not random quirks; they are relics, fossilised responses forged under pressure, shaped by circumstance, and preserved by necessity. To treat them purely as routines to be broken or reprogrammed is to overlook their deeper significance. Before a habit becomes a problem, it is a solution—often one aimed at something invisible.

Contemporary productivity culture tends to flatten habits, treating them as if they exist in isolation, disconnected from psychology or lived experience. You pick them up, you repeat them, and eventually, they stick. Yet this perspective cannot explain why certain habits remain immovable long after they cease to serve any rational purpose. Many behaviours are etched into our nervous systems not merely through repetition but through emotional resonance. We do not overeat, procrastinate, withdraw, overwork, or people-please simply because our routines were poorly designed. We do these things because, once, they helped us cope. They alleviated anxiety, warded off rejection, or softened the impact of overwhelming experiences—and the body remembers what worked.

To grasp this, we must begin seeing habits as emotional artefacts rather than solely behavioural scripts. A child who learns to stay silent during family conflict may grow into an adult who struggles to speak up at work. That silence is not a flaw—it is a safety mechanism. Someone who internalised the lesson that achievement secured approval may develop an unrelenting work ethic, not from ambition, but from fear: If I do not succeed, I will not matter. Outwardly, these behaviours may appear disciplined—or dysfunctional—but internally, they were adaptive responses, frozen in time.

These emotionally encoded patterns often remain invisible because they were acquired before language could articulate them. They operate as subterranean scripts: automatic, unconscious, self-reinforcing. And because they once helped regulate intense feelings—shame, grief, fear—they are associated not just with action, but with relief. This is why abandoning them is so challenging. You are not merely giving up a habit; you are relinquishing a strategy that once made life survivable. Mainstream change literature, focused on triggers, rewards, and repetition, often misses this nuance. Those mechanics matter, but they cannot explain the grip of behaviours that persist despite consequence and intention.

The question shifts from Why can't I stop this? to What was this behaviour originally trying to solve? Approached with genuine curiosity, patterns that once seemed shameful begin to make sense. Loops that appeared senseless reveal their architecture. The binge-eating was not about food; it was about comfort when no one else could provide it. Avoidance was not irresponsibility; it was protection against overwhelm and exposure. Chronic busyness was not ambition; it was an escape from stillness, stillness that once meant confrontation with unbearable thoughts.

This perspective heralds a profound reframing: from pathology to strategy. Our most stubborn behaviours were not failures—they were context-specific solutions. The problem arises when the context changes but the behaviours endure. What once protected becomes maladaptive—not because the strategy was flawed, but because the nervous system continues to respond to a threat that no longer exists.

This tension—the past shaping present action—is why superficial interventions often fail. One cannot simply discipline a nervous system that perceives danger. One cannot shame a strategy out of existence when it was designed to protect. The only viable route is understanding, followed by renegotiation.

Renegotiation is neither purely cognitive nor linear; it is emotional, embodied, and often disorienting. To relinquish a long-held behaviour is to confront what might return in its absence. If I stop overachieving, will I become irrelevant? If I stop caretaking, will anyone stay? If I stop numbing, will the pain be too intense? These are not hypotheticals; they are internal calculations, unspoken yet profoundly influential. They explain why people remain in discomfort even when they know better—the alternative feels riskier than the familiar pain.

Traditional models seldom acknowledge this, treating behaviour as separate from identity. Yet many habits are entwined with self-concept. Those whose coping strategy has been control may fear change as collapse. Control becomes scaffolding for self-worth; without it, they feel exposed. Similarly, identities entwined with competence, independence, emotional detachment, or self-sacrifice render behavioural change a perceived betrayal of self. Habits are not merely difficult to break—they are difficult to grieve. Letting go often means letting go of a part of oneself that once ensured survival.

Complicating matters, these behaviours are rarely conscious choices. They emerge reactively, automatically, and contextually. You may not notice until you are deep in the pattern—checking your phone for the tenth time, pouring another drink, deferring your own needs again. In those moments, shame floods in, collapsing reflection into self-blame. Yet the work is not in punishment; it is in understanding the emotional contract sustaining the behaviour. What is this doing for me? What would happen if I stopped?

That latter question—What would happen if I stopped?—is a litmus test for emotional attachment. If the answer is "I'd feel free," change is conceivable. If the answer is "I'd feel lost, exposed, unlovable, unsafe," the behaviour still carries protective weight. Change is still possible, but the groundwork must shift. A habit cannot be removed while it still feels protective. First, the safety the habit created must be reconstructed, a process requiring precision, patience, and often support.

Contextual reflection is a particularly effective tool. Noticing when the behaviour intensifies can reveal its underlying purpose. Does it spike under criticism, risk, or invisibility? These cues are not incidental—they point to the root system beneath the habit. Once identified, the work shifts from merely changing actions to addressing underlying fears. Sustainable change begins not through effort alone, but through understanding.

Not all emotional habits are loud or obviously harmful. Some are socially rewarded—overworking, perfectionism, hyper-independence—admired even. Yet if driven by unresolved emotional contracts—I must prove my worth, I must never need anyone, I must never fail—they strain the system just as severely as overtly damaging habits. Understanding their roots remains essential.

Ultimately, habits are neither good nor bad—they are meaningful. They bear the imprint of our past, map our emotional development, and shape our responses to the world. Altering them demands more than surface-level intervention; it requires inquiry, humility, and willingness to experience what the habit has shielded us from. The reward is not merely behavioural change—it is emotional integration. A habit is often a lifeline; recognising its origin transforms blind repetition into conscious choice.

This chapter guides you through that process. Not as a linear checklist, but as excavation. You will explore not just what you want to change, but why the behaviour exists, what it protects, and what it fears. You are encouraged to approach your habits not with force, but with precision—mapping roots before designing new routines. Without such a map, even the best intentions falter. With it, you do more than change behaviour; you expand what feels possible, safe, and deserved. That is the kind of change that endures.

Habits Are Emotional Fossils

The most enduring habits are not formed by repetition alone. They are carved into our psyche through emotion—often intense, unresolved, and hidden from our conscious understanding. We think of habits as behavioural loops, but this is only partially true. A more accurate framing is that many habits are *emotional fossils*—remnants of once-necessary adaptations, preserved in behaviour long after the original context has disappeared. They are traces of former selves, encoded through experiences where a specific action resolved, prevented, or muted an internal threat. To dismantle a persistent habit, we must first ask not *how* it formed, but *why it mattered at the time it did.*

Behavioural psychology has long emphasised the role of reinforcement: the idea that behaviours repeated in the presence of reward are more likely to persist. But reward is not a fixed construct. In the emotional life of a child, a "reward" may not be pleasure, but relief. Safety. Attention. Coherence. Consider a child who learns that performing perfectly earns affection from a critical parent. The immediate reward is not the praise itself—it is the temporary suspension of disapproval. The child internalises a connection between flawlessness and safety. Perfectionism, then, is not merely a work ethic. It is a survival strategy. Years later, when deadlines loom and the stakes feel high, that same drive is activated—not by reasoned ambition, but by an implicit warning: *If you don't do this perfectly, something bad will happen.*

This emotional imprinting is why early behaviours become rigid over time. Habits that emerge in emotionally significant moments are not simply remembered—they are *relived.* The nervous system does not distinguish clearly between past and present when survival is at stake. If a behaviour once alleviated distress, the brain stores it as a reliable escape route. And when a current situation vaguely resembles the original context—even symbolically—the body retrieves that map and follows it. What looks like irrational repetition is often an echo: the past masquerading as the present.

These echoes often originate in environments where emotion was overwhelming, unprocessed, or invalidated. A child who had to suppress sadness to avoid shaming might develop a reflexive detachment from emotional states. That detachment, rehearsed over years, becomes a default mode—one that feels less like a choice and more like a personality trait. Or take someone who learned to appease an unpredictable caregiver; their instinct to people-please will feel automatic, even moral. It's not that they enjoy being deferential—it's that compliance once meant safety. And the alternative, no matter how trivial it may seem now, still registers as a potential threat.

This logic also applies to avoidance. Procrastination, often framed as laziness, is frequently a by-product of emotional association. If past efforts were met with criticism or failure, the brain may come to link effort with pain. Delaying action is not about incompetence; it is about reducing the anticipated discomfort. The habit persists because it works—not in terms of outcome, but in terms of emotional regulation. It reduces immediate anxiety, even if it creates long-term stress. This trade-off—relief now, consequence later—is the hallmark of emotionally driven habits.

The emotional utility of these behaviours often remains hidden because their origins are obscured by time and shame. Adults rarely connect their compulsive overworking to a childhood fear of being deemed lazy. They don't see the link between chronic defensiveness and a history of having their feelings invalidated. The present-day habit is seen in isolation, stripped of its backstory. But context is everything. Without it, behaviours appear to be moral failures. With it, they begin to make sense. And when something makes sense, it becomes possible to change—not through punishment, but through understanding.

The process of tracing a habit back to its emotional origin is not simply a reflective exercise; it is an act of psychological precision. It requires asking: *When did this behaviour start serving a purpose? What internal state was it helping me avoid? What role did it play in preserving my sense of safety, identity, or connection?* These questions dismantle the illusion that habits are random. They reveal that what we call a "bad habit" may once have been the only available form of self-regulation. That reframe matters. Because you cannot replace a habit until you acknowledge what it has been doing for you.

This insight is particularly relevant in cases of trauma. When someone has lived through chaotic or neglectful environments, their behaviours are often not habits in the traditional sense, but *automatic defences*. Hypervigilance, dissociation, overcontrolling tendencies—these are not quirks. They are solutions. They reduce threat, preserve function, and allow the person to keep moving forward in contexts that would otherwise overwhelm. The problem arises not because the strategy was misguided, but because it calcifies. What worked at twelve does not work at thirty-five. But the body doesn't update the code unless invited to. It repeats what it knows.

Importantly, not all emotional fossils are obviously maladaptive. Some are outwardly functional. A person who copes by becoming relentlessly competent, for example, may be praised for their achievement while privately burning out. The underlying driver is often unacknowledged: the need to earn safety through performance. These individuals often struggle to rest, not because they lack time, but because stillness activates internal alarm bells. Rest is not neutral—it is associated with vulnerability, irrelevance, or shame. In such cases, the habit—constant productivity—is not merely behavioural. It is existential. It sustains an identity built on *doing*, rather than *being*.

To shift these deeply embedded patterns, the emotional logic must be replaced, not erased. The question is not *How do I stop doing this?* but *What else could offer the safety or relief this habit provides?* This is not about behavioural substitution alone. It is about *emotional substitution*. The nervous system must be given evidence that a new strategy is not only available but *safe enough* to trust. Otherwise, change will be interpreted as a threat, not an opportunity.

This is where insight meets intervention. Recognising a habit as an emotional fossil allows for greater empathy—but it also demands precision. What need was this behaviour meeting? How did it prevent overwhelm, humiliation, or disconnection? What associations does the body hold with the behaviour's absence? This level of inquiry allows for the construction of new behaviours that are not simply rational, but *resonant*. They speak to the emotional need beneath the surface. Only then does the new habit stand a chance of sticking.

Even the language we use around habit must evolve. Terms like "breaking a habit" imply destruction. But many of these patterns are not obstacles—they are protectors. You do not break a protector. You thank it. You acknowledge its role. And then, gently, you reassign it. This shift from adversarial to relational transforms the entire process of change. You are no longer trying to defeat yourself.

You are trying to update a strategy that no longer matches your current capacity or context.

Ultimately, emotionally rooted habits are not signs of failure. They are evidence of adaptation. The fact that they persist, despite your awareness of their cost, means they are still serving a purpose—however outdated. Treating them as mere behaviours to be corrected will always miss the point. They must be *decoded* before they can be *revised*. And that decoding begins not with condemnation, but with curiosity.

The past lives in the present not just through memory, but through behaviour. Habits that frustrate or confuse us are rarely about the thing itself. They are about what the thing once prevented, soothed, or resolved. Seen through this lens, the question shifts: from *Why can't I change?* to *What part of me is still afraid to stop?* This is the work—not of willpower, but of awareness. Not of erasure, but of integration. And only through that process can emotional fossils be unearthed, understood, and gently laid to rest.

What Was This Habit Trying to Solve?

Few questions are as deceptively simple—or as psychologically revealing—as this: *What was this behaviour trying to solve?* It invites a shift away from blame and toward understanding, from condemning an unwanted habit to decoding its original emotional logic. Behaviours that we now call destructive, compulsive, or dysfunctional were rarely born in chaos. They were formed in context, under pressure, as strategic responses to internal or relational threats. Before they became problems, they were *solutions*. They offered relief, protection, or agency in a world that felt overwhelming, unpredictable, or unsafe. And though the context may have changed, the original need they addressed often has not.

This line of inquiry matters because people do not repeat difficult behaviours out of ignorance. They repeat them because, at some point in their developmental history, those behaviours worked. A child who learns to disappear when their parents argue may grow into an adult who shuts down during conflict. An adolescent who found comfort in food during periods of emotional neglect may become an adult who eats compulsively in response to stress. A teenager who achieved approval only through performance may develop an adulthood shaped entirely around achievement and productivity. In each case, the behaviour is not random or illogical—it is a form of *emotional problem-solving*, frozen in time.

Yet when individuals attempt to change these habits, they often start at the surface. They ask: *How do I stop procrastinating? How do I stop lashing out? How do I stop numbing out at the end of every day?* These are understandable questions, but they are also incomplete. They assume that the behaviour is the issue, rather than the symptom. More often than not, the behaviour is an answer to a question the person no longer remembers asking: *How do I stay safe? How do I feel less alone? How do I stop feeling like too much or not enough?*

To trace a habit back to its emotional origin, specificity is essential. General labels—stress, boredom, anxiety—are insufficient. What kind of stress? What situation activates it? What belief about the self or the world is triggered in that moment? For example, procrastination might stem not from disorganisation but from an internal narrative that says: *If I don't try, I can't fail.* Emotional eating might be less about appetite and more about containment—soothing feelings that were once unsafe to express. Avoiding intimacy may not be about disinterest, but about protection from engulfment, learned in a family system where boundaries were chronically violated. These distinctions matter because they reveal the *function* of the behaviour—not just its form.

The reflective process begins with pattern recognition. When does the behaviour occur most reliably? What precedes it—not just externally, but internally? Is there a common emotional thread? Does the behaviour tend to follow criticism, rejection, stillness, praise, or perceived loss of control? For example, someone who finds themselves snapping at their partner every time they feel unseen might trace that irritation back to a younger part of themselves that learned protest was the only way to get attention. In childhood, this part may have protected them from emotional invisibility. In adulthood, it disrupts connection. But the core need—to be seen—is not problematic. The strategy, now outdated, is.

This is the pivotal insight: *the behaviour is often a flawed solution to a valid emotional need.* The need may be for safety, connection, autonomy, validation, predictability, control, or emotional regulation. The original behaviour emerged to meet that need using whatever tools were available at the time—usually under conditions of limited support or awareness. Over time, the behaviour became automatic, even ritualised, while the underlying need remained unspoken, unmet, and unexamined. Without conscious reflection, the original function is lost, and the behaviour becomes pathologised. But when the function is recovered, the behaviour can be reframed as a protective adaptation—misapplied in the present, but intelligent in its inception.

This reframing is not just comforting—it is transformational. It allows for self-compassion rooted in clarity, not excuse. It moves the individual from internal warfare to internal negotiation. The question becomes not *How do I kill this habit?* but *How do I meet this need in a way that no longer costs me my wellbeing?* This shift invites replacement, not repression. It allows new behaviours to emerge organically, not through force, but through emotional alignment.

Yet this work is not without resistance. The act of identifying the original function of a habit often brings up grief—grief for the unmet need, for the years spent coping instead of healing, for the relationships shaped by unconscious patterns. There is also fear. Letting go of a longstanding behaviour can feel like stepping into vulnerability. If your irritability has always protected you from feeling dismissed, what will replace it? If your hyper-productivity has always buffered you from feelings of inadequacy, who are you without it? These are not rhetorical questions. They are emotional calculations the nervous system makes in every moment of attempted change.

Change that ignores this calculus is fragile. It may produce short-term compliance, but it lacks internal buy-in. The emotional system does not relinquish a protective strategy without evidence that a new one is safer. That evidence is rarely verbal. It is experiential. It must come through lived moments in which a new behaviour leads not to punishment or shame, but to safety, connection, and coherence. This is where the therapeutic process, trusted relationships, and intentional self-reflection become indispensable—not as abstract support systems, but as *corrective emotional experiences* that allow the nervous system to revise its expectations.

The process of reflection can also be facilitated by writing. Journaling prompts like *When did I first remember doing this?* or *What feeling does this behaviour protect me from?* or *If this behaviour could speak, what would it say it's afraid of?* are not simplistic self-help exercises. They are cognitive invitations to emotional memory. They create access points to the origins of habits that otherwise appear senseless. For many, simply naming the emotional logic behind a behaviour reduces shame by half. The rest is learning how to meet the need differently.

It is worth noting that not all functions are obvious or conscious. Some behaviours serve *relational* purposes rather than emotional ones. A person may continue minimising their needs because that was how they stayed connected to a narcissistic parent. They learned: *My needs endanger the relationship.* Others may use humour, charm, or helpfulness as socially rewarded masks to keep others at a distance. These habits are not about emotional regulation per se, but about relational strategy—how to stay attached, accepted, or invisible. These strategies are harder to detect because they are externally reinforced. But their function is no less protective, and their cost no less significant.

To ask what a habit was trying to solve is to honour the complexity of the human mind. It is to recognise that even our most confusing behaviours were born in service of something. They are not enemies to be eradicated, but strategies to be understood, updated, and, when necessary, retired. This perspective does not excuse harmful patterns, but it does explain them. And explanation is a prerequisite for integration. Without it, we remain trapped in loops of shame and resistance, trying to change without knowing what we are truly up against.

Change begins not when we declare war on a habit, but when we decode its function. Only then can we ask the right questions. What do I need now that this behaviour is trying to deliver? What safer, more effective ways can I meet that need? And what part of me still fears that letting go means being unprotected? These are not abstract reflections. They are the foundation of sustainable behavioural transformation—not because they make the habit disappear, but because they finally answer the question that was buried inside it all along.

From Coping to Controlling

One of the most paradoxical features of human behaviour is that the very strategies we once used to survive can become the structures that keep us stuck. Coping mechanisms, by definition, are adaptive. They emerge in response to overwhelm, scarcity, trauma, or emotional invalidation, and they serve a critical function: they help us reduce immediate pain. In the moment they arise, they are intelligent, creative, and efficient. They allow us to stay afloat in environments where our needs cannot be fully expressed, processed, or held by others. But coping has a shelf life. And when a strategy outlives the context that called it into being, it doesn't dissolve—it hardens. It becomes control.

Control, in this sense, is not limited to external rigidity or micromanagement. It refers to the internalisation of coping strategies as fixed identities and default behaviours—automatic, unconscious, and emotionally non-negotiable. What was once a flexible response to distress calcifies into a rule: *I must never be vulnerable. I must always be productive. I cannot trust anyone fully.* These internal commandments do not feel chosen; they feel like reality. And as the emotional logic behind the behaviour fades into the background, the behaviour itself remains, driven less by need and more by habit—less by adaptation and more by fear of relinquishing control.

This shift from coping to controlling is rarely conscious. It usually unfolds gradually, reinforced by a life that rewards outward competence, self-sufficiency, and emotional restraint. A child who learned to anticipate parental mood swings by becoming hyper-vigilant and pleasing may grow into an adult whose people-pleasing becomes chronic—driven not by generosity but by anxiety. The function has changed, but the behaviour persists. What once kept the child emotionally safe now traps the adult in cycles of resentment, burnout, or relational imbalance. The original context—the chaotic household, the unpredictable caregiver—is gone. But the coping strategy has been repurposed as a control strategy: *If I just meet everyone's needs, no one will abandon or criticise me.* That belief, though invisible, governs choices, boundaries, and self-concept.

This dynamic becomes even more entrenched when the strategy is socially validated. Controlling behaviours that mask as virtues—like perfectionism, over-responsibility, or stoicism—often escape scrutiny because they align with cultural ideals. A person who copes with inner chaos by becoming obsessively organised is praised for their discipline. Someone who manages relational anxiety by remaining emotionally distant is viewed as independent. The overachiever is admired; the hyper-rational thinker is seen as calm under pressure. But these are not always signs of wellbeing. Often, they are evidence of hyper-adapted nervous systems trying to hold themselves together in the absence of emotional safety. The problem is not that the strategy worked. It's that it *never got to retire.*

When coping becomes controlling, the nervous system is no longer responding to real-time input. It's operating on outdated templates. Control strategies rely on *prevention logic*: If I anticipate everything, I won't be surprised. If I never ask for help, I can't be let down. If I don't express how I feel, I won't be rejected. But prevention is not presence. It is not a response to the moment—it is a defence against the past repeating itself. And that defence, while once adaptive, becomes costly. It restricts emotional range, narrows relational authenticity, and undermines spontaneity. You don't get to feel peace; you get to feel *in control.* And often, they are mutually exclusive.

A particularly revealing expression of this transition is the loss of flexibility. Healthy coping is responsive—it adapts to different circumstances and evolves as needs change. Controlling behaviour, by contrast, is rigid. It insists on predictability, clings to routine, and resists ambiguity. It mistakes structure for safety. This rigidity is not characterological—it is protective. It signals that the person's internal world feels too volatile to risk improvisation. In such cases, even minor deviations from plan can provoke outsized distress. A cancelled meeting, an unexpected question, a hint of emotional intimacy—any of these can trigger a system primed to feel endangered by the unfamiliar.

Another marker is *emotional intolerance.* When coping becomes controlling, there is often a refusal—not just a difficulty, but a refusal—to engage with certain emotional states. Anger is shut down before it surfaces. Grief is minimised. Neediness is reframed as weakness. These are not mere preferences; they are learned constraints. Emotional suppression becomes an internal governance system. The controlling part says: *We don't do that here.* And because it has been protecting the psyche for so long, it is rarely challenged. The cost, however, is profound: when whole categories of feeling are exiled, the person becomes alienated not only from others, but from themselves.

Ironically, many people come to realise the cost of their control not through breakdown, but through success. The strategy worked—it brought achievement, order, social approval. But it didn't bring fulfilment. It didn't resolve the anxiety underneath. And eventually, the emotional suppression that sustained the strategy begins to crack. The person may find themselves overwhelmed by feelings they've long buried, confused by behaviours they thought they'd outgrown, or haunted by a chronic sense of flatness. These are not signs of regression. They are signs of the nervous system attempting to reclaim its full range. They are *the body saying: enough.*

The work, then, is not to discard the strategy outright. That would be destabilising and disrespectful to the part that created it. The work is to *contextualise* it—recognise when it arose, what it protected, how it helped, and where it no longer fits. That recognition requires nuance. The strategy may still be useful in certain domains. The high-functioning executive who manages stress through structured routines may benefit from that approach in work but suffer from it in intimacy. The insight lies in asking: *Where is this helping? Where is this hurting? And what am I afraid would happen if I did it differently?*

That last question is especially important. Control strategies are often powered by *catastrophic expectation.* The person doesn't merely believe that relinquishing control is uncomfortable—they believe it is *dangerous.* That belief is often rooted in real experiences: moments when vulnerability led to pain, openness led to betrayal, or stillness led to emotional abandonment. These are not imagined fears. They are memory-encoded truths. To shift the behaviour, then, is not just to change a habit. It is to challenge a belief system. And belief systems, especially those that kept us safe, do not collapse under pressure. They shift under *new evidence*—evidence that safety is now possible without the old defences.

Creating that evidence is a relational and emotional process. It often begins in spaces where vulnerability is met with attunement rather than dismissal. In therapy. In secure friendships. In moments of honest self-reflection. It also requires a new internal contract: to honour the original function of the coping strategy while making space for more nuanced, present-day responses. That might mean softening perfectionism without abandoning excellence. It might mean opening to intimacy while retaining discernment. The goal is not to dismantle the entire system, but to give it an update. To acknowledge that the conditions have changed—and therefore, the rules can, too.

Control is seductive because it offers the illusion of certainty. But emotional life is not a spreadsheet. It is dynamic, unpredictable, and relational. Coping strategies that demand total predictability will inevitably clash with reality. And when they do, the person faces a choice: double down on control, or begin the more difficult, more rewarding work of loosening their grip.

That loosening is not a betrayal of strength. It is a redefinition of it. True resilience is not the ability to hold everything together at all times—it is the capacity to stay present and responsive even when things fall apart. The person who can adapt, feel, and reconnect without defaulting to rigid control is not weak. They are integrated. They are whole. And that wholeness was never available through coping alone.

What begins as coping does not have to end in control. But the transition requires clarity. It requires the willingness to name where the old strategy helped, and where it now hinders. It requires emotional fluency, internal negotiation, and the slow cultivation of safety where fear once ruled. Only then can we stop living as though the past is still present—and begin to act as if we are safe enough to choose differently.

The Risk of Letting Go

Most people who seek change are not short on insight. They often know exactly what needs to shift. They can name the behaviour, map the pattern, articulate the cost. They can quote research, recall therapy sessions, and repeat mantras with impressive fluency. And yet, they remain stuck—held in place by a force more potent than logic: *fear*. Not fear of failure, as is commonly assumed, but fear of what will be lost if the old behaviour is relinquished. Letting go is not just a cognitive decision. It is an existential one. It confronts us with the terrifying ambiguity of who we become when we are no longer defined by our protective strategies.

This is not a theoretical concern. Emotional habits—especially those formed early—are deeply tied to identity. A person who has spent years coping through self-sacrifice may come to see themselves as generous, reliable, even morally superior. Their worth becomes synonymous with their usefulness. To stop overgiving is not just to shift behaviour; it is to risk being seen as selfish, expendable, or irrelevant. Similarly, someone who copes through perfectionism may fear that releasing control will expose them as incompetent or ordinary. The behaviour may be painful, but it offers something profoundly stabilising: a coherent sense of self.

This stabilising function is why many destructive patterns persist even when they are consciously disavowed. The part of the psyche that maintains them is not illogical—it is loyal. It believes, often rightly, that without the behaviour, the person may feel exposed, groundless, or emotionally unsafe. The suffering produced by the habit is weighed against the *threat of transformation*, and the latter often feels riskier. Not because the future is necessarily worse, but because it is *unknown*. The nervous system prioritises familiarity over flourishing. It does not ask what will help in the long term; it asks what will *hurt least* in this moment.

The concept of "secondary gain" in clinical psychology touches on this dynamic. It refers to the hidden benefits a person derives from a behaviour that appears self-defeating. These benefits are rarely conscious. They may include maintaining emotional distance in relationships, avoiding vulnerability, gaining sympathy, or preserving a specific social role. But the term itself can be misleading. It implies manipulation or dysfunction. In truth, the "gain" is usually survival. It is emotional containment. It is control in an otherwise uncontrollable world. When people hesitate to change, they are not clinging to suffering—they are clinging to the *structure* that suffering provides.

This is particularly relevant in cases of trauma, where coping strategies are often encoded as identity structures. A child who learned to stay silent during volatile arguments may grow into an adult who equates passivity with safety. Their self-concept may be deeply entwined with being accommodating, agreeable, non-threatening. To assert a need, to express anger, to stand one's ground—these are not simple behaviours to adopt. They are violations of the original survival script. The risk is not just rejection—it is annihilation of the known self. Change, in this context, does not feel empowering. It feels dangerous.

The same principle applies to high-functioning individuals who rely on hyper-competence to mask deep shame or fear of inadequacy. Their relentless drive is often applauded by society, which makes the habit harder to challenge. But underneath the success is a rigid bargain: *I am only acceptable if I am exceptional.* To slow down, to fail, to rest—these are not neutral choices. They threaten to unmask what the person believes will be revealed as deficiency. Letting go of the behaviour requires not just a change in action, but a radical revaluation of worth. And that revaluation cannot happen abstractly. It must be *felt*—relationally, emotionally, somatically. Until then, the habit remains the lesser evil.

This dynamic explains why even therapy, coaching, or insight-rich environments can fail to produce change. People do not resist change because they enjoy their patterns. They resist because the alternative requires a level of vulnerability they have not yet been resourced to tolerate. The nervous system does not respond to logic.

It responds to *felt safety*. And until the new behaviour is associated with safety—not just intellectually, but experientially—it will be rejected, no matter how sensible it appears.

This process is further complicated by the grief embedded in change. Letting go of a coping strategy often means acknowledging what it once protected you from—and, by extension, what you never received. The person who used food to regulate abandonment anxiety must face the original loneliness. The person who used control to manage chaos must confront how unsafe the world once felt. The person who used humour to deflect pain must sit with the rawness they've kept hidden. These are not just difficult emotions. They are foundational. They live in the architecture of the self. And they do not surface politely.

Letting go, then, is not merely about stopping. It is about *mourning*. It is about acknowledging the years spent in a particular strategy and honouring what it helped you survive. It is about grieving the self you had to become to feel okay—and the selves you never got to be. It is not uncommon for people on the brink of transformation to feel a strange emptiness, even as they move closer to what they say they want. That emptiness is the space where the old pattern once lived. It is not a sign that something is wrong. It is a sign that something is being released.

To move through this space requires not motivation, but containment. Motivation speaks to outcomes. Containment speaks to *capacity*—the ability to hold discomfort without collapse or reversion. Without containment, the nervous system interprets change as threat and regresses to familiar behaviours. This is not failure. It is unmetabolised fear. The solution is not more willpower. It is more *emotional architecture*—practices, relationships, environments, and narratives that support the self as it reshapes. Letting go without scaffolding is not courage; it is coercion.

One of the most disorienting aspects of change is that progress often feels like loss. As the old identity weakens, nothing immediately replaces it. The person is not yet who they are becoming, but no longer who they were. This liminal state is psychologically demanding. It can produce anxiety, fatigue, and existential questioning. *Who am I if I'm not this? What happens to my relationships if I change? What do I do with the pain that now has no container?* These are not detours—they are *core material.* And they must be engaged with compassion and precision.

The challenge is not just to let go, but to stay *present* as you do. The temptation is to rush—to adopt a new habit, identity, or role as quickly as possible. But integration cannot be fast-tracked. The nervous system needs repetition, consistency, and reassurance. This is not regression. It is calibration. The psyche is asking: *Is this new way of being safe? Will I still be loved? Can I survive the uncertainty?* When those questions are met with attunement—internally or interpersonally—real change becomes not only possible, but sustainable.

This is why many people do not change until they *must.* Not because they were lazy or unaware, but because the cost of the old strategy finally outweighs the fear of the new. It is a tipping point, not a choice. And even then, the shift is rarely linear. It is halting, fragile, and often accompanied by guilt, doubt, or sadness. These are not obstacles to change. They *are* the change—evidence that the emotional system is reorganising. If those feelings are met with self-judgment, the system retreats. If they are met with patience, something new begins to emerge—not just a new behaviour, but a new internal equilibrium.

Letting go is not just about relinquishing a harmful habit. It is about *trusting that who you are without it is enough.* That trust is not cultivated through discipline alone. It is built through small moments of risk and safety—speaking a truth and not being punished, expressing a need and having it met, resting without losing your value. Over time, these moments form a new map. They tell the nervous system: you are safe now. You do not have to grip so tightly. You are not that helpless child anymore.

What keeps people stuck is not ignorance. It is the unspoken belief that the cost of letting go is too high. That belief must be honoured, not argued with. Because underneath it is a story about survival—and only when that story is heard can it be updated. Letting go is a risk. But it is also a return: to a self that was never broken, only shaped. And once the shape is no longer needed, it can soften. Not because it was wrong. But because *you no longer need it to be right.*

Chapter 3
The Hidden Reward

Most attempts at behaviour change falter not because of a lack of motivation, but because we overlook what the existing behaviour provides. A habit that seems destructive rarely lacks purpose. It may be harmful, unsustainable, or misaligned with one's values, yet beneath that surface lies a framework—emotional, neurological, often relational—that has kept the pattern alive. We talk readily about addiction, procrastination, avoidance, or overconsumption, but far less often do we ask what these behaviours are actually protecting. The uncomfortable truth is that the behaviour we judge is often meeting a need we've never named. And when that need is ignored, any attempt to change the behaviour risks becoming an act of self-abandonment masquerading as self-discipline.

This chapter confronts a central paradox: we repeat what hurts us, not because we crave pain, but because pain wrapped in familiarity feels safer than freedom without a guarantee. There is always a reason someone reaches for wine, the screen, the silence, or an extra shift. These are not merely lapses in impulse control or moments of weakness. They are complex strategies to soothe, regulate, and orient ourselves—to meet needs that may remain entirely unconscious. Behaviour that seems irrational from the outside often follows a coherent emotional logic within.

To understand this logic, behaviour must be reframed as a response to an internal condition: unmet need. These needs are rarely extravagant; they form the scaffolding of psychological safety: the need to feel loved, understood, competent, seen, or capable of exerting agency. When these needs are chronically unmet, the psyche adapts. It finds workarounds—patterns that may later appear dysfunctional. But dysfunction is often the residue of adaptation, not evidence of disorder.

Habit reward cannot be comprehended in isolation from emotion. Too often, habit science defaults to dopamine, the shorthand for reinforcement. Yet the dopamine spike is merely a cue that something significant occurred. The real reward lies deeper—emotional resolution: relief, containment, a sense of belonging or control. Someone who lashes out after feeling dismissed may experience a fleeting sense of power or visibility; someone who remains silent in conflict may gain temporary safety. These are not ideal solutions, but they work—and that is why they endure.

Counterintuitively, the brain does not seek pleasure so much as predictability. Familiar discomfort often trumps unknown freedom. Neuroscience repeatedly demonstrates that the human nervous system favours the familiar, even when it is distressing. Known as "status quo bias," this tendency means the protective parts of the mind favour pain with a script over joy without guidance. Behaviour that once aided survival—even dysfunctionally—becomes encoded as the safe choice.

This explains why attempts at change can provoke intense emotional reactions. A person may resolve to stop overfunctioning in their family, only to experience panic, guilt, and intrusive thoughts. This is not irrational; it is predictive coding. The nervous system expects upheaval, having learned that deviation from established roles risks rejection or chaos. Overfunctioning may now be exhausting, but it has reliably preserved emotional order, even at personal cost.

Complicating matters, most of these reward structures remain invisible to the person enacting them. The binge, the scroll, the overwork is experienced as failure, not as a form of self-regulation. Enter shame: it obscures function and frames behaviour morally—What is wrong with me?—precisely when inquiry is most necessary. A more productive question is: What is this behaviour doing for me? And, crucially, what would I lose if I let it go?

The latter question exposes the hidden economy of unmet needs. People do not fear losing the behaviour itself—they fear losing the benefit: the emotional buffer, the illusion of control, the temporary relief. Take someone who repeatedly chooses emotionally unavailable partners. It appears irrational on the surface. Yet the hidden reward is clarity: distance preserves safety from engulfment, obligation, or being truly known—threats that may have felt unbearable in early relational experiences. Dysfunction, in other words, is often adaptive.

Attempting to remove these behaviours without addressing the underlying need triggers deficit in the nervous system. Relapse is common—not due to lack of commitment, but because the mechanism of emotional regulation has been stripped without replacement. The system reverts to what it knows. This is not regression; it is the natural consequence of subtraction without substitution. Change is not too hard; need is too strong to ignore.

The consequences of unmet need are subtle yet persistent. People may become irritable, disengaged, chronically fatigued, or numb. Progress may feel destabilising, precisely because it removes a coping mechanism before a replacement exists. The hidden cost of change without emotional fluency is often invisible but profound.

The solution is not to romanticise harmful behaviours but to approach them with respectful precision. Identify what the behaviour regulates, what threat it mitigates, what story it sustains. Is it offering control in a chaotic environment? Shielding from vulnerability? Damping emotions not yet processed? These are diagnostic questions for emotional mapping.

Once the core need is identified, structures can be built to meet it sustainably. Integration requires more than stopping behaviour; it requires replacing the reward. Safety may be restored through ritual, predictability, or grounding practices. Visibility may be cultivated through creative expression or authentic dialogue. Control may be managed through agency over one's schedule or environment. These are not lifestyle hacks; they are scaffolds for emotional containment.

The work, then, is not punitive. It is to dissolve the necessity of the behaviour by meeting the need it once compensated for. Change becomes durable when the nervous system learns that need can be fulfilled in a new way. This process is slow, relational, and non-linear—but it is the only route that does not rely on suppression or force.

This chapter navigates that terrain. Habits are examined not as problems, but as strategies with hidden architecture. You will see why the familiar feels compelling even when painful, distinguish surface payoffs from deeper emotional functions, and understand the consequences of unmet need—not as moral failure, but as a system responding to deprivation. By chapter's end, behaviours may not yet appear different—but they will make more sense. In the landscape of change, that is the crucial first step.

The Behaviour You Judge, the Need You Ignore

Most people misunderstand their worst habits. They believe they're acting against their own interests, betraying their values, or succumbing to weakness. In reality, they're negotiating with unmet needs—needs that have learned to speak the only language they were allowed. When someone lashes out, shuts down, binge eats, overworks, or emotionally withdraws, they're not trying to sabotage themselves. They're attempting to *solve something*—something that hasn't been spoken, perhaps even understood. The tragedy is that in judging the behaviour, we almost always miss the need it's trying to meet.

This is the blind spot of both popular self-help and performance psychology: the tendency to treat behaviour as if it exists in a vacuum. We isolate the action—procrastination, avoidance, reactivity—and focus on how to remove it or replace it. But behaviours don't arise in a vacuum. They arise in context, and they survive because they *work*. Maybe not rationally. Maybe not long-term. But emotionally, in the moment they're chosen, they offer something. *Relief. Control. Soothing. Escape. Connection.* Until we understand what that "something" is, any effort to change the behaviour risks becoming a form of internal violence—tearing down a structure without understanding what it was holding up.

The needs behind our destructive behaviours are not extravagant. They're profoundly ordinary—foundational to human development and stability. The need to feel safe. The need to feel in control. The need to belong. The need to feel real in another's eyes. The need to not be overwhelmed. The need to express pain without being punished. These are not signs of weakness. They are signs of life.

But when those needs are unmet or consistently violated—by trauma, neglect, shaming environments, or relational instability—they don't disappear. They go underground. And from there, they begin to drive behaviour from behind the curtain.

Take emotional eating, for instance. The behaviour is often framed as gluttony, lack of control, or addiction. But when unpacked, it frequently reveals a need for comfort, self-soothing, or momentary relief from shame. The food isn't the problem; the problem is *what the person had to learn to tolerate without help*. Similarly, the person who constantly interrupts or dominates conversations may not be egotistical—they may be seeking a felt sense of visibility after a lifetime of being emotionally sidelined. What appears as rudeness is actually an urgent protest against invisibility. Again and again, what looks irrational from the outside makes emotional sense when traced to its origin.

The mind is skilled at disguising needs as traits. Someone who always takes on more than they can manage may be seen as ambitious or driven. But dig deeper, and you often find a compulsion powered by fear: *If I stop achieving, I'll stop mattering.* The external behaviour gets rewarded—praise, promotions, admiration—while the underlying need goes ignored. Over time, the individual may become so identified with the behaviour that they lose the ability to distinguish it from who they are. The self becomes the strategy. And when that strategy starts to break down—burnout, resentment, physical illness—they are left not only depleted, but disoriented. Because what they've lost isn't just a habit. It's the scaffolding of their worth.

Understanding behaviour through the lens of need is not an excuse. It's a recalibration. It allows us to engage with habits, not as symptoms of a broken self, but as messages from a system trying to regulate itself without adequate resources. The person who procrastinates isn't necessarily lazy. They may be overwhelmed by an internal expectation of perfection—paralysed by the belief that anything less than flawless will invite rejection or ridicule. The procrastination, then, is an avoidance of *pain*, not an avoidance of effort. But without naming the emotional need for safety and reassurance, we target the wrong layer. We slap on time-blocking systems and focus apps without ever asking *What part of you is scared to begin?*

This shift in framing also helps explain why habits resist change. When a behaviour is meeting an emotional need, even dysfunctionally, the system protects it. The nervous system doesn't prioritise success—it prioritises familiarity and survival. If a behaviour—no matter how self-defeating it looks—keeps a person regulated, it becomes fused with safety. And until that underlying need is met in another way, the system won't release the behaviour, no matter how much insight or intention is applied. You can't shame or discipline a habit out of existence when it's doing the emotional labour your environment never did.

This is especially true in relational dynamics. Consider someone who habitually avoids conflict. They may appear passive, evasive, or disengaged. But often, the underlying need is safety—psychological or even physical. In their past, expressing anger may have led to violence, abandonment, or being emotionally iced out. Avoidance becomes a protective reflex. To stop avoiding would require the belief that anger is safe and connection won't be withdrawn. Until that belief is tested and confirmed in real relationships, the avoidance won't yield. And it shouldn't—because to the inner system, it's still the best available protection.

The core problem is not the behaviour. It's the disconnection between the behaviour and the *need it was built to serve.* As long as that need remains unnamed, the behaviour becomes both compulsive and misinterpreted. We fight the behaviour instead of feeding the need. And in doing so, we create internal conflict: one part of us pushing for change, another part resisting for survival. This creates a cycle of shame and sabotage—trying harder, failing again, feeling worse, and doubling down on the same pattern. All the while, the original need remains untouched.

Naming the need does not instantly dissolve the behaviour. But it reframes the project. Instead of self-improvement, it becomes self-integration. You stop asking *How do I fix this?* and start asking *What's missing that this behaviour is trying to supply?* This shift invites compassion without complacency. It creates a space in which the self can be both held and challenged—where you can honour the intelligence of your adaptations while building more sustainable ways to meet your emotional requirements.

Of course, many people struggle to identify their underlying needs, especially if they were raised in environments that discouraged emotional awareness. If your needs were ridiculed, pathologised, or ignored, you may have learned to bury them. But buried is not gone. Needs are not optional. When they aren't expressed through language, they are expressed through behaviour—often destructively. The body keeps asking, through symptoms, compulsions, addictions, or shutdowns. And until those needs are brought into conscious awareness, behaviour remains the only way they know how to speak.

To move from judgement to understanding, we must develop emotional granularity—the ability to name not just what we're doing, but *what we're needing.* That might be safety, control, rest, recognition, connection, autonomy, or expression. The more precisely we name the need, the more accurately we can address it. And the more accurately we address it, the less we rely on behaviours that once stood in for the care we didn't receive. This is how change happens—not from pressure, but from *precision.*

Ultimately, the behaviours we judge most harshly are often the ones that once protected us the most. They carry the imprint of what we learned to do when our needs weren't being met directly. That doesn't mean they should run our lives forever. But it does mean they deserve to be understood before they are changed. Because beneath the coping is a human need. And beneath the need is a person who deserves to have it met. Not in secret. Not through sabotage. But with clarity, dignity, and choice.

Comfort in the Familiar

The brain does not crave pleasure nearly as much as it craves predictability. While we are evolutionarily wired to seek reward, our deeper neurological imperative is to reduce uncertainty. The brain is a prediction machine—not just in the cognitive sense of anticipating outcomes, but in the deeper, embodied sense of sustaining coherence across time. From this perspective, it becomes easier to understand why people cling to patterns that actively harm them. Why someone stays in an emotionally draining job, returns to a toxic relationship, or continues habits they've vowed to quit. The explanation lies not in a lack of discipline or desire, but in the brain's preference for *known discomforts over unknown freedoms*.

This principle sits at the heart of behavioural neuroscience: the familiar is neurologically stabilising, even when it's emotionally dysregulating. It provides a sense of control, of continuity. And the neural architecture that supports this is the habit loop—a mechanism that, once encoded, functions largely outside of conscious awareness. Every habit has a cue, a routine, and a reward. But crucially, in many destructive patterns, the "reward" is not pleasure—it's *relief*. A momentary drop in tension, a slight return to coherence, a shift away from overwhelm. This distinction is subtle, but it changes everything. If the brain has to choose between a predictable coping mechanism that brings relief and a novel behaviour that promises long-term growth but no immediate familiarity, it will choose the former. Every time.

To understand why, we must look at the basal ganglia, the brain structure central to habit formation. Once a behaviour is repeated enough times in response to a consistent cue and delivers a predictable outcome, it becomes routinised. The brain then stores this behavioural sequence as a kind of default script. This allows the cortex—the brain's centre of executive function and conscious decision-making—to conserve energy. Habits are metabolically efficient. They reduce cognitive load. They are, in effect, neurological shortcuts designed to increase survival by decreasing the need for constant deliberation.

But here's the rub: the brain encodes behaviours based on *efficacy*, not morality. It doesn't ask whether a behaviour is good for your long-term wellbeing. It asks only: *Does this reliably reduce discomfort?* If the answer is yes, the habit is reinforced. Over time, this reinforcement becomes so automatic that even when a person consciously rejects the behaviour, their body pulls them towards it. This is the tug of war so many people feel when they say, *I know this isn't good for me, but I can't stop doing it.* What they're describing is not a moral failing. It is a conflict between cortical intention and subcortical automation.

This conflict is magnified when the familiar behaviour serves an emotional regulation function. For instance, someone who habitually overworks may say they're driven by ambition, but under the surface, the pattern often functions as a way to avoid internal stillness—which might evoke feelings of inadequacy, loneliness, or anxiety. The work, however unsustainable, becomes a buffer. It occupies the space that would otherwise be filled by emotional content the person doesn't yet know how to hold. This is the hidden reward: not advancement, but *avoidance.* And avoidance, while costly, is familiar. It follows a script. It confirms what the person already believes about themselves and the world.

This is also why freedom can feel threatening. A person who has always coped through control—be it through dieting, rigid routines, or emotional detachment—may consciously desire spontaneity, intimacy, or rest. But when presented with the opportunity to experience those states, they recoil. Not because they don't want them, but because those states represent *unmapped terrain.* The nervous system has no script for them. And the brain does not interpret this as opportunity—it interprets it as threat. Novelty, in the absence of safety, triggers stress.

The amygdala, the brain's threat detection centre, plays a central role here. It doesn't distinguish between physical and psychological danger. It simply flags uncertainty as something to be cautious of. And because habits provide a buffer against uncertainty, they are inherently reassuring. Even if the habit results in pain, that pain is *known.* It's coded into the person's identity. They know how to manage it, narrate it, make sense of it. This is why people often describe dysfunctional patterns in strangely affectionate terms: *That part of me kept me alive. It got me through.* The discomfort is not just tolerated—it's *trusted.*

This trust in discomfort is reinforced socially and culturally. In environments where vulnerability is pathologised or success is idealised, habits that prioritise control and suppression are often rewarded. The person who copes by staying emotionally distant is praised for being stoic. The one who copes through perfectionism is called high-achieving. The one who copes through hyper-independence is seen as resilient. These habits become socially sanctioned identities, making them even harder to challenge. Letting them go is not just a neurological shift—it's a relational risk. The person doesn't just fear change. They fear disconnection.

Moreover, many people have internalised a model of safety that is built around *familiar pain.* If your earliest experiences taught you that love comes with emotional inconsistency, that success demands self-erasure, or that asking for help leads to humiliation, those patterns become your baseline. And your brain, committed to maintaining coherence, will seek to reproduce them. Not because they feel good, but because they feel *normal.* In this context, healing can feel like disloyalty—to the family system, to the self you had to become, to the identity that gave you structure.

This is why behaviour change must be understood not just through the lens of motivation or discipline, but through the lens of *safety.* Change isn't hard because it's unfamiliar. It's hard because the unfamiliar feels unsafe. And until safety is redefined—not as sameness, but as *resourced novelty*—the brain will retreat into what it knows. This is not stubbornness. It is neurobiology.

The path forward is not to shame the brain's preference for familiarity, but to work with it. This means building what researchers call "predictable novelty"—introducing new behaviours in consistent contexts, so the nervous system can encode them as safe. It means creating emotional rituals around change, so the unfamiliar becomes scaffolded by relational or sensory cues. It means learning to sit with the discomfort of not knowing—not as a flaw, but as a developmental threshold.

It also means reinterpreting resistance not as a sign of failure, but as a sign of intelligent adaptation. The person who keeps going back to the old pattern isn't failing to evolve. They are *doing exactly what their brain believes will keep them safe.* That belief must be engaged, not overridden. Because only when the nervous system *feels* that the new path is safe will it release the old one. And that feeling doesn't come from logic. It comes from repetition, resonance, and relational trust.

The real challenge, then, is not to break the habit, but to *update the story* the habit was telling. The story that says discomfort is safer than change. That old pain is preferable to new possibility. That the self, to be secure, must remain unchanged. This narrative is deeply embedded—not just in our brains, but in our bodies, our relationships, our sense of identity. To shift it requires not just intention, but precision. Not just willpower, but *emotional fluency.*

Comfort in the familiar is not weakness. It is survival logic. But survival is not the same as living. And when the cost of safety becomes the erosion of vitality, something deeper must be reckoned with. The nervous system will always choose what it knows—until it knows something better. The task, then, is not to demand change, but to *make safety bigger than the habit.* Only then does the familiar lose its grip. Not through force, but through obsolescence. Because once the system learns that something else works, it stops reaching for what once did.

The Reward Is Not What You Think

The behaviour you're trying to stop might not feel good, but it almost certainly *does* something. And that "something" is where the real reward lives—not in the fleeting chemical hit, but in the emotional architecture that behaviour supports. Too often, change efforts fail because people target the surface-level reinforcement—the dopamine spike—while completely overlooking the *underlying emotional resolution* the behaviour provides. But unless that deeper reward is identified and addressed, the nervous system will continue to demand it, even as the mind insists it's time to move on.

To understand this tension, we must first dismantle a common misrepresentation of how habits work. Much of the popular literature on behaviour change fixates on dopamine—as if every habit, good or bad, begins and ends with a chemical reward loop. While it's true that dopamine plays a key role in reinforcing behaviour, the story is more complex. Dopamine is not pleasure; it is *prediction*. It signals to the brain that a certain cue led to a certain outcome, which might be worth repeating. It's a flag for potential importance, not a confirmation of satisfaction. This distinction matters, because it reveals how easily our internal systems can become miscalibrated—pursuing momentary relief rather than true resolution.

The most persistent behaviours are often those that resolve something emotionally, not merely chemically. Consider the person who chronically overcommits. The immediate reward may look like social approval or a feeling of accomplishment, but underneath lies a deeper payoff: the avoidance of guilt, rejection, or the terror of seeming dispensable. In another example, the individual who scrolls compulsively at night may appear to be chasing distraction or entertainment, but the true reward is likely the brief suspension of internal pressure—the dissolution of responsibility, however fleeting. These aren't dopamine-driven decisions in the reductive sense; they are *emotionally stabilising rituals*. The chemical cue only reflects a deeper need being momentarily acknowledged.

This principle reframes the core question in behaviour change from *What am I getting out of this?* to *What am I trying to solve through this?* That shift moves the conversation out of behavioural economics and into emotional intelligence. Because while the surface-level reward may be a temporary high, the *functional reward* is relief: from shame, from disconnection, from overwhelm, from the sense of being too much or not enough. That relief may last seconds, but if it consistently returns the person to an emotional baseline they've been trained to crave, the habit will stay alive—regardless of its external consequences.

The challenge, then, is not simply to resist the behaviour, but to deconstruct the *emotional contract* it upholds. Every entrenched habit says something like this: *When I feel X, I do Y, because it makes me feel a little less broken.* These contracts often form early. A child who learns that emotional needs are met with criticism may find ways to self-soothe through food, control, withdrawal, or people-pleasing. As that child grows up, the surface of the behaviour changes, but its core reward remains consistent: *I do this because it makes me feel safe, in control, invisible, acceptable.* The specifics differ. The logic does not.

This explains why some habits feel so irrational to the outside observer. The person who repeatedly returns to toxic relationships may, on the surface, appear unaware or self-destructive. But internally, the behaviour may be meeting a vital need: the need for familiarity, or the need to re-enact a dynamic that once defined love. The emotional reward is coherence—however painful it may be. The nervous system is not chasing pleasure. It is chasing *predictability*. And in the absence of conscious intervention, it will continue to choose what it recognises over what might actually heal.

To interrupt this cycle, precision is required. We must identify not just what the behaviour does, but what it *represents*. This means going beyond symptom management into symbolic decoding. For instance, someone who procrastinates might assume the behaviour is laziness, or a fear of failure. But if the behaviour is mapped with care, the core reward might be something entirely different: protection from exposure, preservation of autonomy, or a way to reclaim time in an otherwise controlled life. The procrastination is not about the task—it's about the *meaning* of doing the task. Unless that meaning is addressed, all the time-management strategies in the world will fall flat.

This is where many change models collapse under their own simplicity. They assume that removing the behaviour is enough. But a vacuum is rarely tolerable. If the underlying need remains unmet, the system will find another way to meet it—often by creating a new behaviour with a similar emotional signature. This is the cycle of "symptom substitution": one addiction becomes another, one avoidance strategy morphs into a different distraction. Without identifying the true reward, we never actually change—we just *rebrand* the habit.

To change behaviour at the root level, we must answer two deceptively complex questions: *What does this behaviour protect me from?* and *What need does it try to meet—however poorly?* These questions invite honesty, not just about pain, but about *pleasure*—or more accurately, the pleasures we are ashamed to admit. The pleasure of control. The pleasure of being right. The pleasure of zoning out. These are not immoral. They are intelligible responses to overwhelming conditions. But until we stop moralising them, we can't transform them. Because what we moralise, we suppress. And what we suppress, we repeat.

Understanding the emotional reward also allows for a more humane approach to relapse. When someone returns to an old pattern, the assumption is often that they're weak or undisciplined. But relapse is frequently the result of an *unmet need reasserting itself*. The person didn't just slip—they lost access to the strategy that was holding something in place. If the behaviour is the only mechanism the nervous system has for managing a particular emotion, it will return. Not out of defiance, but out of *necessity*. Change that ignores this will be fragile. Change that incorporates it becomes resilient.

So how do we meet the underlying need differently? The answer is not to seek a perfect replacement, but to *broaden the nervous system's library of options*. If a habit has been the only way you've known to self-soothe, then the first step is not elimination, but expansion. What else helps you feel safe, in control, seen, soothed, or stable? These alternatives must not only be intellectually satisfying—they must be *emotionally believable*. That believability comes through repetition and trust. And until the new reward is neurologically and emotionally encoded, the old one will feel more compelling, even if it's more damaging.

This is why sustainable change is slow. It requires more than insight. It demands the cultivation of new rituals, the building of new associations, the testing of new narratives. It is not just a rewiring of behaviour—it is a *revision of what safety and satisfaction mean*. And that revision cannot happen in abstraction. It must be lived, often awkwardly, often inconsistently, but with increasing fidelity to a new internal logic: *I can meet this need without betraying myself*.

The reward is not what you think. It is not the buzz, the high, the laugh, or the rush. It is the sense—however faint—that something inside you has been temporarily soothed, stabilised, or made bearable. Once you recognise this, the conversation around change transforms. You stop asking, *Why can't I stop doing this?* and begin asking, *What part of me still needs what this gives me?* That question is not just a key to behavioural insight. It is the beginning of emotional integration. And only through that integration can we replace compulsion with choice—not by removing the reward, but by learning to seek it in ways that honour both our need and our growth.

What Happens When the Need Goes Unmet

Removing a destructive behaviour without understanding—and replacing—the emotional function it serves is not just ineffective; it's destabilising. What appears on the surface as a habit—drinking, scrolling, overeating, avoiding, overachieving—is, more often than not, a carefully wired system of emotional regulation. These behaviours do not exist in isolation; they exist in relation to the needs they soothe, conceal, or negotiate. Take away the behaviour without addressing the underlying need, and you don't get freedom. You get fallout: resentment, fatigue, panic, and an unspoken sense that something vital has gone missing. Not because the behaviour was good, but because it was *doing something essential.*

This is the quiet failure of many change models—especially those that equate success with abstinence, discipline, or willpower. The assumption is that if a person stops the "bad" behaviour, the problem has been solved. But in truth, behaviour is only the visible expression of a hidden calculus. Beneath the act lies an emotional contract: *I do this because it helps me manage something I haven't learned to face directly.* Break that contract without renegotiating the terms, and the system doesn't heal—it revolts.

Consider someone who uses food to self-soothe. Perhaps it's late at night, after a day of managing everyone else's needs, suppressing difficult conversations, and navigating silent shame. The person knows the habit isn't ideal. They've read about intuitive eating, tried fasting apps, followed nutrition influencers. And for a time, they might stop. They might assert control, set boundaries, "take charge." But if nothing replaces the original comfort the behaviour provided—if there's no new mechanism for self-nurturance, containment, or recognition—then the body rebels. Cravings intensify. Irritability spikes. Emotional volatility creeps in. And when they inevitably "slip," they don't just experience guilt. They experience *confirmation* of failure. But it's not a failure of effort. It's a failure of substitution. The need was never met. It was simply silenced.

This principle holds across domains. A high-functioning individual who drops their perfectionistic tendencies might initially feel lighter, more relaxed. But if their perfectionism was serving as a buffer against childhood chaos or internalised shame, removing it without offering a new form of safety quickly backfires. The emotional tension reemerges, unfiltered. And without the scaffolding of their old strategy, they feel raw, exposed, and emotionally disorganised. In such cases, relapse is not regression—it is *rescue*. The system returns to the behaviour not out of weakness, but out of necessity. Because the alternative is psychological collapse.

When emotional needs are not met—especially those that were never met consistently during development—the nervous system does not remain neutral. It shifts into survival mode. Depending on the person's relational and psychological history, this might manifest as resentment (the internal protest of unmet autonomy or recognition), fatigue (the physiological exhaustion of prolonged self-monitoring), or panic (the acute activation of the body's threat detection system when safety is withdrawn). These reactions are not overreactions. They are proportional to the unmet need's significance.

Resentment, in particular, is one of the clearest indicators that a behaviour change has failed to honour an emotional need. A person may say yes to fewer commitments, set boundaries more often, or become more assertive in relationships. But if those shifts are not paired with genuine inner permission—to rest, to prioritise self, to tolerate disappointment—resentment builds. Not because the boundaries are wrong, but because the emotional cost of maintaining them has not been properly processed. The need for respect or reciprocity remains unmet, and so the change becomes performative rather than transformative.

Fatigue is another common consequence. When a behaviour is removed without a replacement, the brain must work overtime to regulate emotional and physiological states without its usual shortcuts. This demands significant energy. The prefrontal cortex, responsible for conscious decision-making, has to stay online far longer than it's built for. This is why early stages of behaviour change often feel exhausting. But when that fatigue is paired with unmet need, the person doesn't just feel tired—they feel *depleted*, emotionally anaemic. The behaviour used to deliver quick access to relief. Without it, everything feels harder.

And then there is panic. Not the kind that always registers as an acute anxiety attack, but the more subtle version—an internal jitteriness, an inability to settle, an exaggerated sense of urgency or danger when confronted with ordinary stimuli. This is the body's protest against unmet regulation. If the removed behaviour once helped to down-regulate stress, signal safety, or provide a sense of control, its absence creates an internal void. The amygdala, hypersensitive to patterns of deprivation or emotional abandonment, begins to overfire. What was once a strategy to maintain equilibrium has now become a destabilising absence.

One of the great misunderstandings in behaviour change discourse is the idea that eliminating a bad habit creates a neutral baseline. It doesn't. It creates a *deficit*—unless the emotional function of the behaviour is explicitly acknowledged and directly addressed. This is why traditional behaviourism, while effective for short-term habit training, often fails at deeper emotional rewiring. It measures success through visible outputs—how often the behaviour occurs—without tracking what's happening *internally* when the behaviour is withdrawn.

Change is not just about stopping. It is about *reallocating*. The need doesn't disappear because the behaviour does. And if that need remains unmet, it will find a way to speak—through mood, through impulse, through relational rupture. The system is wise in this way. It refuses to be ignored.

The solution is not to cling to the behaviour or to fear change, but to engage in what psychologists call "functional replacement." This means identifying the *precise* emotional or relational need the behaviour was meeting—however imperfectly—and crafting a new method of addressing that need directly. If the old habit was regulating anxiety, what practices, people, or environments can now provide containment? If it was securing connection, how can that connection be sought more consciously, more sustainably? If it was providing a sense of control, where else can control be grounded in real agency rather than symbolic ritual?

This requires slowing down the change process, not rushing it. It demands not just awareness, but experimentation—testing new ways of meeting old needs until the nervous system begins to trust them. Because trust is not built through insight. It is built through *consistency*. The body learns safety by repetition. And until the new behaviour proves itself emotionally credible, the old one will remain more compelling—even if it's simultaneously self-destructive.

It also requires emotional honesty. Many people are ashamed of what their behaviour does for them. They don't want to admit they need soothing, or control, or reassurance, or to feel powerful. But those needs are not shameful. They are *human*. Naming them doesn't make you weak. It makes you capable of choosing a strategy that meets the need without harming the self. That's not indulgence. It's *maturity*.

To change a behaviour sustainably, the need it served must be respected—not demonised, not dismissed, not bypassed. Because when a need goes unmet, the behaviour it was tethered to becomes more than a habit. It becomes a placeholder for something vital. And when you remove that placeholder without care, what follows is not freedom, but fallout. The key is not to fear this fallout, but to use it as feedback. It's telling you something essential: *The body still remembers what it's waiting for.* The task, then, is not to suppress that message, but to finally respond to it. Not with control, but with care. Not with shame, but with precision. Not with force, but with the kind of insight that dares to ask, *What was I really trying to get from this? And how can I offer it to myself—fully, finally, and without compromise?*

Chapter 4
Shame: The Lock on the Chain

Shame is rarely just an unpleasant feeling; it operates as a quietly formidable organising principle. It does not simply visit the psyche in passing; it rewires it, subtly sculpting how we perceive our actions, our relationships, and ultimately, our sense of worth. It is intensely private, yet deeply conditioned by social expectation. Unlike guilt, which murmurs I did something wrong, shame asserts—sometimes shouts—I am wrong. This distinction is not trivial. It is structural. Where guilt can guide repair, shame ensnares, driving secrecy, paralysis, or self-punishment. Within the context of behaviour change, shame rarely encourages growth; it fosters fear, and fear discourages trying.

The influence of shame on entrenched habits is often misinterpreted or overlooked entirely. Conventional frameworks treat it as a moral compass or a motivational device, as if sufficient self-reproach could compel behavioural cessation. In reality, the dynamic is far more insidious. Shame fuels the very actions it condemns. Someone drinks to quiet self-loathing, only to awaken to intensified self-hatred. Another withdraws from intimacy, convinced they are too broken, then chastises themselves for emotional unavailability. The behaviour generates shame, and shame perpetuates the behaviour—a feedback loop airtight in its logic. Shame punishes the crime it creates.

This recursive structure is what makes shame so resistant to interruption. It acts simultaneously as trigger and consequence. Unlike anger or sadness, which typically move through the body when acknowledged, shame lingers. It is quiet, but vigilant, shaping posture, tone, and inner dialogue: I'm such a mess. I always screw up. I'm just not built for this. These utterances are not confessions of accountability—they are admissions of internal collapse. And for many, that collapse begins early, before language or insight can name it. In high-pressure, punitive, or emotionally inconsistent environments, shame becomes the default survival strategy. It offers a semblance of coherence: If I feel unloved, it must be because I am unlovable. The logic is flawed, but emotionally economical.

By adulthood, this economy is entrenched. Shame has become not merely a feeling, but an identity. When that identity is challenged—by success, compassion, intimacy, or even rest—the system reacts with suspicion. Self-compassion, seemingly straightforward, often feels hazardous to those most in need of it. For someone raised where love was conditional or achievement never sufficient, gentleness with oneself can trigger anxiety rather than relief. Shame is not merely an emotion to be overcome; for many, it is the scaffold of selfhood. Remove it hastily, and the psyche does not feel liberated—it feels untethered.

This is precisely why shame must be recognised as an adaptive strategy, not a character flaw. Its function is inhibitory: it curtails expression, need, exposure. It shields the system from humiliation, rejection, and the pain of unmet longing. In doing so, however, it blocks access to authenticity, connection, and healing. Shame silences grief, transmutes vulnerability into perceived weakness, and exiles emotions: neediness becomes childish, anger dangerous, envy disgusting. The result is fragmentation—managing the self, rather than meeting the self.

Clinically, shame often operates as a secondary emotion, a protective veneer over primary feelings. Deep sadness at exclusion is intercepted by self-contempt: No wonder they didn't invite me; I'm annoying. Envy of a friend's success is masked as disgust: I shouldn't feel this way; I'm pathetic. Shame amplifies suffering while obscuring its source, confusing the emotional data—the longing, pain, and desire—that could otherwise guide resolution.

The camouflage of shame is especially obstructive in behaviour change. Progress may occur—boundaries set, compulsions reduced, autonomy exercised—yet the individual feels little reward. Instead arises guilt for perceived selfishness, fear of losing control, or anxiety about being "too much." These responses do not necessarily indicate a problem; they signal that the shame system has been disrupted. Like any threatened system, it resists.

This resistance often manifests as a shame spiral. A perceived misstep triggers shame, which is then outrun through distraction, overcompensation, or deeper self-criticism. A momentary lapse escalates into a sweeping self-condemnation: this is not merely a bad day; I am a bad person. Prolonged spirals desensitise the nervous system to feedback; even therapeutic insight or praise is deflected. Shame metabolises evidence of failure, not guidance.

What is required is precision, not more critique. Shame cannot be countered with vague affirmation. It must be approached with differentiation: What am I actually feeling? What am I protecting myself from? Whose voice is embedded in this judgment? What does this story omit? These are practical tools, allowing the self to distinguish internalised shame from legitimate accountability, defensive habit from authentic value.

Interrupting shame does not mean eradicating it. It involves conscious presence, supported by both cognitive reappraisal and somatic awareness. Shame resides in the body—in the lowered gaze, tensed shoulders, constricted breath. Recognising these cues is resistance; naming them is acknowledgement; choosing not to collapse under them is agency. This triad—notice, name, choose—operates as a form of reparenting, signalling to the nervous system that distressing feelings can be tolerated without dictating action.

The goal of this chapter is not to eliminate shame, but to disentangle it from identity and behaviour. To illuminate how it functions as both lock and chain—maintaining toxic patterns by convincing us they are unavoidable—and to invite a nuanced engagement: shame as signal, with history, function, and alternatives. When shame loses its monopoly on meaning, options emerge. Taken seriously—not as platitudes but as viable pathways—these options render genuine change not only possible, but inevitable.

The Double Trap of Shame

Shame does not simply whisper that something is wrong—it declares that *you* are what is wrong. And unlike guilt, which invites repair, shame demands silence, self-monitoring, and withdrawal. It does not aim to make you better; it convinces you that you already are worse. But its influence doesn't stop at internal judgment. Shame also becomes the architect of behaviour. It drives patterns of hiding, appeasing, controlling, or self-sabotaging—only to then punish the self for engaging in those very patterns. This is the double trap of shame: it fuels the actions it later condemns, locking people into cycles they don't know how to exit.

At first glance, shame seems like an emotional by-product—something that arises *after* a perceived failure or social misstep. But functionally, shame often acts as a *driver*, setting into motion the very behaviours that later reinforce it. Take, for example, the person who overeats in secret. The act is not simply impulsive—it often begins with an internal narrative of inadequacy, loneliness, or stress. Eating becomes a coping mechanism, a short-term form of comfort or self-soothing. But once the moment has passed, shame floods in. *Why did I do that again? I have no control. I'm disgusting.* This cascade doesn't lead to change. It leads to a renewed sense of internal disgust, which in turn increases emotional stress—making the next binge more likely. The original action wasn't born of indulgence; it was born of pain. But that pain is compounded by shame until it becomes unbearable.

This feedback loop is not exclusive to food. It exists in the perfectionist who procrastinates on a project for fear it won't be good enough, then shames themselves for "being lazy." It lives in the person who lashes out at a partner, then retreats into self-loathing rather than repair. It fuels the overachiever who says yes to everything, only to resent themselves for never resting. In each case, shame plays two roles: the instigator and the judge. And because both roles operate internally, they remain largely unchallenged.

Part of what makes shame so insidious is that it presents itself as self-awareness. A person caught in this cycle might believe they're being "realistic," "disciplined," or "hard on themselves because they care." But underneath this narrative is a misunderstanding of how change actually works. Shame does not enhance self-regulation. It disrupts it. Neurobiologically, shame activates the same areas of the brain associated with physical pain and social exclusion. It heightens stress responses, narrows perspective, and reduces access to the prefrontal cortex—the very part of the brain needed for reflection, decision-making, and behavioural adjustment. When someone is steeped in shame, they are not learning. They are bracing.

This bracing state is deeply familiar to those who grew up in emotionally volatile, high-pressure, or invalidating environments. For them, shame often became a survival strategy. Criticise yourself before someone else can. Keep your feelings small so they won't be used against you. Push yourself harder because anything less invites disappointment. These adaptive strategies may have served a protective function in childhood, but when carried into adulthood, they begin to implode. The inner critic becomes a constant saboteur. The fear of being exposed becomes a barrier to intimacy. The compulsion to prove oneself erodes any sense of internal rest. And the shame that once shielded now suffocates.

Crucially, the double trap of shame thrives on the illusion of control. It offers the fantasy that if you just shame yourself enough, you'll finally behave differently. That if you punish yourself harshly enough, you'll prevent future mistakes. But the opposite is true. Shame doesn't prevent transgressions—it preconditions them. By turning internal experience into evidence of failure, it reduces the capacity to regulate those experiences. The more you feel bad, the more shame interprets it as proof of your unworthiness. This circular logic makes it nearly impossible to intervene without precision.

What complicates this even further is how shame masks itself as moral conscience. It mimics the voice of accountability, but it does not offer the same outcomes. Accountability focuses on actions and their consequences. Shame collapses actions into identity. Accountability says, *I made a poor choice—what can I learn?* Shame says, *I am a poor choice—why would I even try?* This distinction is not just semantic—it is predictive. People who can distinguish shame from accountability are more likely to change their behaviour. People who conflate the two are more likely to stay stuck.

And so the trap tightens. The person begins to anticipate shame before any mistake has occurred. They avoid opportunities, relationships, and challenges not because they lack capability, but because they fear the internal backlash if things don't go perfectly.

The behaviour becomes risk-averse, guarded, or compulsively managed. Not as a form of care, but as a form of *shame pre-emption.* This is not growth. It is emotional containment masquerading as self-discipline.

To escape the double trap of shame, the system must be rewired. Not by removing shame entirely—an impossible and misguided goal—but by disrupting its monopolistic role in self-perception. This begins with naming. *What does shame sound like in my mind? When does it tend to show up? What behaviour does it follow or precede?* Naming is not a performative act. It is an act of clarity. Because shame thrives in generality: *I'm not enough. I always screw up. I'm just like this.* Precision undermines its power. Specificity gives you something to examine rather than internalise.

Next comes differentiation. The ability to recognise when shame is disguising itself as self-awareness is crucial. If a thought leaves you hopeless, paralysed, or unable to act with care, it is likely shame. If a thought leaves you clearer, more motivated to repair, and more willing to engage relationally, it is likely accountability. This litmus test isn't perfect, but it can break the spell. Because once you see that shame is a mechanism—not a truth—you are no longer obligated to obey it.

But perhaps the most subversive move is one of permission. To allow yourself to hold complexity. To admit that your behaviour may have caused harm *and* that you are worthy of repair. To acknowledge that you felt out of control *and* that there's a reason your system reacted that way. To believe that softness is not complacency, but context. These permissions don't excuse harm. They locate it within the broader frame of human adaptation. And only from within that frame can sustainable change emerge.

Shame's promise is seductive: that if you feel badly enough, you will finally become good. But the promise is hollow. Shame can compel compliance, but it cannot cultivate integration. It can silence, but it cannot soothe. And as long as it remains unchallenged, it will continue to fuel the very behaviours it later punishes—trapping people in cycles of self-judgement, relapse, and withdrawal.

Breaking that cycle requires more than self-esteem. It requires structural literacy. It requires learning to identify when shame is masquerading as insight, when it is hijacking behaviour in the name of protection, and when it is punishing you for a wound it never allowed you to name. This is the first step to liberation—not from mistakes, but from the compulsion to see those mistakes as evidence of your defectiveness.

Because once you know what shame is doing—and why—you can stop following its instructions. And when you stop following its instructions, you don't just change your behaviour. You reclaim your agency. Not by becoming perfect, but by becoming *present.* With your fallibility, your story, and your rightful permission to grow without being shamed into submission.

Why Self-Compassion Feels Dangerous

Self-compassion is often framed as the antidote to shame, the balm for burnout, the missing key to resilience. Yet for many people, especially those raised in high-pressure, punitive, or emotionally volatile environments, kindness directed inward feels neither intuitive nor safe. It feels disorienting. Even threatening. They may recognise the intellectual value of compassion, understand the research that supports it, and even encourage it in others—yet when it comes to applying it to themselves, they recoil. Not because they don't want relief, but because their nervous systems have been conditioned to equate softness with exposure, indulgence, or moral failure. For them, self-compassion is not simply unfamiliar; it is *emotionally hazardous.*

This aversion does not stem from stubbornness or immaturity. It stems from the deep architecture of early relational learning. If a child grows up in an environment where love is conditional—contingent on achievement, obedience, emotional suppression, or perfection—then internal kindness becomes associated not with safety, but with danger. The logic is primitive but coherent: *If I let myself off the hook, I'll fall apart. If I stop pushing, I'll be punished. If I show myself grace, I'll become weak or unlovable.* These internalised beliefs are not always conscious, but they are powerfully embodied. They show up in a person's inability to rest without guilt, in their reflexive self-criticism after making a mistake, in the unease they feel when someone compliments their progress. Praise doesn't land. Reassurance feels slippery. Stillness makes them anxious. And attempts at self-compassion trigger defensive suspicion rather than ease.

For such individuals, their entire motivational framework is often built around internal pressure. They achieve by criticising. They perform by bracing. They avoid rejection by pre-emptively shaming themselves into compliance. Remove the internal whip, and there's a fear of collapse. As a result, self-compassion is not interpreted as soothing—it is interpreted as risky deregulation. The mind may say, *This is what I need*, but the body says, *This isn't safe.* And the body always wins.

Neuroscience supports this. When a person practices self-compassion, they activate brain regions associated with care, bonding, and parasympathetic regulation—such as the insula and the vagus nerve. But for people with a trauma history, particularly developmental trauma, these same pathways are often dysregulated. The activation of safety cues can paradoxically trigger arousal, as the nervous system misinterprets calm as vulnerability. In such cases, attempts at self-compassion can induce more stress, not less. This response is confusing, even humiliating, for those who assume that healing should feel good. But healing, when you're wired for vigilance, often feels like loss of control.

This physiological confusion is mirrored in internal dialogue. For those raised in environments of emotional scarcity, the inner critic often became an early survival tool. It protected the child from external judgment by internalising it first. It helped them anticipate danger, avoid mistakes, maintain approval. Over time, it became fused with their sense of identity. To remove it feels like removing a part of themselves that kept them alive. And so when self-compassion asks that person to replace that critical voice with one of warmth, patience, or understanding, it's not a simple cognitive shift. It's a reorganisation of loyalty. They are not just being asked to speak kindly—they are being asked to *betray the part of them that protected them.*

This internal betrayal is rarely articulated consciously, but it often emerges in the form of emotional backlash. A person might try self-compassion for a day and then feel unusually irritable, numb, or ashamed. They might reject the practice altogether, dismissing it as "cheesy" or "unrealistic." Or they might intellectualise it—studying it, talking about it, teaching it—without ever allowing it to reach the core. This pattern isn't resistance for the sake of resistance. It's resistance as an expression of loyalty to the original survival system. A system in which harshness equalled protection and kindness signalled risk.

The cultural context exacerbates this problem. Many Western societies valorise grit, stoicism, and individualism. Emotional self-discipline is mistaken for maturity. Toughness is admired. Self-sacrifice is glorified. These values reinforce the idea that softness, especially towards oneself, is weakness. In corporate environments, in educational systems, even in some therapeutic models, performance is often rewarded over presence. And so the internal resistance to self-compassion is not just personal—it is institutional. It is built into the very scaffolding of what people are taught to admire.

To dismantle this resistance, self-compassion must be reframed not as indulgence, but as *precision.* It must be presented not as the opposite of accountability, but as its foundation. Because without compassion, accountability collapses into punishment. Without compassion, growth becomes a trauma reenactment—always trying to earn safety by being good enough, disciplined enough, healed enough. But compassion says: *You are already worthy of care, even as you change.* And for those who have spent their lives trying to *deserve* kindness, that message is radical.

This reframing must also account for how self-compassion feels in the body—not just what it means intellectually. Practicing self-compassion is not always soothing at first. For some, it will feel hollow. For others, it will feel like failure. That doesn't mean it isn't working. It means it's touching a part of the system that has never been met before. The work is not to *force* self-compassion to feel good, but to allow it to feel *strange*, *awkward*, even *unsafe*—and to keep going anyway. Because it is through repeated exposure to compassion that the nervous system begins to recalibrate. And only with time, and consistency, does the body start to believe what the mind has always hoped: *I can be kind to myself and still be safe.*

But this recalibration cannot occur through bypass. One of the most common misapplications of self-compassion is its use as a numbing strategy—an attempt to silence discomfort rather than understand it. This is not compassion. This is avoidance disguised as care. Real self-compassion does not sugar-coat. It does not placate. It sits beside the shame. It tolerates the rage. It holds the grief without trying to fix it. It says, *Yes, you were hurt. Yes, this is hard. And yes, you are still deserving of gentleness.* This kind of compassion is not sentimental. It is fierce. It is demanding. It requires maturity. Because it insists on seeing the whole self—not just the curated self, the improved self, or the socially acceptable self.

To develop this kind of compassion, especially for those raised in punitive systems, often means grieving. Grieving the years spent believing pain was deserved. Grieving the relationships that only responded to excellence. Grieving the parts of the self that were exiled to survive. This grief cannot be rushed. It must be witnessed. And self-compassion becomes the witness: not pushing for transcendence, not demanding transformation, but simply staying present. Again and again. Until the system learns that presence itself is a form of safety.

Why does self-compassion feel dangerous? Because it threatens the identity that was built to survive without it. It challenges the belief that only self-punishment prevents collapse. It interrupts the lie that the only way to matter is to be flawless. And it dares to suggest that even in imperfection, there is something lovable. For someone whose worth has always been conditional, this is not just a comforting idea. It is a *revolution.* And revolutions are rarely calm.

But they are necessary. Because no system built entirely on shame, pressure, or vigilance can sustain growth. At some point, the organism needs to rest—not in apathy, but in *integration.* Not in fantasy, but in *truth.* And the truth is this: you do not have to earn your own kindness. You do not have to wait until you're healed to treat yourself with dignity. The very act of offering compassion, especially when it feels unsafe, is itself a sign that something deep is shifting. Something more honest. Something more whole. Something finally *free*.

Shame as Emotional Camouflage

Shame is often mistaken for the core wound, the final emotion in the sequence of internal suffering. But shame is not the origin—it is the cover. It is the gatekeeper that stands between a person and the more tender, more disorganising truths they are not yet ready or permitted to feel. It does not simply announce "I am bad"; it interrupts a deeper message: *I am hurting, I am lonely, I am afraid, I am grieving, I am longing.* Shame inserts itself between stimulus and honesty, between pain and articulation, and calls itself insight. But in reality, it is an evasion mechanism—an emotional camouflage that obscures the most vital material for healing.

This role is both protective and paradoxical. Shame offers structure in moments of internal chaos. When a child feels abandoned or overlooked, shame provides a reason: *You are the problem. You are the cause.* The logic is cruel but coherent. It gives the mind something to do when reality feels incomprehensible. It gives the body something to hold when helplessness is intolerable. In this way, shame offers what grief, need, or envy cannot—control. And for many, control feels safer than truth.

To understand shame as camouflage is to recognise that much of what appears as self-loathing is actually displaced vulnerability. Beneath the narrative of "I'm not enough" may live a quiet, unspoken grief: *I was never allowed to be fully seen.* Beneath the declaration "I'm disgusting" may sit unresolved envy: *Why do they get to have what I always wanted?* Beneath the loop of "I'm a burden" may pulse the raw need for attachment: *Please don't leave me alone.* These aren't just different emotions—they are different *risks.* Grief demands surrender. Envy threatens social standing. Neediness invites shame if the environment has not been responsive. So shame steps in. It offers a shortcut: condemn the self and you don't have to experience what lies beneath.

This substitution is not incidental. It is learned. In many families, emotional honesty is punished, pathologised, or ignored. Anger is called disrespect. Sadness is dismissed as weakness. Desire is framed as entitlement. Over time, children absorb the message that their emotional reality is too much, too dangerous, or too inconvenient. In response, they build internal systems of censorship. Shame becomes the first responder to any feeling deemed unpalatable. The result is an emotionally inverted world: the person appears contrite, apologetic, or self-effacing—not because they have wronged anyone, but because they were never taught how to feel without fearing rupture.

This emotional inversion becomes particularly dangerous when it calcifies into personality. Adults who chronically lead with shame often appear humble or hyper-accountable, yet struggle with intimacy, authenticity, or joy. Not because they are incapable of those states, but because accessing them requires vulnerability—and vulnerability has long been coded as a liability. Shame, in contrast, feels strangely familiar. It may hurt, but it does not expose. It contracts, it contains, it organises. And because of this, it is often preferred over feelings that stretch the self toward openness or relational risk.

In therapeutic contexts, this pattern shows up as emotional mislabelling. A client may say they feel ashamed of having lashed out at a friend, but closer examination reveals underlying hurt: *I felt betrayed. I felt left out.* Another might speak of being ashamed for not performing well at work, when beneath that sits a deeper fear: *If I am not exceptional, I am invisible.* These substitutions are not dishonest—they are habitual. They reflect a nervous system trained to route vulnerable experience through the only channel it believes is allowed: *self-condemnation.*

There are also cultural amplifiers. In many societies, shame is institutionalised as a method of control. In schools, it is used to enforce conformity. In families, it maintains hierarchy. In religion, it polices morality. In media, it sells correction. These collective norms reinforce the idea that shame is not only valid, but *virtuous*. As a result, people often wear their shame as evidence of depth, self-awareness, or moral integrity. But shame, as a moral compass, is deeply unreliable. It does not tell us what is right—it tells us what will keep us hidden.

This is why people can feel deep shame about emotions that are, in fact, morally neutral. Take envy: an evolutionarily conserved signal of comparison and lack. In many environments, especially those steeped in scarcity or competition, envy is taboo. So instead of acknowledging it, people shame themselves for feeling it. The result is a double bind: the original envy remains unexamined and unresolved, and now the person feels *bad* for feeling bad. Or consider neediness. In attachment theory, the need for closeness is a sign of relational intelligence. But in shame-bound systems, need is equated with weakness, and independence with virtue. So when someone longs for reassurance, they pre-emptively shame themselves: *I'm too needy. I should be able to do this alone.* Again, the emotion is disallowed, and shame is deployed to police it.

The consequences of this pattern are profound. When shame disguises other emotions, it impairs self-understanding. Emotional granularity—the ability to identify, name, and interpret emotions with specificity—is a critical predictor of psychological wellbeing. But shame flattens nuance. It turns everything into a referendum on the self: "I feel this, therefore I am wrong." Without the ability to distinguish sadness from disappointment, loneliness from rejection, or desire from entitlement, the person becomes emotionally illiterate—not because they lack capacity, but because shame has hijacked their internal vocabulary.

Moreover, this camouflage effect makes healing far more complex. Because shame is often the first emotion to surface, both client and clinician can be misled into thinking it is the true target of intervention. But if shame is approached as the problem rather than the cover, the work stalls. The person may gain insight into their patterns, may even learn to speak about shame with fluency, but unless the protected emotions underneath are accessed and integrated, change remains performative. The internal wound stays intact.

To interrupt this camouflage, the therapeutic stance must shift from interrogation to invitation. Instead of asking, "Why are you ashamed?" a more fruitful inquiry is, "*What might this shame be protecting you from feeling right now?*" This reframes shame not as an enemy to be eradicated, but as a signal—an adaptive signal pointing to emotional content that has not yet been metabolised. And just as importantly, this inquiry must be accompanied by an environment of relational safety. People do not release shame because they are told to. They release it because they are *held well enough to risk what lies beneath.*

Practically, this means slowing down emotional narratives, watching for places where shame shortcuts the story, and gently circling back to the moment before self-judgement took over. What was happening then? What did you notice in your body? What did you wish you could have said? These are not mechanical questions—they are acts of re-entry. They allow the person to reverse-engineer their defences and reconnect with the truth that was there all along, buried beneath the reflex of self-blame.

Understanding shame as camouflage also opens up space for greater compassion—not just for others, but for oneself. When a person sees that their shame was not a failing, but a strategy, they can begin to disengage from the moral framework that kept them trapped. They can begin to view envy, need, and grief not as signs of deficiency, but as signals of life: *I want something. I care about something. I lost something.* These recognitions are not easy. They are emotionally expensive. But they are also essential. Because what we fail to name, we are doomed to mislabel. And what we mislabel, we cannot change.

So the next time shame shows up—swift, loud, convincing—the invitation is not to argue with it, nor to obey it. The invitation is to pause and ask: *What might this feeling be standing in front of? What am I not yet allowed to know?* That is where the real work begins. Not in silencing shame, but in decoding its message. Not in erasing it, but in tracing its outline—until the shape of a forgotten grief, an unspoken longing, or a valid anger emerges behind it. And in that emergence, something sacred happens: the self that has been hiding behind shame steps forward—not for judgment, but for understanding. And perhaps, at last, for healing.

How to Interrupt the Shame Spiral

A shame spiral is not a singular emotional event; it is a patterned psychological process—a sequence of reactions that begins with perceived failure and ends in self-collapse. It is fast, recursive, and often invisible until the person is already submerged in it. One moment of imperfection—missing a deadline, eating off-plan, forgetting a name—sets off a chain reaction. The internal narrative flares: *I've done it again. I never learn. What's wrong with me?* This isn't just self-criticism. It's *identity indictment.* The spiral tightens, reducing a specific error to a globalised sense of defectiveness. And with each loop, the person becomes not more self-aware, but less capable of change.

What makes the shame spiral particularly corrosive is its false promise: that self-punishment will lead to self-correction. But shame does not produce insight. It produces overwhelm, rigidity, and emotional paralysis. Neurologically, it hijacks the brain's regulatory systems. It floods the body with stress chemicals, narrows cognitive flexibility, and deactivates the very neural networks required for adaptive decision-making. In this state, reflection is nearly impossible. The person is no longer relating to the mistake—they are fighting for psychological survival.

Interrupting this spiral is not about erasing shame altogether. Shame, when metabolised properly, can play a signalling role. It alerts us when we've violated our own values. But in a spiral, shame ceases to be a compass and becomes a cage. The task is to *reposition shame from centre stage to the periphery*, and re-engage the cognitive and emotional faculties that allow for movement, nuance, and repair.

The first critical intervention is *noticing.* Shame thrives in ambiguity. It relies on speed, generalisation, and internalised scripts. To interrupt it, the person must learn to detect it early—not just in thought, but in physiology. Shame often manifests as heat in the face, a drop in the stomach, a desire to disappear. It can also present as mental fog, hypervigilance, or withdrawal. The ability to name these sensations not as failure but as *shame cues* creates distance between the emotion and the identity. This is not mere mindfulness; it's neurobiological self-recognition. It marks the moment where reactivity can become reflection.

Once identified, the next step is *naming with precision.* Vague self-judgements like "I'm a mess" or "I ruin everything" must be translated into specific, emotionally accurate language. What exactly happened? What was the belief triggered? Was it embarrassment, disappointment, guilt, envy? These distinctions matter. They return emotional granularity to an experience that shame seeks to flatten. A person might discover that beneath their shame is not a sense of moral failure, but a feeling of being unseen, unheard, or misunderstood. Precision disrupts the automaticity of shame and reintroduces choice.

But clarity alone is not enough. Shame spirals are driven by *narrative loops*—habitual stories about the self that feel absolute: *I always ruin things. I'm unlovable. I'll never get it right.* These are not truths. They are inherited scripts, often learned through repetition in childhood, social conditioning, or trauma. To challenge them, a new form of inner dialogue must be developed—one that combines accountability with *context.* For example: "Yes, I made a mistake, and I understand why. I was exhausted. I was scared. I didn't know how to respond." This is not self-justification. It is *emotional integrity.* It allows the person to stay in relationship with their values without collapsing into self-attack.

This distinction is vital. Shame spirals are often mistaken for accountability because they involve a harsh moral tone. But true accountability requires *agency*, not annihilation. It asks, *What matters to me here? What would it mean to repair?* It keeps the focus on behaviour and consequence—not identity. In contrast, shame says: *Because you failed, you are a failure.* The goal in interrupting the spiral is to reorient the person from judgment to curiosity: *What is this reaction protecting me from? What story am I defaulting to? Whose voice is this?*

The practice of disrupting shame spirals also requires temporal awareness. Shame distorts time. It makes past mistakes feel present and future consequences feel inevitable. A missed opportunity ten years ago becomes a living wound. An imagined criticism from next week becomes an emotional certainty. Learning to *time-stamp* shame helps separate historical trauma from current context. Asking "Is this about now, or is this about then?" restores orientation. It allows the person to locate their reaction within a broader emotional timeline, reducing the grip of old narratives.

Another critical skill is *containment*. When shame floods the system, the impulse is often to confess, collapse, or compensate—to seek immediate relief through apology, withdrawal, or perfectionism. These behaviours can appear responsible, but often they are attempts to *escape* the discomfort, not integrate it. Containment means learning to sit with the feeling *without obeying it*. This might involve grounding techniques, breath work, or simply narrating the internal experience in real time: *I'm noticing a wave of shame. I want to disappear. My chest feels tight. I'm going to stay with this feeling for a moment.* This practice strengthens emotional endurance and teaches the system that shame is survivable.

Importantly, none of these tools work in isolation. Shame spirals are relational by nature. They often originate in relationships where vulnerability was punished, and they require *new relational experiences* to fully unwind. This means that while cognitive tools are necessary, they are not sufficient. At some point, shame must be *witnessed*. Whether in therapy, trusted friendship, or reflective writing, the process of having shame seen and *not shunned* is what ultimately reshapes the internal landscape. Because shame, at its core, is about exclusion. And the antidote to exclusion is not analysis—it is belonging.

Yet care must be taken not to bypass the valuable information shame sometimes carries. Interrupting the spiral does not mean dismissing discomfort. It means staying long enough with the feeling to discern what it is actually about. Sometimes shame is alerting us to a value we've compromised, a boundary we've ignored, or a truth we've avoided. The goal is not to silence shame, but to *decode* it. To ask: *Is this shame telling me something useful—or is it replaying an old fear in new language?* This reflective stance turns shame from a tyrant into a messenger.

Finally, shame spirals can only be disrupted sustainably when integrated into a larger *emotional ecosystem*—one that includes practices of self-trust, emotional literacy, and compassionate boundary-setting. No single intervention will prevent shame from arising. But with consistent, embodied awareness, its power can be significantly reduced. It becomes a signal, not a sentence. A moment, not a mandate.

To live without being governed by shame is not to live without remorse, error, or discomfort. It is to live with *access*—to one's values, one's choices, and one's full emotional range. And it is this access that makes transformation possible. Because change does not begin with judgment. It begins with the courage to see oneself clearly—without collapsing—and to choose, again and again, not punishment, but presence.

Chapter 5
The Cultural Chains We Wear

Culture does more than influence behaviour; it shapes our values, dictates how we manage difficulty, and signals who we must become to be deemed acceptable. It prescribes which emotions to suppress, which achievements to pursue, and which identities are safe to inhabit. Much of what we perceive as personal struggle often reflects a tension between our inner reality and the roles culture demands we perform. Culture is not inherently oppressive—it can provide meaning, belonging, and structure—but it frequently rewards dysfunction when that dysfunction aligns with prevailing ideals. The individual who overworks is lauded for diligence. The one who suppresses emotion is applauded for strength. The person who adapts constantly for approval is described as flexible. In such a landscape, suffering is sanctioned—so long as it is productive.

At the root of many toxic behavioural patterns lies more than individual psychology; collective conditioning is equally at play. What we internalise as moral discipline is frequently social compliance cloaked in virtue. From childhood, we are taught that worth must be earned through performance, sacrifice, and self-effacement. The quiet child is called "mature." The employee who works long hours without complaint is "dedicated." The adult who subordinates their emotions for harmony is deemed "emotionally intelligent." Yet beneath these commendable veneers exists a harder truth: patterns of self-abandonment have become normalised and celebrated under the guise of responsibility.

Nowhere is this more apparent than in the exaltation of discipline. At its core, discipline is neutral—a capacity to act according to one's values, regardless of shifting moods. Contemporary narratives, however, particularly in productivity and fitness spheres, have weaponised it into a performance of control. To be "disciplined" is to override, deny, and suppress. It is to ignore hunger, rest, emotional strain, and relational fatigue in pursuit of visible success. And when such suppression falters, judgment follows—not only from others, but from the internalised voice shaped by these external pressures: You're weak. You don't want it enough. Try harder. Discipline, thus, ceases to be a skill and becomes a test of moral worth.

This veneration of self-denial intersects with a cultural disdain for emotional transparency. Though slogans such as "mental health matters" circulate widely, social currency continues to favour stoicism. The unspoken rule is clear: emotions may be processed—but privately. Public vulnerability is permissible only if it is articulate, aesthetically presented, and concludes with redemption. Messier displays—prolonged grief, disruptive anger, insistent need—are labelled unstable, indulgent, or manipulative. Here, toxic positivity emerges as the emotional enforcer of cultural perfectionism. Phrases like "everything happens for a reason" or "good vibes only" masquerade as encouragement, but often serve as denial. They do not validate emotional reality; they silence it. For those enduring genuine pain, forced optimism reflects back inadequacy: Why can't I be grateful? What's wrong with me for not moving on?

This pattern of emotional bypass is far from harmless. It trains individuals to fear their internal landscape, to question the legitimacy of their reactions, and to dismiss discomfort before it can teach. Even more insidiously, it reinforces the notion that healing is performance rather than process—growth must look like resilience, composure, and cheerfulness, even while the body braces, the nervous system remains alert, and emotional wounds are fresh. People curate their inner lives for external approval, performing wellness instead of integrating it. The cost is not merely unresolved pain, but increasing estrangement from the self.

Overfunctioning, culturally reinforced, compounds self-abandonment. Societal systems equate busyness with purpose, output with value, and efficiency with virtue. Compulsive activity is lauded without interrogating what is being avoided. Many high-functioning individuals are chronically dissociated, moving through a blur of meetings, errands, workouts, and content creation, rarely pausing to feel the emptiness that motion conceals. They are not thriving—they are distracting. Society rewards this. Overworking is framed as ambition. Boundarylessness is praised as dedication. Fatigue is glamorised as hustle. Restlessness becomes entrepreneurial spirit. Beneath the accolades, however, is a nervous system that never feels safe enough to rest.

This compulsion to act is not arbitrary. It is learned in contexts—familial and societal—where mere being was insufficient. Love was conditional, attention contingent on excellence, safety dependent on appeasement. Many who overperform as adults were children who had to earn their place through helping, pleasing, or excelling, while their internal worlds were neglected or shamed. As adults, rest provokes guilt, spaciousness panic, pleasure requires justification. Stillness is intolerable because it confronts muted aspects of the self.

Perhaps the most subtle yet corrosive effect of cultural conditioning is the demand for belonging through self-betrayal. In collectivist or competitive societies, conformity often requires suppressing authenticity. Individuals learn to adapt, mirror social expectations, dilute needs, nod instead of speak, conform rather than risk exile. Approval is earned at the expense of integrity. Over time, adaptation becomes identity. One may no longer remember who they were before contorting for acceptance. Awareness of this loss may exist, but fear of rejection—being too much, too emotional, too idle, too intense—maintains the shape deemed worthy.

Such socialisation reshapes emotional architecture. Parts of the self threatening group inclusion—anger, desire, grief, dissent—are exiled internally, not merely externally. Self-policing emerges; feelings are censored before expression. Yet suppressed emotions persist, manifesting sideways as resentment, burnout, anxiety, or compulsive behaviour. The system cannot contain what it refuses to name. Naming, however, feels hazardous: cultural visibility remains risky, particularly for marginalised, policed, or commodified identities.

Liberation from these cultural chains requires more than behavioural change; it demands excavation. Which parts of myself exist to gain approval rather than reflect truth? Which values do I perform without conviction? Which pains have I silenced to accommodate others? These questions are not abstract—they are relational, embodied, and destabilising. To unlearn cultural conditioning is to confront the grief of having lived under it.

This chapter does not indict culture, but invites scrutiny of its unconscious influence. We are not isolated agents; we are shaped by familial, educational, political, and economic systems, each with its own logic and reward structures. Until these are understood, adaptation may be mistaken for authenticity. The goal is not wholesale rejection of cultural norms, but conscious choice: which values to retain, which to challenge, and who emerges when applause is no longer the guide.

Autonomy begins not with rebellion, but with awareness. Compulsions may not signal personal flaws but cultural artefacts. Shame may be socially implanted rather than self-generated. Exhaustion may reflect systemic distortion rather than mismanagement. Healing is not merely behavioural—it is reclamation: retrieving from the systems that demanded surrender what was denied to the self.

Discipline Worship and the Fear of Being Seen

The modern world has canonised discipline. It is no longer merely a useful trait or a marker of maturity—it has become a moral identity. The disciplined person is not only efficient, they are *good.* They are serious, superior, admirable. They are the ones who rise at dawn, who out-train fatigue, who override distraction, who do not need motivation because they have mastery. They do what others won't, and because of this, they are celebrated. Yet the story beneath this admiration is rarely questioned. What happens when the disciplined self becomes a mask? When restraint replaces self-understanding? When punishment masquerades as progress?

We are conditioned to believe that self-denial is synonymous with growth. That to become someone of value, we must say no—to pleasure, to rest, to softness, to spontaneity. Especially within productivity and fitness culture, this narrative is amplified: results belong to those who *suffer better.* But what if the reverence for suffering isn't about resilience at all? What if it's about fear—of losing control, of being ordinary, of being seen as weak or indulgent? And what if the disciplined persona is not an expression of personal power, but a socially sanctioned way to disappear behind performance?

The cultural worship of discipline is deeply gendered, racialised, and classed. In corporate environments, discipline is often conflated with compliance: punctuality, deference, endurance. In athletic contexts, it is linked to aesthetic outcomes—leaner, harder, faster. In both, the body becomes an object to be optimised, a battlefield where one's worth is negotiated. There is rarely space for the complexity of the human experience—for the messy, the emotional, the inconsistent. The disciplined person must appear as a machine, and any deviation—any need, desire, or emotional fluctuation—is interpreted as failure.

This is not a rejection of discipline per se. Discipline can be deeply nourishing when it is anchored in self-respect, curiosity, and freedom. But what we often see in modern culture is not true discipline—it is *restriction.* It is the compulsive suppression of inner life in favour of outer approval. The student who studies past burnout. The entrepreneur who glorifies 100-hour weeks. The gym-goer who trains through injury. The parent who never pauses to ask what they need. These behaviours are praised not because they are healthy, but because they conform to a system that equates exhaustion with effort and effort with virtue.

What we call discipline is often a trauma response—specifically, a form of *strategic invisibility.* For many, the disciplined self was constructed early, in environments where love was conditional and visibility was unsafe. They learned to earn affection by being useful, quiet, efficient. They discovered that softness invited criticism, that mistakes triggered punishment, that asking for help led to shame. So they adapted. They excelled. They over-functioned. They built identities around performance. And in doing so, they learned to disappear—behind achievements, behind routines, behind hyper-competence.

In adulthood, these adaptations persist. The fear of being seen—not just noticed, but *emotionally perceived*—drives people to double down on structure. They regulate their vulnerability through rituals of productivity. They numb uncertainty with over-planning. They replace emotional expression with measurable output. And because these behaviours are rewarded by peers, employers, and social media, the inner crisis is never addressed. The world sees discipline. But what they do not see is the anxiety, the isolation, the hollowness of a life built on perpetual striving.

This fear of being seen runs deeper than performance. It touches the very architecture of identity. Many people have spent decades suppressing aspects of themselves—creativity, sexuality, sensitivity, rage—because they were taught these parts were too much, too chaotic, too embarrassing. Discipline, in this context, becomes a strategy of containment. It offers predictability. It offers control. It offers safety. But it also limits spontaneity, joy, connection. The self becomes manageable, but it also becomes malnourished.

Nowhere is this more visible than in fitness culture, where discipline is tied to morality. "Clean eating," "no excuses," "beast mode"—these phrases are not simply motivational; they are ideological. They promote a binary: strong or weak, committed or lazy, worthy or shameful. But behind many "fit" bodies is a complex emotional reality—one in which food becomes a proxy for control, movement becomes punishment, and rest becomes betrayal. The fear is not just of gaining weight—it is of being undisciplined, of being seen as someone who cannot self-regulate, who does not deserve admiration.

The consequences are significant. Chronic stress, hormonal disruption, disordered eating, social withdrawal—all can emerge from a lifestyle disguised as "healthy" discipline. And because the symptoms often present alongside public praise ("You're so committed!" "I wish I had your willpower!"), they are rarely challenged. In fact, they are reinforced. This creates a painful paradox: the more a person suffers to maintain the disciplined image, the more validation they receive. The more validation, the more they fear letting go. And so the performance continues—at the cost of authenticity, health, and relational intimacy.

Breaking this cycle requires redefinition. What if discipline were measured not by how much we suppress, but by how consciously we *choose*? What if restraint included the ability to rest, to soften, to listen? What if self-trust replaced self-denial as the measure of maturity? This would require a cultural shift—from glorifying extremes to respecting nuance, from praising appearance to honouring alignment.

It also requires confronting the fear of visibility. Many people fear not just failure, but *exposure*—the exposure of mess, of need, of confusion. To be seen in this way feels unbearable, especially for those who have used discipline as a shield. But true maturity is not found in rigidity. It is found in *integration*—in the ability to hold strength and softness, clarity and uncertainty, autonomy and connection. Discipline can be part of that integration, but only if it is reclaimed from performance culture and returned to the self.

This reclamation involves a practice of discernment. Is this behaviour truly serving me—or is it serving my image? Am I acting from alignment—or from fear of being judged? Would I still choose this if no one were watching? These questions do not vilify discipline—they refine it. They ensure that what we call growth is not secretly self-abandonment.

To move beyond discipline worship is not to reject structure or effort. It is to reclaim wholeness. It is to stop measuring maturity by how well we disappear behind control. And it is to remember that being fully seen—not just for what we achieve, but for who we are—is not a risk to manage, but a freedom to reclaim.

Toxic Positivity and Emotional Bypassing

Not all positivity is healing. While optimism can be an invaluable psychological resource—fostering resilience, motivation, and hope—its counterfeit form, toxic positivity, does the opposite. Beneath the sugar-coated affirmations and Instagram-friendly mantras lies a cultural discomfort with emotional reality. The "good vibes only" ethos, far from being harmless encouragement, functions as a form of emotional gaslighting: it suggests that painful experiences are only tolerable if they are quickly reframed, aesthetically packaged, or ultimately redemptive. And in doing so, it makes entire swathes of the human experience unspeakable.

This phenomenon is not confined to self-help circles or social media trends. It has permeated workplaces, schools, families, and even clinical settings. It sounds like: "Everything happens for a reason," "Just stay positive," "Don't dwell on the negative," or "Happiness is a choice." These phrases are rarely malicious. Most are well-intentioned, offered with the hope of cheering someone up or helping them move forward. But intention does not negate impact. When used reflexively, such comments invalidate emotion, silence distress, and communicate that only curated feelings are acceptable.

At its core, toxic positivity is a defence mechanism—a culturally endorsed method of avoiding discomfort. In a society that prizes efficiency, composure, and emotional self-management, difficult feelings are often seen as inconvenient interruptions. Anger, grief, fear, envy, sadness—these emotions are cast as problems to be fixed rather than signals to be understood. The discomfort they evoke is not just personal; it is social. People struggle not only to feel these emotions themselves, but to witness them in others. The result is a widespread inability to sit with pain—our own or anyone else's.

This intolerance breeds *emotional bypassing*, a concept introduced in the realm of spiritual psychology but relevant far beyond it. Emotional bypassing refers to the use of surface-level positivity, rationalisation, or spiritual platitudes to avoid engaging with underlying emotional truth. For example, a person who feels devastated after a breakup may force themselves to say, "It's for the best," or "I'm better off anyway," before they've even begun to process the loss. Another might suppress rage or resentment by insisting, "I forgive everyone. I don't hold grudges," even as their body tightens and their voice strains. These statements may sound mature—but without integration, they become masks, not healing.

What makes toxic positivity so insidious is that it often masquerades as progress. In reality, it short-circuits growth by encouraging premature closure. Emotions have a lifespan. When honoured and metabolised, they rise, crest, and pass. But when dismissed or buried under forced cheerfulness, they fester. The person may appear composed, even thriving, while internally they are numb, confused, or exhausted by the performance. Over time, unresolved emotion often re-emerges in disguised forms—somatic symptoms, anxiety, irritability, compulsive behaviour, or relational dysfunction. The system seeks expression. If it cannot do so directly, it will find another way.

The cultural roots of toxic positivity are deep and intersecting. In Western societies especially, emotional restraint has long been associated with strength and moral superiority. This stoic ideal is reinforced through parenting ("Don't cry," "Be brave"), education (rewarding quiet compliance), and media representations of success (resilient heroes, unfazed CEOs, emotionally flat leaders). Meanwhile, the consumerist marketplace has commodified positivity into a product. Wellness brands, lifestyle influencers, and pop-psychology authors often push curated happiness as a metric of success—if you're not glowing, you're failing. This creates a pressure not only to *feel* good, but to *look* like you feel good—publicly, consistently, and convincingly.

Even therapeutic language is not immune. Cognitive reframing, mindfulness, and gratitude practices—all valuable tools in themselves—can become instruments of bypass when misused. A client may be encouraged to find silver linings before their anger has been validated. Or they may be told to "observe their feelings without judgement" when what they really need is to scream into a pillow. Healing is not a clean process. Sometimes it's ugly, loud, contradictory. But when therapeutic methods are used to sanitise rather than support, they reinforce the very narratives they were meant to disrupt.

Of course, the problem is not positivity itself. Hope, humour, perspective—these are essential aspects of psychological resilience. The issue is *when* they are introduced and *why*. Positivity becomes toxic when it is wielded to avoid discomfort, rush healing, or secure social approval. It becomes dangerous when it denies lived experience or reinforces shame about emotional depth. It becomes alienating when it implies that happiness is a sign of virtue, and suffering is a personal failure.

The consequences extend beyond the individual. In groups—whether workplaces, families, or communities—enforced positivity can create cultures of silence. Employees may avoid giving critical feedback for fear of being seen as negative. Friends may hesitate to share struggles lest they be labelled "draining." Communities may dismiss valid outrage as divisive or ungrateful. Over time, this erodes trust. People begin to hide their truth, censor their speech, or internalise shame about perfectly human reactions. The result is not cohesion, but fragmentation—masked by smiles and motivational quotes.

There is also a deeper philosophical cost. By overemphasising personal mindset and underemphasising context, toxic positivity individualises what are often collective problems. Structural inequality, systemic injustice, intergenerational trauma—these are not issues that can be solved by positive thinking. Yet when positivity is framed as the primary solution to all suffering, it reinforces the myth that our circumstances are solely a reflection of our attitudes. This not only invalidates real hardship; it protects the systems that perpetuate it.

So what is the alternative? Emotional honesty. Relational authenticity. The willingness to hold both light and dark in the same frame. It's the friend who says, "That really sucks. I'm here," not "Look on the bright side." It's the therapist who allows grief to unfold without fast-forwarding to reframe. It's the leader who says, "This is hard," rather than pretending everything is under control. These responses do not fix the pain—but they dignify it. And dignity is the foundation of healing.

This also means developing greater emotional literacy. Not every painful emotion is negative. Not every difficult conversation is destructive. Discomfort is not the opposite of growth; often, it is the doorway. We must learn to distinguish between harmful rumination and meaningful emotion, between paralysis and presence. This requires nuance, humility, and the courage to feel what is true before reaching for what is hopeful.

Ultimately, the cost of toxic positivity is relational disconnection—first from self, then from others. It teaches people to curate their emotions rather than explore them. It shames their sadness, edits their grief, and silences their rage. And while it may create the illusion of harmony, it comes at the expense of intimacy. Because intimacy—

whether with ourselves or others—requires truth. Not just the truth of joy, but the truth of struggle. Not just the hope of light, but the wisdom of shadow.

To move beyond emotional bypassing is not to abandon positivity. It is to root it in reality. It is to trust that our emotions, however unwelcome, have something to teach us. And it is to believe that healing is not found in suppressing the storm—but in learning how to stay present while it passes.

Addicted to Doing, Numb to Being

Modern culture has mastered the art of being busy. In fact, for many people, busyness is not just a schedule—it is an identity. Days are filled with tasks, goals, metrics, routines, checklists, optimisation strategies. People brag about how much they've done, how little they've slept, how full their calendars are. The phrase "I'm just so busy" has become both badge and armour: proof of one's value, and an implicit excuse for not being present. But beneath this surface of productivity often lies something more fragile—a subtle but profound disconnection from self. The external rush conceals an internal vacancy. We are, increasingly, addicted to doing and numb to being.

This addiction is not merely behavioural. It is emotional. It functions not as a time-management flaw, but as an avoidance strategy—a culturally sanctioned method of escaping discomfort. For many, constant motion offers relief from anxiety, grief, boredom, shame, or existential unease. Stillness threatens to unearth feelings that have long been buried. The mind learns: if you don't stop moving, you don't have to feel. The result is a society that rewards hyper-functioning while pathologising introspection. People who pause to reflect, rest, or question are seen as inefficient, self-indulgent, or lacking ambition.

The neuroscience of compulsive doing adds another layer of insight. Every time we complete a task, respond to an email, tick a box, or hit a goal, the brain releases a small amount of dopamine—a chemical associated with reward and motivation. These micro-rewards reinforce the behaviour, gradually wiring the brain to equate productivity with pleasure. But this neurological loop becomes dangerous when it is severed from emotional self-awareness. The person may continue performing, achieving, building, and fixing—even as their inner world deteriorates. The outside may look impressive. The inside feels hollow.

This is particularly prevalent among high-functioning individuals—those who appear to be thriving professionally while silently suffering emotionally. Their competence becomes a kind of camouflage, a way to keep others (and themselves) from seeing the loneliness, numbness, or fear beneath the surface. They may be celebrated for their output while privately struggling with burnout, relationship strain, or a persistent sense of alienation. And because their suffering does not fit the usual profile of dysfunction, it often goes unnoticed—by friends, by therapists, by the person themselves.

The cultural backdrop cannot be ignored. Capitalist systems reward output, speed, and scalability. The language of worth is inseparable from the language of productivity: "Make yourself valuable," "Hustle harder," "Earn your rest." In this paradigm, rest is not a right—it is a prize you must deserve. Identity becomes transactional: *you are what you produce*. And if you stop producing, who are you then? This existential question is not theoretical. It sits quietly beneath the anxiety of the overworker, the perfectionist, the burnout survivor. The busyness is not just about time. It is about meaning.

What complicates matters further is that hyper-efficiency is often misread as emotional maturity. People who are always in control, who never break down, who manage crises with grace, are admired. But often, what we call "resilience" is actually repression. The person has learned to suppress distress not because they are emotionally robust, but because it was never safe to be vulnerable. As children, they may have been praised for being "so responsible" or "so easy"—when in fact they were silently dissociating from unmet needs. As adults, this pattern hardens. The ability to stay composed becomes synonymous with being good. Emotional suppression becomes the gold standard.

There is also a social currency to busyness. In professional circles, the appearance of being in demand is often conflated with competence. In parenting culture, hyper-scheduling is seen as devotion. In spiritual communities, constant doing can masquerade as service. In all these domains, motion is mistaken for meaning. And because the rewards—social approval, economic gain, internal validation—are so immediate, few people stop to ask: *What is this activity protecting me from?*

One of the most troubling effects of this dynamic is the erosion of inner life. People become so externally oriented—focused on deadlines, performance metrics, social optics—that they lose touch with their internal signals. They struggle to name their feelings, locate their needs, or detect the subtle shifts in mood or energy that could guide more intentional choices. Silence becomes uncomfortable. Slowness feels wasteful. Presence becomes unbearable. The nervous system, wired for alertness and anticipation, cannot find rest. And the soul—the deeper sense of aliveness that comes from feeling connected, creative, spontaneous—begins to fade.

This emotional numbing is not accidental. It is adaptive. For those who have experienced trauma, loss, or chronic invalidation, doing becomes a shield. It offers control in a world that once felt unsafe. It offers certainty in the face of chaos. It offers identity in place of confusion. In this light, overworking is not simply a behavioural habit—it is a survival strategy. And like all survival strategies, it makes sense until it doesn't. What once protected now imprisons.

Recovering from compulsive doing is not a matter of time-blocking or better self-care. It requires a fundamental shift in self-concept. It asks us to disentangle value from output, to trust that being—not just doing—is enough. This is not an easy transition. When a person slows down, what often rises first is not peace, but panic. Without the buffer of constant motion, the buried emotions begin to surface—grief, rage, fear, loneliness. These are not signs of regression. They are signs of thawing. The system is waking up.

But this awakening must be handled with care. It is not enough to tell someone to "just relax" or "do less." That advice, however well-meaning, can feel shaming to those who have built their identity on doing. Instead, we must offer frameworks that honour the intelligence of the pattern while inviting new possibilities. What does it mean to feel safe while resting? How do we distinguish between purposeful activity and anxious reactivity? What rituals, relationships, or environments support genuine presence rather than performance?

Answering these questions requires more than insight. It requires practice. Moments of stillness must be cultivated—not as aesthetic experiences, but as acts of courage. Mindful breathing, unstructured time, gentle movement, creative play—these are not luxuries. They are lifelines. They reintroduce the self to itself. They make space for what has been silenced. And over time, they reveal that aliveness is not found in perpetual motion, but in full presence.

This reorientation is not about rejecting ambition or discipline. It is about reclaiming wholeness. Doing and being are not enemies—they are partners. But when doing is driven by fear, and being is dismissed as indulgent, the system becomes lopsided. The task, then, is not to stop doing, but to *inhabit* the doing differently—to act from alignment rather than compulsion, to work from fullness rather than lack, to produce without forgetting how to *feel.*

To be addicted to doing is to live in exile from the self. To recover is not to abandon action, but to return—slowly, deliberately, tenderly—to the parts of ourselves that cannot be measured, monetised, or performed. In a world that rewards performance and punishes presence, this is a radical act. But it is also a necessary one. Because without presence, we do not live—we only function. And we were made for more than that.

Belonging Through Betrayal

Most acts of self-abandonment don't begin with malice or neglect. They begin with a longing—to belong, to be accepted, to feel safe among others. This longing is universal, evolutionarily encoded, and deeply human. But in environments that prize conformity, obedience, or competitive performance, that longing can quietly become a trap. Individuals begin to internalise a dangerous bargain:

to be loved, I must not be fully myself. The cost of admission into a group—whether a family, a workplace, a school, or a society—is the rejection of parts of the self that don't fit the prevailing script. This is not always a conscious decision. Often, it is an emotional adaptation. But over time, it creates a schism between one's public identity and private truth—a betrayal of authenticity in exchange for approval.

Cultural systems, particularly those steeped in collectivism or performance-based worth, are often constructed in ways that make this betrayal seem not only logical, but necessary. In collectivist environments, the group's needs are elevated above the individual's, often under the banner of harmony, respect, or duty. In competitive environments, value is determined by visible success, efficiency, or excellence. In both cases, deviation is perceived as a threat—whether to unity or to status. The person learns, explicitly or implicitly, that authentic needs—like rest, disagreement, emotional expression, or even spiritual questioning—must be suppressed if they conflict with the prevailing ethos. The unspoken message is clear: *be who we need you to be, or risk exile.*

This psychological trade-off begins early. A child who senses that sadness is unwelcome may smile when they feel like crying. A student who absorbs that obedience equals worth may stop asking difficult questions. A professional who observes that burnout is rewarded with praise may wear exhaustion like a badge of honour. These behaviours are not random—they are emotionally strategic. They are methods of securing safety and attachment in environments where unconditional acceptance is not guaranteed. In this context, *belonging becomes contingent*, and identity becomes modular—shaped by what gains favour, not what reflects inner truth.

Over time, this adaptation becomes internalised. People begin to curate their personalities in anticipation of others' expectations. They downplay emotions deemed too intense, hide desires considered inappropriate, silence values that contradict the mainstream. This isn't limited to overtly oppressive cultures; it happens just as easily in families that value politeness over honesty, companies that prize output over well-being, or religious communities that sanctify conformity over exploration. And because these compromises are often subtle and socially rewarded, they rarely register as betrayals. They are framed as maturity, professionalism, or loyalty. The erosion of authenticity is framed as a noble sacrifice.

But the psychological cost is profound. When the self is consistently edited to preserve harmony or success, emotional dissonance accumulates. The person may appear functional, even admirable, but internally they carry a gnawing sense of emptiness, resentment, or disconnection. Over time, this can manifest as burnout, identity confusion, depression, or relational difficulties. The very strategies that once secured belonging now create isolation—from others and from the self. And because these dynamics are often invisible—normalised by social reinforcement—the individual may blame themselves for feeling unfulfilled, without recognising the structural betrayal they've endured.

The neuroscience of social safety lends additional clarity. Human brains are wired for connection, but not just any connection—*authentic* connection. When a person receives approval for a false self, the reward circuitry lights up momentarily, but the deeper emotional brain—the part that registers safety through resonance and attunement—remains unsatisfied. The person may feel socially successful but emotionally starved. This mismatch creates a feedback loop: perform more, feel less. It's not a matter of insufficient affirmation, but of misplaced identity. Praise directed at a persona does not nourish the soul.

This is not to suggest that social cohesion is inherently oppressive, or that all cultural norms are harmful. Boundaries, rituals, shared values—these are essential to community. The issue arises when these norms become rigid, unexamined, or weaponised to suppress difference. In such contexts, dissent is interpreted as defection, and authenticity as selfishness. People are encouraged to be themselves—*but only within acceptable limits*. This pseudo-inclusivity breeds confusion. One can never be quite sure where the line is. The result is chronic self-surveillance and a growing suspicion that one's real self is somehow unacceptable.

In particularly high-pressure or image-conscious environments, the betrayal of self is often codified as success. The employee who never says no is seen as a team player. The child who never questions authority is deemed well-behaved. The partner who never expresses need is praised for being "low-maintenance." These identities may confer external validation, but they often come at the expense of internal coherence. The person becomes divided—living a life that looks right, but *feels* wrong. And the more invested they become in the role, the harder it is to leave. To question the role is to risk losing everything the role has bought them: approval, protection, belonging.

There is also an intergenerational aspect to this phenomenon. Many people who betray themselves for belonging do so because that is what they observed or were taught. Their parents may have modelled suppression in the name of family honour, religious piety, or career advancement. Their ancestors may have learned, through direct trauma or historical oppression, that visibility was dangerous and silence was survival. In such lineages, conformity is not just cultural—it is inherited as a survival script. Breaking that script is not simply a matter of will. It is an act of intergenerational courage.

So what does it mean to reclaim authenticity without sacrificing connection? The answer is not radical individualism, nor is it performative rebellion. It is a slower, subtler process of re-tuning one's internal compass. It means learning to distinguish between approval and attunement, between fitting in and truly belonging. It means asking uncomfortable questions: *What parts of myself have I edited for acceptance? Whose love have I been performing for? What would I say or do if I trusted that I wouldn't be abandoned for it?*

This process may involve grief—the grief of lost time, of unspoken truths, of relationships built on conditionality. But it also opens the door to deeper belonging—the kind rooted not in conformity, but in mutual recognition. True belonging, as Brené Brown famously writes, "doesn't require you to change who you are; it requires you to be who you are." But to arrive there, one must first see where they have been complicit in their own disappearance.

Reclaiming authenticity in a world that rewards betrayal is not easy. It will require discernment, boundaries, and sometimes loss. But it is the only path to genuine intimacy—within ourselves and with others. Because connection that depends on performance is not connection at all. And approval that costs you your truth is not a gift—it is a transaction. The task is not to abandon belonging, but to redefine it. Not as proximity or praise, but as resonance, alignment, and presence. Only then can we stop betraying ourselves for inclusion and begin building communities where the full self is not just tolerated, but welcomed.

Chapter 6
The Attachment Blueprint

No one arrives in the world already equipped to regulate their emotions, establish boundaries, or trust others. These capacities are not innate, nor do they follow any predictable distribution according to temperament or intelligence. They are learned—or missed—through the earliest bonds with those charged with our care. Our attachment blueprint does more than guide relationships; it lays the foundation for how we relate to ourselves, navigate stress, tolerate vulnerability, and respond to threat. The habits we label as destructive, self-sabotaging, or irrational frequently trace back not to flaws in character but to developmental patterns formed long before language or agency could shape them differently.

Attachment theory, while well established, remains as urgent now as ever. From John Bowlby's foundational insights to Mary Ainsworth's meticulous observations, the concept has evolved from a model of child–caregiver interaction into a lens for understanding adult emotional life. At its essence, attachment describes how we seek safety and soothe distress in the presence—or absence—of others. Secure attachment does not demand constant proximity; it requires reliable attunement, the capacity to feel seen, understood, and comforted when it matters most. Disruptions—neglect, inconsistency, criticism, enmeshment—force adaptation. Children learn strategies designed not for flourishing but for survival. Over time, these adaptations crystallise into patterns: perfectionism, emotional avoidance, hypervigilance, compulsive caretaking. Habits, in turn, harden into identity.

As adults, we rarely connect present difficulties to the unmet needs of infancy. We fixate instead on symptoms: the overreactions in relationships, the reluctance to seek help, the harsh inner critic, the chronic fear of failure. Logic and willpower may seem like remedies, yet insight alone seldom dissolves entrenched behaviours. These patterns are not irrational; they are emotionally encoded memories, stored in the nervous system. They echo the logic of a child who learned that crying invited danger, that independence was demanded prematurely, that love arrived only on condition. In adulthood, such individuals may appear high-functioning or even successful, yet their emotional habits remain tethered to these old relational templates. They may fear intimacy yet crave it, over-function to stave off shame, numb to forestall grief—and when these strategies impede growth, self-blame follows, often without recognition of the embedded wisdom in these reactions.

Understanding your attachment blueprint is not an exercise in self-diagnosis but in contextualisation. It offers explanation without excusing behaviour, inviting a lens of compassion. An avoidant attachment style, for instance, may manifest as resistance to closeness—not from coldness, but from an early lesson that emotional needs were burdensome. Anxious attachment does not signify neediness or drama; it reflects hypersensitivity to abandonment born of inconsistent caregiving. Disorganised attachment, frequently stemming from trauma, may oscillate between longing and fear, producing inner chaos that resists tidy categorisation. None of these are pathologies—they are strategies that once served a purpose.

The challenge emerges when these strategies become unconscious defaults, applied long after their original context has vanished. A child who remained invisible to avoid punishment may grow into an adult unable to advocate at work. A teenager who found control through disordered eating may continue decades later to micromanage every calorie as a stand-in for emotional stability. What once protected becomes rigid, eventually self-defeating. Outdated attachment strategies persist not because they are effective now, but because they were necessary then—and the body remembers.

One of psychology's most counterintuitive lessons is that insight does not equal change. A person may map their patterns meticulously—naming, explaining, understanding—and yet remain powerless to shift them. Attachment patterns are not merely cognitive; they are somatic, emotional, relational. Someone who intellectually knows they are safe may still experience panic in intimacy. Someone who trusts their partner in thought may still feel abandonment in practice. These are not failures of reason; they are echoes of emotional memory. Transformation demands new experiences—corrective emotional feedback that rewires the nervous system.

This is why some people shed harmful behaviours with seeming ease while others remain trapped despite years of effort. The distinction is rarely about discipline or intelligence—it is about emotional safety. Those with secure or repaired attachment foundations tolerate discomfort, seek support, and integrate feedback more readily. Those with attachment wounds often perceive change itself as threat: familiarity, even if painful, feels safer than novelty. They may sabotage progress, resist kindness, or reject rest because it challenges an internal model of security.

A particularly insidious manifestation of attachment patterns is repetition compulsion: the unconscious drive to recreate past emotional injuries in pursuit of resolution. Adults criticised as children may gravitate toward subtly demeaning partners. Those unseen in early life may chase unresponsive authority figures, hoping to finally earn recognition. These patterns are not conventional choices—they are enactments of unresolved longing. Until the original need is named, felt, and grieved, the cycle endures.

Yet this chapter is not about blame. It is about understanding—how past experiences inform present behaviours, and how compassion, rather than coercion, opens the door to change. Emotional regulation is not a moral feat; it is a skill often acquired through co-regulation with emotionally attuned others. If no one modelled how to name feelings, tolerate distress, or soothe the system, struggles are relational inheritance, not personal failure. Skills can be learned at any age, and when they are, habits rooted in avoidance begin to loosen.

Transforming entrenched patterns requires viewing the self not as a project to fix, but as a system to understand. This chapter invites exploration of how attachment styles shape behaviour, self-concept, and emotional reflexes. It offers insight into why some aspects of oneself resist change—not from sabotage, but from loyalty to the only strategies ever available. It examines the emotional architecture of habits, tracing how old pain drives present action, and provides tools, reflections, and frameworks for constructing a new internal scaffolding—one founded on trust, repair, and presence rather than vigilance or performance.

This work is neither simple nor linear. It asks you to look back—not to linger, but to decode; to feel—not to collapse, but to integrate. Ultimately, it asks a choice: the self that survived is not the only self allowed to live. You are not broken, nor bound to repeat inherited patterns. With clarity, compassion, and new emotional experience, the script can be rewritten—not by erasing the past, but by understanding its logic and choosing to meet present needs authentically.

How Childhood Bonds Shape Adult Habits

By the time we reach adulthood, many of our habits seem automatic. We avoid confrontation, over-apologise, chase perfection, struggle to rest, or repeatedly attach to emotionally unavailable partners. These patterns are often described in behavioural terms—bad habits, poor coping skills, self-sabotage—but their origins rarely begin in adulthood. Long before these behaviours become conscious choices, they are rehearsed in the emotionally formative theatre of our early relationships. What we call "adult dysfunction" is often the matured version of a child's adaptation. Understanding this is not a poetic notion or a vague therapeutic platitude—it is an empirically supported truth grounded in decades of psychological and neurobiological research: *our earliest attachment experiences shape our nervous system, relational blueprints, and emotional reflexes for life.*

Attachment theory, first articulated by British psychoanalyst John Bowlby in the mid-20th century, was a radical departure from prevailing views of child development. Bowlby posited that a child's relationship with their primary caregiver—typically the mother—was not just about food or physical safety but a deep biological imperative to form emotional bonds. From this foundation, Mary Ainsworth's "Strange Situation" research helped categorise attachment into three major styles: secure, avoidant, and anxious, with a fourth, disorganised, added later through subsequent trauma studies. These categories are not fixed boxes but living tendencies that guide how a person seeks closeness, manages distress, and perceives threat. Crucially, these attachment strategies are not chosen—they are shaped through lived experience and then internalised into behaviour.

Consider the child whose parent responds predictably, empathically, and consistently to their needs. That child learns that others are safe, that emotions can be shared, and that they themselves are worthy of care. They develop *secure attachment*, a relational template that fosters trust, emotional flexibility, and resilience. In adulthood, these individuals are more likely to self-soothe effectively, engage in balanced relationships, and recover from setbacks with less internal drama. Their behavioural habits are often underpinned by a foundational sense of safety.

Now contrast that with the child whose caregiver is emotionally absent, physically present but inattentive, or consistently rejecting of neediness. This child may learn that expressing emotion invites disappointment or shame. They adapt by *suppressing need*, minimising vulnerability, or becoming highly self-reliant. This gives rise to *avoidant attachment*—not a fear of people per se, but a deep-seated mistrust in the availability of others. In adulthood, this may manifest as the compulsive need for control, emotional detachment, or habits that prioritise independence even when closeness is available. Their avoidance isn't a flaw; it's an emotional scar tissue—a strategy that once served survival.

Then there is the child who experiences inconsistency. Sometimes their caregiver is attuned and warm; other times distracted, anxious, or withdrawn. The emotional landscape becomes unpredictable. To restore connection, this child may amplify their distress—cry louder, cling harder, or obsessively seek reassurance. From this instability emerges *anxious attachment*. As adults, these individuals may fear abandonment, over-analyse social interactions, and form compulsive relational patterns. Their behaviours—texting repeatedly when ignored, ruminating on perceived slights, collapsing under relational ambiguity—are often driven not by neurosis, but by a nervous system wired to monitor safety through hypervigilance.

These early adaptations shape more than romantic patterns. They influence our work ethic, our stress responses, our capacity for emotional regulation, and our sense of self. A securely attached person might experience workplace feedback as constructive. An avoidantly attached person may interpret it as a threat to autonomy. An anxiously attached person might spiral into shame or overcompensation. These reactions are not solely about mindset—they are *embodied scripts* rooted in developmental wiring. Thus, the adult who avoids resting is not merely a productivity addict; they may have learned that slowing down invites criticism. The person who becomes the social chameleon in every room may not be attention-seeking but rather survival-trained to attune to others' needs at the expense of their own.

Importantly, attachment is not destiny. Patterns forged in childhood are not immune to revision. They are *neuroplastic*, meaning they can be updated—but only through emotionally corrective experiences. Insight alone is not enough. Telling yourself you are safe does not rewire a system that was taught the opposite. You must *feel* safety, *experience* stability, and *receive* attunement over time for new patterns to take root. This is why therapy, secure friendships, and emotionally available partners can be so transformative—they serve as relational dojos where new emotional habits can be trained.

Yet this process is rarely linear. Adults with insecure attachments may find that even when they cognitively understand their habits, they feel *compelled* to repeat them. A person might know that overfunctioning at work is draining, yet find themselves unable to stop. This isn't weakness—it's familiarity. The nervous system often prefers *predictable discomfort* over *uncertain change*. This is the paradox of attachment injury: the strategies that once protected you now prevent the very connection or peace you long for.

Moreover, attachment styles rarely exist in isolation. People often exhibit *earned security*, where a previously insecure style shifts through corrective experiences. Others develop *contextual attachment*, where they are secure in friendships but anxious in romantic relationships, or avoidant at work but needy with a parent. These patterns are flexible, not fixed, but recognising their variability requires reflection and nuance—not self-judgement.

In modern settings, these early patterns are frequently misunderstood. A colleague labelled as "cold" may be emotionally self-contained out of necessity. A friend who never initiates plans may fear rejection, not lack interest. A partner who needs constant reassurance may be responding to deeply ingrained abandonment anxiety, not manipulating for attention. When we interpret these behaviours without historical context, we tend to moralise them. But when we understand them through the lens of attachment, we see that what looks like dysfunction is often *a map of past pain.*

This insight is not merely interpersonal—it is profoundly intrapersonal. Many of our toxic habits are self-directed versions of attachment responses. We abandon our own needs. We criticise ourselves to avoid others' judgement. We ignore our pain until it erupts. These internal dynamics mirror early patterns. The child who was invalidated may grow into an adult with an invalidating inner voice. The teen who learned to please to earn love may become a boundaryless adult, burned out from over-accommodation. The habits we want to break are not just behavioural—they are *relational imprints*, played out within the self.

Recognising these patterns allows us to ask better questions. Not "Why am I like this?" but "Who taught me it wasn't safe to be otherwise?" Not "How do I fix myself?" but "What version of me is trying to stay safe through this behaviour?" These are not sentimental questions. They are clinical, grounded, and psychologically precise. They shift us from blaming to understanding—and from understanding to healing.

Ultimately, the task is not to eliminate attachment patterns, but to bring them into awareness. Once we see the logic behind our loops, we can disrupt them. We can catch ourselves before withdrawing, pausing to ask if safety is truly under threat. We can soothe ourselves before overreaching, reminding the nervous system that we are not seven years old anymore. We can learn to parent the inner child without performing for the inner critic.

How childhood bonds shape adult habits is not a sentimental idea. It is a call to precision. The task is not to wallow in the past, but to study it with clear eyes and open awareness—to locate the emotional blueprints that built our scaffolding and decide, with agency, what to preserve, what to mourn, and what to rebuild from the inside out.

Emotional Regulation Is a Learned Skill

A regulated adult is not someone who feels less—it is someone who has learned how to feel *well.* This distinction is vital. In a world that too often equates composure with suppression, many people walk through life mistaking emotional numbness for maturity, stoicism for strength. But the truth is both more humane and more demanding: emotional regulation is not the absence of emotion, but the ability to stay present with it—without becoming dominated by it or dissociating from it. And contrary to what many believe, this is not an innate trait one either possesses or lacks. *Emotional regulation is a learned, trainable skill.* And when it is not taught—or worse, when it is punished—people find other ways to cope. These compensatory strategies may look like addiction, perfectionism, chronic busyness, emotional outbursts, or toxic self-talk. But at their core, they are *makeshift technologies for managing internal distress* in the absence of healthier tools.

Modern behavioural science and affective neuroscience confirm what many clinicians have long observed: that the ability to regulate emotion is not a fixed capacity, but a developmental outcome. The brain's emotion-regulating structures—such as the prefrontal cortex, anterior cingulate cortex, and amygdala—are shaped by early relational experiences. When a child's emotional expressions are consistently met with attuned responses—comfort when distressed, mirroring when joyful, co-regulation when overwhelmed—their nervous system learns a fundamental truth: *emotions are survivable.* But when a child is shamed, dismissed, punished, or left alone with their big feelings, a different lesson is encoded: *emotions are dangerous, shameful, or disruptive.* That lesson may become invisible with age, but it remains active. And in adulthood, it shows up not as a memory but as a reflex.

This is why so many seemingly irrational adult behaviours—binge eating, self-isolation, compulsive achievement, rage outbursts—make perfect sense when viewed through the lens of emotional regulation. They are not random or self-sabotaging. They are the body's improvised solutions to intolerable affect. When the nervous system has not internalised the skills to metabolise sadness, soothe anxiety, or tolerate shame, it reaches for what *works*—even if that solution is maladaptive in the long run. In this sense, *many destructive behaviours are simply emotional strategies performed in disguise.*

Consider the example of emotional numbing through overwork. On the surface, the high achiever appears disciplined, productive, even admirable. But dig deeper and you may find that busyness is a way to outrun the stillness in which grief might surface. The habit of constant doing becomes a way to regulate what cannot yet be safely felt. Or take the case of someone with volatile anger. Behind the explosion is often a nervous system in threat mode—unable to contain the rising swell of helplessness, fear, or rejection. Anger becomes a primitive regulatory response: it transforms vulnerability into force.

It is not enough to label these behaviours as "bad habits." We must understand what they are trying to solve. *The angry outburst is the exhale of a body that never learned to self-soothe.* The emotional eating is the only reliable moment of comfort in a day full of self-denial. The self-harming behaviour is often a last-ditch attempt to escape psychic chaos, to convert emotional pain into something visible and physical. These acts are tragic not because they are irrational, but because they are *logical in a system that lacks alternatives.*

One of the greatest myths surrounding emotional regulation is the idea that it is controlled by willpower. But neuroscience paints a more nuanced picture. Regulation is not about forcing feelings into submission—it is about developing the capacity to *stay with* them without being hijacked. This requires interoception (the ability to sense internal states), emotional labelling (naming what is felt), tolerance of discomfort, and eventually, modulation. Each of these steps relies on specific neural circuits that are developed over time and with practice—ideally through secure relationships and later through intentional training.

Furthermore, regulation is not merely an individual capacity. It is co-created. Infants cannot regulate themselves. Their early experience of being soothed by caregivers creates the foundation for internalising that regulation later. This is why emotionally neglectful or chaotic households don't just produce "sensitive kids"—they produce *dysregulated systems* that never had the chance to learn stability. In adulthood, healing often begins not with solitary effort but with *co-regulation*: being in the presence of someone else who can hold space for distress without amplifying or minimising it. Only from that safe base can a person begin to practise self-regulation on their own.

It is also crucial to separate regulation from repression. To regulate emotion is not to silence it. It is to be in dialogue with it. Repression, by contrast, pushes emotion out of awareness, only for it to return in disguised forms—chronic tension, migraines, autoimmune flare-ups, compulsive behaviours, or mood volatility. The body keeps the score, as Bessel van der Kolk famously wrote, because *it is the last place emotion has to go when it cannot be processed consciously*. Effective regulation means *making space*, not shutting down.

So why is this skill so rarely taught? Partly because our culture still rewards emotional suppression. In many professional, educational, and even familial environments, stoicism is equated with strength. Children are told to "toughen up," "stop crying," or "get over it." Adults are praised for "keeping it together" even when their internal world is falling apart. In this context, emotional regulation is confused with emotional denial. But the cost is profound. When people are not taught to feel safely, they develop elaborate systems to *not feel*. And those systems become the architecture of dysfunction.

This is not just a personal tragedy—it is a collective one. Workplaces, families, institutions, and entire cultures suffer when emotional regulation is absent. Leaders make reactive decisions. Parents pass on their own unprocessed trauma. Partners communicate through defence mechanisms instead of vulnerability. And beneath it all lies a nervous system in survival mode, doing its best to manage what was never modelled.

Fortunately, emotional regulation can be learned at any age. But like any skill, it requires practice, feedback, and patience. The tools are simple in theory but profound in practice: naming emotions without judgement, using breath and posture to signal safety to the body, distinguishing between primary and secondary emotions, building tolerance for distress, cultivating compassionate inner dialogue, and creating relational spaces where all feelings are welcome—even the messy ones.

It also requires a shift in framing. Instead of pathologising our compensatory behaviours, we must learn to *interrogate them with curiosity*. What is this behaviour trying to solve? What feeling is it trying to regulate? And what might I offer myself instead that is both more effective and more kind?

Ultimately, emotional regulation is not a performance skill—it is a survival skill. And when it is cultivated with care, it becomes a liberation skill. Because once we are able to be with our full emotional range, we are no longer controlled by it. We can respond rather than react. We can rest rather than run. We can stay present rather than shut down. And in that presence, real change becomes possible—not because we are fighting ourselves harder, but because we are finally *with* ourselves fully.

To understand emotional regulation as a learned skill is to remove shame from struggle. It is to replace blame with precision, confusion with insight. And it is to give ourselves—and those around us—the grace to learn what was never taught. Because no one is born knowing how to hold sadness, metabolise fear, or soften shame. But anyone can learn. And it is never too late to start.

Why Some People Can Let Go—and Others Can't

Cognitive insight is not always the key that turns the lock. Many people know *exactly* why they struggle. They can articulate their patterns, trace their triggers, and reference research on trauma and behaviour with fluency. And yet—they remain stuck. Not because they lack knowledge, but because *knowledge alone does not undo attachment wounding*. The reason some individuals seem to move forward with relative ease while others tread water, even in therapy or self-work, often lies not in motivation or intelligence, but in the architecture of their earliest relational bonds.

To understand why letting go proves elusive for so many, we must begin with what's really at stake: *psychic survival*. In the context of secure attachment, a child internalises the message that safety is available, that repair follows rupture, and that connection can be maintained without self-abandonment. This gives rise to what developmental psychologists call a "secure base"—a felt sense of stability from which exploration, risk-taking, and letting go become possible. When this base is absent, fragmented, or conditional, the individual learns a different lesson: *attachment must be preserved at any cost—even at the cost of authenticity, autonomy, or change.*

This conditioning doesn't vanish with adulthood. It becomes the template through which we relate to ourselves, others, and even our habits. A person with a history of avoidant attachment, for example, may intellectualise their problems with clinical precision yet remain emotionally disengaged from them—treating self-awareness as a shield rather than a doorway. On the other hand, someone with anxious attachment might chronically ruminate on their issues, desperate to understand and please, but terrified of what change might rupture in their relationships. In both cases, the stuckness isn't a failure of will—it's the residue of an internalised contract: *stay small to stay safe.*

Letting go, in this light, is not a simple act of decision. It is a *relational risk*. To release a harmful behaviour, even one that is causing pain, is to relinquish the strategy that once preserved connection—however dysfunctional that connection may have been. For the child who learned that compliance brought warmth, saying no can feel like exile. For the child who was only noticed in crisis, calm feels invisible. Letting go isn't difficult because people are resistant. It's difficult because it *threatens to rewrite the very terms of attachment their nervous system still believes are non-negotiable.*

The phenomenon of repetition compulsion, first articulated by Freud and later expanded in trauma theory, offers additional insight. This is the tendency for people to unconsciously recreate unresolved early dynamics in adult life—not because they enjoy suffering, but because the psyche attempts mastery through reenactment. The mind returns to the familiar pain not to indulge it, but to *finally fix it.* If a person was never emotionally attuned to as a child, they might unconsciously pursue relationships, jobs, or environments that mirror that early neglect—hoping that this time, it might go differently. And when it doesn't, they interpret the failure as further proof of their defectiveness, reinforcing the cycle. It's not the logic that's flawed—it's the *framework of expectation* rooted in attachment trauma.

Even behaviours that appear purely self-defeating often have an underlying relational logic. A person who clings to perfectionism may not merely fear failure—they may fear what failure represents in their internalised schema: rejection, abandonment, withdrawal of love. Another might resist letting go of anger because it is the only boundary they've ever known. To release it would be to risk collapse into vulnerability without any guarantee of safety. These behaviours are not irrational. They are protective structures—emotional exoskeletons formed in environments that lacked sufficient containment, attunement, or repair.

This is where the frustration of cognitive insight becomes particularly painful. A person might fully *understand* their pattern—why it exists, how it plays out, what it costs—and still find themselves unable to stop. This dissonance can lead to shame: "I know better. Why can't I do better?" But the more accurate question is: "What *threat* does doing better activate in my nervous system?" Often, the answer is some variant of: "If I let go of this, I will lose my place in the world—or I will lose myself." That fear is not irrational; it is *learned.*

Understanding this allows us to shift from blaming resistance to *befriending it.* Stuckness is not laziness or failure. It is often a form of loyalty—to early caregivers, to survival strategies, to unspoken family rules. Some individuals cannot let go because letting go feels like betrayal: of the mother who needed them to stay small, of the father who only responded to anger, of the culture that equated need with weakness. These attachments—however toxic—are laced with emotional debt. To break the pattern is to risk breaking the bond.

The therapeutic task, then, is not to force change through logic or behavioural hacks. It is to create enough relational safety—whether with a therapist, partner, friend, or within oneself—for the nervous system to *consider a different outcome.* Neuroscience supports this. The brain's plasticity means that with consistent, embodied experiences of safety, new pathways can form. But they cannot be willed into existence through insight alone. They must be *lived*, co-regulated, and reinforced over time.

In clinical practice, this often involves making contact with the part of the self that is afraid. Not shaming it. Not bypassing it. Not trying to evict it with affirmations. But *meeting it*, gently and repeatedly, until it begins to trust that its job is no longer required. This inner reconciliation is slow, often nonlinear. But it is the heart of trauma-informed healing.

Real letting go does not feel like discarding a burden. It feels like saying goodbye to a protector. And until a new protector—a more adaptive internal structure—is in place, the psyche will not relinquish its old strategies. This is why trauma work, and by extension, deep habit change, is not about eradication. It is about *integration.* The goal is not to remove the past but to build enough inner safety to live *beyond* its rules.

In this context, some people are more able to let go not because they're more motivated, but because their attachment blueprint makes flexibility *less threatening.* They have a lived template for rupture and repair, for safe autonomy, for emotional presence. Others do not—and they deserve compassion, not comparison. The work of letting go is not simply about release. It is about *replacing the function* that the old behaviour served, without replicating the wound it was protecting.

To truly support those who feel stuck, we must stop asking, "Why aren't you changing?" and start asking, "What has change cost you before?" For some, the answer will be connection. For others, identity. For many, both. Only by honouring those losses—and creating a space where new forms of safety can be felt—can the nervous system begin to uncurl its grip on the past.

Letting go, then, is not a heroic leap. It is a slow, dignified act of emotional reparenting. It begins not with strategy, but with understanding. And it succeeds not through pressure, but through safety. Because in the end, the body won't let go of what it believes it still needs to survive. And to honour that truth is not weakness—it is wisdom.

The Repetition of Familiar Pain

The human psyche, for all its complexity, is often governed by a quiet but relentless drive: the need to resolve what was once unbearable. This drive explains one of the most puzzling paradoxes in behavioural psychology—why people, despite insight and suffering, often return to situations that hurt them. They recreate the very emotional injuries they long to escape, not because they desire pain, but because, at some fundamental level, they hope this time will be different. This unconscious return to emotional wounds is not masochism. It is what Freud termed *repetition compulsion*—an attempt not to relive the past, but to *rewrite* it.

Repetition compulsion doesn't announce itself with clarity. It operates subtly, often disguised as choice. A person repeatedly dates emotionally unavailable partners, each time convinced this one is different. Another chronically overcommits, secretly hoping their exhaustion will finally earn admiration. Someone else might recreate the chaos of their childhood home through workplace conflict or financial volatility—not because they enjoy instability, but because that landscape is *familiar*. The pain is known. Predictable. Containable in its own distorted way. And, more importantly, it offers the illusion of mastery—if I can endure it again, maybe this time I'll win.

But the deeper mechanism is not victory—it's longing. The child who was dismissed emotionally becomes the adult who seeks attention through performance or provocation, hoping not just to be seen, but to rewrite the ending of the story. That child is not trying to repeat the pain, but to transform it—this time to finally receive the attunement that was missing. That effort, however, is usually unconscious. It is not reflected in logic or declared in words. It lives in patterns. In selection. In habit.

Attachment theory intersects here with precision. Our earliest relationships form blueprints for how we expect to be treated and how we believe we must behave in order to be loved, safe, or worthy. If those relationships were inconsistent, conditional, or harmful, the blueprint is not erased with time—it becomes a framework. The adult continues to seek out dynamics that match the emotional tone of those early attachments, not because they are satisfying, but because they are *coherent with the self-image built in that original context.* It's not the event that repeats—it's the *emotional logic*: "I must earn love." "I must be perfect." "I must not need."

In this sense, repetition compulsion can be understood as a covert loyalty to early emotional terms. It's as if the psyche is saying: "I didn't get to resolve this then, so I'll keep creating conditions where I might." But this logic is fraught. The adult may now have more agency, but the old dynamic still rules the script. And when the present fails to heal the past—as it often does—the result is not growth, but deepened wounding. The person does not interpret the repeated failure as a fault of circumstance, but as confirmation of their defectiveness. The wound grows, while the hope that it might someday be healed grows more desperate.

Neuroscience offers complementary insight here. The brain is a prediction machine. It relies on past data to interpret the present and forecast the future. Emotional memories, particularly traumatic or unresolved ones, are encoded in neural networks that remain activated until they are reprocessed. When the brain detects a match—someone's tone of voice, the power dynamics of a situation, a bodily sensation—it may trigger a full emotional memory even if the context is entirely different. This is not recall. It's *reliving*. The person reacts, not to the now, but to the echo. And without awareness, they may not realise they are trying to *complete a loop that began decades earlier*.

One of the more subtle dangers of repetition compulsion is that it can be reinforced by temporary relief. For example, a person who always overfunctions in relationships may experience a fleeting sense of control or worth when they are needed—momentarily satisfying the inner child's need to be indispensable. But when that role leads to resentment or burnout, they feel used or unseen. The cycle begins anew, and the cost accumulates. What started as an effort to resolve unmet needs becomes a form of self-sabotage that *feels like love but acts like harm.*

Breaking this pattern requires more than recognition. Many people understand their tendencies and yet still repeat them. What's needed is *emotional resolution*—a willingness to grieve what never was and to stop asking the present to repair what the past withheld. This is not resignation. It is reclamation. It involves separating the *original need*—to be safe, to be valued, to be seen—from the *current strategy* that seeks to achieve it. And it requires offering that need new avenues of expression, grounded in the adult self's real agency rather than the child's emotional scarcity.

This process is painful. It asks the individual to stop hoping that the next relationship, job, achievement, or sacrifice will finally earn what their younger self was denied. It asks them to sit with the sadness, the rage, the longing—not to bypass these emotions but to integrate them. Only then does the compulsion lose its urgency. Only then can the behaviour become a choice rather than a reflex.

Therapeutic approaches such as Internal Family Systems, psychodynamic therapy, and trauma-informed somatic work are particularly effective here. They help individuals identify the part of themselves that is carrying the wound and the part that is reenacting it. They build a bridge between the impulse to repeat and the possibility to repair. And they do so not by forcing change but by *increasing internal safety*—so the nervous system can begin to believe that resolution is possible *without reenactment.*

Importantly, repetition compulsion is not pathological. It is profoundly human. It reveals how devoted we are to healing, even when our strategies are misaligned. It shows the lengths to which the psyche will go in pursuit of closure. And it reminds us that most self-defeating behaviour is not driven by irrationality, but by *unresolved emotional logic.* When that logic is understood, compassion becomes possible. And with compassion, choice returns.

Repetition may be the default, but it is not destiny. Once the compulsion is named and understood, it can be disrupted—not through suppression or willpower, but through grief, insight, and new relational experiences. Those who break the cycle are not simply exercising discipline. They are *honouring the emotional intelligence of the pattern, while refusing to remain hostage to it.* They are choosing to give themselves—deliberately, patiently—what the past could not.

To heal from repetition compulsion is not to reject the past. It is to *release it from the job of directing the present.* It is to say: I see why I chose this before. I see how it made sense. And I no longer need to suffer the same injury to prove I am worthy of healing.

That is not forgetfulness. That is freedom.

Chapter 7
Conflict Within

One of the most pervasive assumptions in contemporary self-help is that we are singular beings: one mind, one self, one coherent identity. Yet anyone who has wrestled with procrastination, self-sabotage, emotional eating, or sudden bursts of anger knows this is far from the truth. Often, people report thoughts like, "Part of me wants to change, but another part just doesn't care," or, "I know what I should do, so why do I keep doing the opposite?" These observations are too readily dismissed as indecision or weakness, when in fact they point to something far deeper—a fractured interior. We are not unitary; we are systems.

This chapter explores a framework that honours and works with this multiplicity: Internal Family Systems (IFS). Though it emerged as a psychotherapeutic approach, its relevance extends beyond the clinic, because it reflects a truth most people recognise intuitively. You know the inner critic, the avoider, the achiever, and the tender child who longs for safety. These are not metaphors, nor simply personality traits—they are internal agents, each carrying distinct histories, responsibilities, fears, and hopes. When they clash, it can feel like being pulled apart from within.

IFS is radical in its refusal to pathologise this internal conflict. No part is labelled "bad" or "irrational." Each part is assumed to be attempting to help, however clumsily. The bingeing voice, for instance, may be trying to soothe pain that no other part can reach. The anger that flares unbidden may be shielding a younger self who once felt powerless or humiliated. Seen this way, what appears as self-sabotage is often a form of misguided protection. Dysfunction is not the problem; disconnection is.

This chapter avoids over-intellectualising IFS. While clinical literature can be dense, the essence of the model is accessible. Anyone can begin to understand their inner fragmentation, replace self-blame with curiosity, and start asking, "Which part of me is acting, and what is it afraid of?" rather than, "What's wrong with me?" That subtle shift in questioning opens a dialogue rooted in listening, not suppression.

Much of our suffering comes not from having multiple parts, but from treating those conflicts as threats to be vanquished rather than messages to be understood. Popular self-improvement culture rarely helps; it celebrates mastery, control, and conquest over the "lesser selves." Yet silencing a part only deepens its fear of rejection. Punishing a habit reinforces the pain it sought to soothe. Healing does not arise from dominance—it comes through relationship.

Working effectively with inner conflict requires internal leadership: the ability to relate to each part with compassion and authority, rather than fusion or rejection. This does not mean indulging every impulse or allowing fear to dictate behaviour. It means recognising the dynamics beneath those impulses and responding with presence, not force. Think of it as convening a roundtable rather than waging a war. Some parts will speak loudly and insistently; others may remain hidden, ashamed, or silent. All of them carry information. None are disposable.

This chapter distinguishes between protector parts—those that manage, control, please, numb, or explode to preserve safety—and exiled parts, which hold the original emotional wounds. Exiles are often buried beneath strategies and self-denial, yet they are the very parts most in need of attention. Until they are acknowledged, protector parts remain active. They are not enemies; they are waiting for guidance.

You will also see why behaviours that appear "irrational" or "out of character" often make perfect sense when viewed from within the system. The part that drags you back into bed after a week of productivity may be exhausted from upholding an image of competence. The part that lashes out at a loved one may fear intimacy. The procrastinator may be guarding against exposure. Seen in isolation, these actions seem to undermine goals; in context, they preserve balance in a nervous system that does not yet trust change is safe.

This perspective reshapes self-development. The aim is not to become someone else but to reintegrate the disowned or distorted parts of oneself. Integration is not achieved by overriding impulses or dismissing objections; it comes through dialogue. Not a voice that declares victory, but one where each part is acknowledged, understood, and gradually aligned with a central Self: calm, clear, curious, and compassionate.

The latter half of the chapter provides practical tools for beginning this dialogue. No gimmicks or quick fixes—just structured prompts that cultivate trust within your psyche. You will learn to identify when a part has commandeered behaviour, differentiate it from your core Self, and respond without shame or aggression. These are practices—simple, repeatable, and potent over time.

Engaging with parts work requires recognising that your psyche is a community, not a problem to solve. Like any community, it needs leadership—not authoritarian command, but relational wisdom. Anger, craving, avoidance, or perfectionism are not enemies to be exorcised; they are messengers to be heard. Ask what they protect. Listen. Lead—not with force, but by inviting each part back into connection with the whole.

Internal conflict is not a failure of selfhood; it is the residue of adaptation. The parts that now clash were once allies, formed under pressure, striving to protect and survive. Their methods may be outdated, but their intent was life-preserving. You owe them curiosity, not control. In that curiosity lies the beginning of healing—not by fixing yourself, but by leading yourself from the inside out.

Parts Work for Everyday People

It is a quietly radical act to stop assuming that all your thoughts, impulses, fears, and behaviours come from a single, unified self. Most people walk around with the vague belief that they are one "I," when in fact they are many. They say things like, "I just don't understand why I did that," or "Part of me wanted to say no, but another part caved." These aren't rhetorical tics. They are clues—

slips of truth that reveal a psychological reality that modern neuroscience, trauma theory, and therapeutic practice increasingly affirm: the mind is not monolithic. It is *modular*. The question is not whether you are made up of parts, but how conscious you are of them.

Internal Family Systems (IFS) provides a clear, compassionate, and intuitive way of exploring this truth. Developed by family therapist Dr Richard Schwartz in the 1980s, IFS began as a clinical approach but has since evolved into one of the most accessible models for self-inquiry available today. The brilliance of the framework lies in its simplicity: all of us have "parts" within us—discrete sub-personalities that carry their own emotions, beliefs, and behaviours. Some are protectors: the controller, the perfectionist, the avoider. Others are exiles: younger, wounded parts that carry grief, shame, longing, or fear. And beneath them all is the Self—a calm, clear, compassionate centre that is capable of leading the internal system, if it is allowed to emerge.

IFS is not about fragmentation. It's about integration. It does not treat parts as pathological but as *adaptive*. That inner critic who won't shut up? It likely developed in childhood to keep you out of trouble. The overeating part? It may have stepped in during adolescence to soothe an emotional wound. Even the procrastinator—the bane of so many professionals—is often protecting against the terror of being judged. When viewed through the IFS lens, these behaviours are not random or irrational. They are *relational*. They make sense within the internal dynamics of your system. And, crucially, they are trying to help—even when they hurt.

For people outside of clinical settings, parts work offers something rare in psychological models: immediacy. You don't need to memorise terminology or study theory to benefit. You simply need to start noticing your inner world with more granularity. Instead of saying "I'm anxious," you might begin to say, "A part of me feels anxious." That linguistic shift alone can de-escalate internal pressure. It creates space. It acknowledges complexity. It invites you to *lead*, rather than collapse into identification.

But what does it mean to lead your internal system? In IFS, leadership comes from Self—not ego, not role, not strategy. Self is the state of being that emerges when protective parts trust they can relax. It's characterised by eight qualities: calmness, curiosity, clarity, compassion, confidence, creativity, courage, and connectedness. Most people don't live from Self all the time—and that's not the goal. The aim is not perfection, but relationship. When a part is activated—when you're hijacked by rage, stuck in despair, or paralysed by indecision—the question is not "How do I get rid of this?" but "Can I connect with this part from Self?" That shift alone can change the trajectory of a reaction.

For example, imagine you're in the middle of a conflict with a colleague. A part of you wants to explode. Another part wants to retreat and avoid. Yet another is performing a calm, diplomatic mask. In the traditional model of behaviour change, you'd try to pick the "right" one and force the others into silence. But in IFS, you'd pause, acknowledge each part, and ask what they're afraid of. You might discover that the angry part is protecting a part that feels unrespected. That the avoidant part fears humiliation. That the diplomatic part is exhausted from constantly smoothing over tension. In that moment of dialogue, new options become available—not because you've conquered the parts, but because you've *listened* to them.

This is not indulgent or inefficient. It's strategic. Systems work best when all parts feel seen and understood. Suppression breeds sabotage. Exile breeds escalation. When a part is ignored, it often intensifies to get your attention. This is why so many self-improvement efforts backfire. People try to bulldoze their way to discipline, only to find themselves bingeing, quitting, or imploding weeks later. The issue isn't lack of willpower—it's *lack of internal trust.*

IFS helps rebuild that trust through a practical, repeatable process: unblending, witnessing, and unburdening. First, you unblend—meaning you notice when a part has taken over your internal state and gently separate from it. This might sound abstract, but it's surprisingly familiar. Have you ever calmed yourself down by saying, "Okay, this is just my anxiety talking"? That's unblending. Second, you witness. You turn toward the part with curiosity, asking what it's afraid of, what it's trying to do for you, and when it first took on its role. This is not an interrogation—it's a respectful inquiry. Third, you support the part in releasing its burden. This may involve visualisation, memory work, or simply acknowledging that the circumstances that required its extreme role no longer exist. Again, no certification required. Just presence.

One of the most healing aspects of parts work is that it removes moralism from the equation. You are not a failure for avoiding hard conversations, numbing out with screens, or pushing people away. These behaviours are not character flaws—they are *strategies*. And like all strategies, they were developed under conditions of constraint. Maybe you learned to fawn to stay safe in a volatile home. Maybe you learned to stay busy to outrun grief. These patterns don't just disappear with insight. They soften with relationship. IFS doesn't ask you to be perfect. It asks you to be *present to what's happening inside*, and to build trust over time.

The practical implications are profound. In moments of overwhelm, you can ask, "Which part of me is driving right now?" In situations of stuckness, you can explore, "What part of me doesn't want to move forward, and why?" These are not tricks. They are invitations. And as parts begin to trust that they don't have to scream to be heard, the system calms. New choices emerge. You don't have to white-knuckle your way through change. You can *lead your way into it.*

IFS also offers a framework for emotional nuance. For example, someone may say, "I'm angry," but with deeper exploration realise there's also a part that's sad, another that's ashamed of feeling sad, and yet another that's trying to keep it all together. Without parts work, this inner chorus gets collapsed into one emotional note. With parts work, you can begin to differentiate. And with differentiation comes dignity. You are no longer reacting blindly. You are relating internally—with respect.

This model also scales across domains. In relationships, it helps partners avoid fusion and blame. In parenting, it allows adults to respond rather than react. In leadership, it cultivates clarity and resilience. And for anyone navigating burnout, addiction, anxiety, or creative paralysis, parts work offers not just relief, but reintegration.

You're not trying to eliminate your symptoms. You're trying to understand what parts are producing them—and why they believe those strategies are still necessary.

The greatest misconception about IFS is that it is overly therapeutic or too abstract for "ordinary" people. In reality, it's one of the most democratic psychological models available. You don't need a diagnosis. You don't need to understand polyvagal theory or attachment styles. You just need curiosity, patience, and a willingness to be honest about what's happening inside. The goal isn't transcendence. It's *wholeness.*

In a culture that rewards performance, perfectionism, and productivity, parts work is subversive. It invites you to slow down, listen internally, and honour complexity. It teaches that the parts of you you've tried to exile—the addict, the procrastinator, the control freak—are not barriers to healing. They *are* the path to healing. They are carrying burdens, not causing problems. And they will soften when you stop treating them like enemies.

You don't need to conquer yourself to become whole. You need to meet yourself—fully, compassionately, and often. That is the essence of parts work. Not because it's fashionable. Not because it's soft. But because it works.

Meet Your Inner Opponents

There's a reason your efforts to "just stop" a behaviour—overeating, snapping at your partner, procrastinating—rarely work for long. It's not because you're lazy or weak-willed. It's because, inside you, there's more than one agenda. One part of you wants growth, clarity, connection. Another part tightens, resists, distracts. This isn't ambivalence; it's inner conflict. And until you understand the nature of your internal opposition—not as sabotage but as protection—you'll keep fighting shadows with no clear target. The first step is to stop asking, "What's wrong with me?" and start asking, "*Who in me is doing this—and why?*"

Internal Family Systems (IFS) offers a rigorous yet humane answer. It reframes what many consider flaws—addictions, avoidance, rage, shutdown—not as pathologies but as the desperate work of *protector parts*: internal agents acting on behalf of your survival. These protectors are not malicious. They are overburdened. And they are often defending what IFS calls *exiles*—parts of you that hold pain too overwhelming to face directly: the grief-stricken child, the ashamed adolescent, the abandoned lover. If the exile is the wound, the protector is the armour.

This internal system is not theoretical. It is experientially verifiable. Most people, when guided gently, can identify these factions within themselves. They'll say things like, "There's a part of me that's always on edge," or "A part of me shuts down every time someone gets too close." These are not metaphors. They are phenomenological truths. Your mind is a living ecosystem, and parts arise in response to what you've lived through. They are shaped by context, not character. And their roles, however disruptive, began with an earnest mission: *keep you safe.*

Understanding protectors is often the entry point. They are the ones you meet most often—sometimes hourly. The inner critic, for instance, is one of the most common protectors. People loathe it, but rarely ask what it's protecting. Often, the critic is guarding against rejection by preemptively attacking you before anyone else can. Or consider the part that numbs with social media, alcohol, food. It may look like sabotage, but in reality, it's interruption. It's keeping you from touching the deeper pain underneath—perhaps unworthiness, shame, or loneliness. These protectors are not the enemy. *They are responders working without adequate support.*

Exiles, on the other hand, are often invisible until protectors soften. These are the parts of you carrying burdens from the past: the panic of being left, the humiliation of being dismissed, the rage of being powerless. Many people have no conscious access to their exiles because their system has deemed it unsafe. A high-functioning executive might feel mysteriously flattened every weekend—until she realises that her driven, perfectionist protector has been shielding a core exile who learned that only achievement earns love. A withdrawn teenager might resist therapy, not because he's oppositional, but because a protective part won't allow anyone near the terror that comes from past violation. The more extreme the protector, the more profound the exile it's defending.

What complicates healing is that these parts often oppose each other. One part wants to speak up; another fears the consequences. One wants rest; another screams about laziness. These internal battles are exhausting—not because they are irrational, but because they are unresolved. Each part is trying to do its job in isolation, with no awareness that others even exist. This is why internal dialogue is not indulgent—it's *organisational.* It brings coherence to chaos. It allows you to become the leader of your system rather than its battleground.

One way to begin identifying your parts is to track patterns in your behaviour. Ask yourself:

When I get overwhelmed, what do I do automatically? That's likely a *protector.*

What emotion does this part try to prevent me from feeling? That's the *exile* it's shielding.

When have I felt this way before? That's your map to origin.

For example, someone who overfunctions in relationships—taking on tasks, fixing others' problems, preemptively managing conflict—might discover a managerial protector who emerged during childhood to maintain order in a chaotic home. This protector may be shielding an exile that felt unseen, scared, or responsible for others' emotions. That inner manager is not trying to control your adult life for no reason—it's still operating in the past.

Importantly, this mapping is not about blame. It's about context. It turns self-sabotage into self-protection. And that shift creates options. Once a protector knows it no longer has to do its job alone, it often relaxes. Once an exile is witnessed by Self—calm, curious, compassionate presence—it no longer has to scream through symptoms to be heard. That's the alchemy of this work. *What you identify and relate to, you transform.*

Still, many people resist the idea of making friends with parts they despise. They'll say, "But this part is ruining my life!" That's valid—and also incomplete. Often, the part we most want to get rid of is the part that most needs compassion. The bingeing part may be feeding a hunger that isn't about food. The avoidant part may be protecting against a flood of grief. The angry part may be holding power on behalf of a part that once felt powerless. Until we stop pathologising these responses, we cannot liberate them. We stay stuck in a loop: react, regret, repress, repeat.

Meeting your inner opponents is not about choosing sides. It's about learning to *mediate*. Self doesn't eliminate parts. It listens, respects, and leads. And once parts feel safe in that leadership, they stop fighting each other and start collaborating. The critic might soften into a discerning advisor. The avoidant might shift into a boundary-setter. Even the most extreme parts—those labelled "toxic" or "addictive"—can take on new roles once they are unburdened from the trauma or beliefs they've carried. But this can't be rushed. It happens at the speed of trust.

One of the great contributions of IFS is the reminder that all parts are welcome. This is not a passive acceptance; it's an active inquiry. Every part, no matter how disruptive, carries a piece of your history, your adaptation, your intelligence. And when you relate to them instead of react to them, healing becomes possible—not as behaviour modification, but as system-wide recalibration.

For those accustomed to high performance and cognitive mastery, this can be humbling. Insight alone doesn't move protectors. Logic doesn't heal exiles. These parts respond to relationship, not reason. They need to be *felt* and *heard*, not argued with. That's why even the most articulate people find themselves stuck in loops they can describe perfectly but cannot exit. The system doesn't shift because the system doesn't *feel* safe.

The invitation, then, is to meet your inner opponents not with force, but with curiosity. You do not need to negotiate peace in one session. You only need to begin the conversation. Ask, "What is this part trying to do for me?" Listen without agenda. Watch what unfolds. You may find that the part you feared most is the one that has worked hardest to protect you. You may find that behind resistance is grief. Behind rage, a cry for help. Behind shutdown, a buried longing to be known.

This is not easy work, but it is humanising. It allows you to make contact with yourself in a way that restores dignity to your experience. And once you stop exiling parts of yourself internally, you become less susceptible to doing it to others. You build capacity—not just for regulation, but for integration.

So when the next internal flare-up arises—when you're flooded with anxiety, defensive in a conversation, caught in a compulsive loop—pause. Ask: *Who's here right now?* That question, simple but profound, is the beginning of a different kind of inner life—one where survival strategies give way to coherence, and where no part of you is left behind.

When Your 'Bad' Self Isn't the Enemy

It's a common but costly mistake: treating the part of yourself that misbehaves as a defect to be eradicated. The binge-eating, the snapping at loved ones, the endless avoidance of that important conversation—these behaviours are rarely random or illogical. Yet we shame ourselves for them with a punishing certainty, as if inner sabotage were a matter of character rather than context. But what if the part of you you've labelled "bad" is not an intruder, but a misunderstood protector? Not a source of your suffering, but a symptom of it? Not the root problem—but the first clue?

This reframing is not mere semantics. It's the difference between self-punishment and self-inquiry. Within Internal Family Systems (IFS) and other parts-based psychologies, seemingly destructive behaviours are often enacted by *protector parts*—internal subpersonalities tasked with shielding you from pain. These protectors do not emerge arbitrarily; they are formed in response to lived experience. A child who endured ridicule for emotional expression may develop a part that numbs feeling. A teenager who learned that silence equals safety may develop a part that avoids confrontation. These parts continue operating long after the original danger has passed. *They are outdated solutions doing the best they can with what they remember.*

The challenge is that most people relate to these parts as adversaries. We resist, suppress, or attempt to overpower them. The bingeing part is met with dietary control, the angry part with shame, the avoidant part with harsh discipline. But control without curiosity hardens the system. The part doesn't go away—it just goes underground. And underground parts tend to escalate. They act out in increasingly extreme ways, not out of malice, but in a desperate attempt to be noticed, or to maintain their protective function. When we treat these parts as enemies, *we deepen the internal war that created them in the first place.*

A striking example can be seen in the common experience of procrastination. Many treat it as a flaw in willpower. But closer inspection often reveals a protective part avoiding the risk of failure, humiliation, or overwhelm. For someone raised in a perfectionistic or critical environment, even small tasks can trigger a cascade of fear. In such a case, procrastination is not laziness—it is risk management. It is the nervous system placing a buffer between the self and potential danger. You cannot eliminate that kind of behaviour through productivity hacks alone. *You must engage with the protector carrying the burden of past experience.*

Similarly, parts that lash out—often vilified in both social and therapeutic spaces—are frequently defending vulnerable exiles underneath. What appears as volatility may be a preemptive strike. It's common for someone with abandonment trauma, for example, to push others away in moments of perceived closeness. The anger says, "I don't need anyone," but behind it is a terrified exile saying, "Please don't leave me again." Until the anger is seen for what it truly is—*a shield*—its function will remain unchanged, no matter how many interpersonal conflicts it creates.

This model also extends to parts that engage in numbing behaviours—overeating, alcohol, compulsive scrolling. These parts are often attempting to dampen the volume on internal pain. They serve as anaesthetics, not saboteurs. A part that reaches for food every night may be silencing an exile that feels unlovable, lonely, or chronically unseen. That food may be the only consistent comfort the system knows. Remove the behaviour without understanding the need it serves, and you don't create freedom—you create panic. The system doesn't just lose a crutch; it loses its only form of pain relief.

To break these cycles, you must stop treating parts as problems and start asking questions. What is this part trying to do for me? When did it first show up? What is it afraid will happen if it steps back? Most parts, when given the chance to speak, don't talk in pathology—they talk in pain. They remember the times you were humiliated, neglected, silenced, or judged. They carry those memories as burdens. And because they are burdened, they overfunction. The bingeing part doesn't *want* to be compulsive—it *has* to be, until something safer is in place.

That distinction between burden and essence is vital. In IFS, all parts are considered inherently valuable. Their current behaviours may be extreme, but their core qualities are often gifts distorted by trauma. The hypercritical part might carry innate discernment. The avoidant part may hold wisdom about boundaries. The rageful part may possess fierce protective instinct. When these parts are unburdened—when they are no longer carrying trauma, fear, or shame—they don't disappear. They transform. *What once felt like sabotage becomes support.*

This isn't instant. Parts that have been active for decades don't relinquish their role overnight. Many don't trust your adult Self yet—especially if you've spent years trying to suppress or override them. They require not domination, but relationship. And that relationship begins with genuine, agenda-free curiosity. Not "How do I get rid of this part?" but "What is this part trying to protect me from?" That shift in inquiry alone can change the internal tone from hostility to leadership. It creates psychological safety—the only condition under which real transformation occurs.

Still, this approach may initially feel counterintuitive. Most cultures pathologise these behaviours. They reward productivity, composure, emotional restraint. They label bingeing, avoidance, or rage as moral failings. Many clients resist the idea that their "worst" part might be doing something right. They are afraid that compassion will lead to complacency. But self-compassion is not a lack of standards—it's a change in strategy. Instead of attacking the symptom, it addresses the source. And when the burden is healed, the behaviour often resolves without force.

Moreover, the act of listening to these parts fosters integration. It collapses the split between the "good" self and the "bad" self, between who you want to be and what you keep doing. It allows you to live less from fragmentation and more from wholeness. When you stop fighting your parts, you recover energy that was spent on internal combat. You gain clarity that was previously clouded by shame. And you develop emotional agility—the capacity to respond from Self rather than react from fear.

Real-world application of this approach requires structured curiosity. When a pattern shows up—be it bingeing, snapping, zoning out—pause. Name it as a part. "Something in me is doing this." Notice it. "Where do I feel it in my body?" Ask it. "What are you trying to protect me from?" And listen—not from the mind, but from the heart. Don't rush to fix. Don't demand it change. Just make space. This, paradoxically, is what begins to loosen the grip. Parts don't relax under pressure—they relax under presence.

There's immense relief in discovering that your inner saboteur is not out to ruin you. It's out to *rescue* you—from danger that may no longer exist, but that was once very real. And once you see that, the urgency to eliminate these behaviours often fades. You begin to work with your system, not against it. And in doing so, you discover something quietly radical: *Your 'bad' self was never the enemy. It was your wounded protector—waiting to be met, heard, and finally relieved of a job it never wanted in the first place.*

Dialogue Instead of Dominance

When most people try to change a behaviour—quit smoking, stop snapping at their partner, reduce doomscrolling—they come at it with force. They declare war on the unwanted part of themselves: I need to get rid of this. I have to stop doing that. I can't let this keep happening. Beneath these statements lies a belief system built on internal dominance: that some parts of us are good and rational, while others are bad, irrational, or weak. Change, under this model, is achieved through suppression, control, and often shame. And yet, most lasting personal change doesn't arise from dominance. It arises from dialogue. Not the command of a general, but the curiosity of a diplomat.

In Internal Family Systems (IFS), this principle is foundational. Every behaviour—no matter how maladaptive it appears—is driven by a *part* of you that believes it is helping in some way. That part may be deeply mistaken, working with outdated data or traumatised logic, but its intent is protective. Even the part that procrastinates until everything collapses is not lazy—it may be terrified of failure or craving safety. Trying to dominate that part into submission not only fails; it often intensifies the behaviour. The real shift happens when you *speak* to the part, not *at* it.

Imagine someone who compulsively rechecks their email at night, despite knowing it disrupts sleep and offers little value. A dominance-based strategy might sound like: "I have to stop this. I'm sabotaging myself. Just turn off your phone and grow up." That tone mimics the critical parenting many people internalised—and it usually backfires. The behaviour may stop temporarily, only to return more forcefully during stress. A dialogue-based approach might begin instead with: "Something in me is checking email. I wonder what it's afraid would happen if I didn't?" That inquiry signals presence, not punishment. It gives space for a genuine response to emerge, often surprising in its emotional nuance.

This is not abstraction. It's a specific, learnable practice. The key is shifting from *interrogation* to *conversation.* One practical tool is the "You're welcome to speak" script: "I notice this behaviour again. I'm not here to silence you. You're welcome to speak. What's going on?" The part may respond with anger, resistance, silence, or even sarcasm—just like a real person who's never been truly listened to. That's fine. Stay in relationship. Respond with: "I hear you. That makes sense. I'd like to understand more." When parts feel heard, they soften. When they're forced, they dig in.

Of course, this requires an inner orientation that many adults never learned: self-leadership. Not the version sold by productivity gurus, but the kind that arises from calm, curious, confident presence. IFS calls this the "Self"—the seat of internal leadership that is not a part, but the grounded observer capable of holding all parts with compassion. When we speak from Self, we don't collapse into the urgency of one part or the contempt of another. We listen, negotiate, and discern. We don't let the anxious part drive, but we don't banish it from the car either. We say: "You can ride up front, but you're not steering."

This relational stance requires practice. Most people's first attempts at internal dialogue are coloured by impatience or scepticism. That's normal. The key is *consistency over performance*. Even brief, two-minute check-ins can start to shift the tone of the internal system. For instance, you might start the day with: "Who's most activated in me right now?" or "Which part of me needs something before I go into this meeting?" These questions don't demand answers; they invite them. Over time, parts learn they are safe to speak—and, more importantly, they are not alone.

It's worth noting that some parts may resist dialogue entirely. They may say, "This is pointless," or "This is just navel-gazing," or even, "I don't deserve compassion." That's another part speaking—the sceptic, the critic, the shamed protector. It, too, can be met with curiosity. "What are you afraid will happen if I try this?" This is where self-dialogue becomes a kind of emotional aikido: *You never fight force with force. You use the momentum of resistance to create connection.* That in itself is transformative.

For people who've been shaped by high-control, emotionally avoidant, or shaming environments, this shift can feel almost dangerous. Internal dominance often mimics what felt safe in childhood: controlling emotions to avoid punishment, suppressing vulnerability to maintain approval. Dialogue, in contrast, opens the door to listening to grief, rage, neediness, or fear—feelings that may have been explicitly or implicitly forbidden. That's why this work is not just psychological; it is, in many ways, political. It reclaims sovereignty from the inherited internal regime of repression. It says:

Every part of me has a place. Every voice deserves to be heard, not obeyed—but heard.

Some practical prompts to begin this process include:
– "What are you afraid would happen if you stopped doing this?"
– "When did you first feel the need to protect me in this way?"
– "What do you want me to understand about you?"
– "If I could help you rest, what would you need from me?"
– "Are you carrying someone else's pain?"

These are not manipulations. They are invitations. You cannot script your way into internal harmony by treating parts like code to be debugged. You have to *relate* to them. And that means being willing to sit with discomfort, to move slowly, to listen beneath the noise. Over time, a remarkable thing happens: parts that once fought for dominance begin to collaborate. The angry part warns you about crossed boundaries. The anxious part helps you prepare without panicking. The avoidant part helps you pace yourself. They don't disappear—they *mature.*

This shift also changes how you relate to others. People who develop internal dialogue skills often become less reactive, more empathic, and more resilient. That's not because they have less emotion—it's because they've built the capacity to hold conflicting feelings without collapsing into them. They can notice that they feel both angry and afraid, both hurt and grateful, both resentful and responsible. That emotional ambidexterity is what makes dialogue—inside and out—possible. It's not about being "healed." It's about being *available*—to your own complexity and to the world's.

This kind of work is not glamorous. It doesn't produce dramatic Instagram quotes or quick-fix checklists. But it is quietly revolutionary. It builds internal infrastructure for long-term growth. It prevents relapse into self-abandonment. It allows for change without coercion. Most importantly, it gives you access to the kind of wholeness that doesn't require erasing any part of who you are.

Dominance might bring temporary compliance. But only dialogue brings durable change. And in a world that rewards control, domination, and suppression, choosing to listen—to truly listen—to your inner life is a radical act. Not because it's indulgent, but because it's honest. You cannot out-discipline what you have not yet understood. You cannot fix what you refuse to speak with. And you cannot lead your internal system if you're still at war with it. *The real revolution starts when you stop shouting at your parts—and start talking to them instead.*

Chapter 8
Emotion as Intelligence

We have been taught, both overtly and subtly, to treat emotion as a liability—something to be managed, suppressed, or bypassed. Listen to the familiar refrains: "Don't take it personally," "Keep your cool," "Get over it." The implication is unmistakable: feelings are distractions from rationality, obstacles to progress, indicators of weakness. This framing is far from neutral; it shapes the very architecture of how we perceive ourselves and others. In professional settings, emotion is often deemed disruptive; in personal growth circles, it is portrayed as a hurdle to spiritual evolution; in medicine, a biochemical nuisance. Rarely, however, are emotions recognised for what they truly are: intelligence in motion. They are not derailments from thinking, but a distinct—and sometimes faster—form of it.

Emotions exist to aid survival, not sabotage it. Biologically encoded by the nervous system, they track safety, anticipate social threats, strengthen connection, and mobilise action. Their intensity is not evidence of irrationality but of significance. Anger signals injustice. Anxiety forecasts uncertainty. Grief marks attachment. Even envy, so often pathologised, illuminates desire disguised as comparison. To ignore emotion is not to become rational; it is to wander blindly through unexamined data.

The brain does not treat emotion and cognition as separate rivers. The limbic system, where affective processing occurs, is not a backwater to the neocortex; it is in continuous dialogue with it. Antonio Damasio's research revealed that patients with damage to emotion-processing regions do not become hyper-rational—they become unable to decide. Without emotional input, the evaluation of value, priority, and consequence collapses. Emotion is not the opposite of reason; it is the soil in which reason takes root. Feelings do not block logic—they nourish it.

Yet for many, especially those with high-functioning intellects or cultural conditioning around stoicism, emotions feel threatening precisely because they are ambiguous. They cannot be quantified, they resist obedience, and expressing them can leave one vulnerable. Sadness risks rejection. Anger risks retaliation. Need risks shame. The result is often hyper-management: avoidance, numbing, or control strategies that appear mature but are neurologically costly. Suppressing emotion does not build resilience; it builds distortion. The body continues to feel even when the mind refuses to acknowledge it.

This disconnection produces what psychologists call emotional incoherence: a misalignment between what we report feeling, what we display, and what the body experiences. It manifests in relapses, miscommunication, and chronic stress. Someone may insist, "I'm fine," while clenching their fists; claim, "I don't care," while obsessively scrolling an ex's social media; believe, "I've moved on," while reacting disproportionately to minor rejection. These contradictions are not hypocrisy—they are signals of emotional data being mislabelled, minimised, or ignored. And they surface, unfailingly, in habitual behaviour.

Habits are never merely actions. They are conclusions drawn by the nervous system: this feeling signals danger, act now; this context echoes abandonment, protect yourself. If the underlying emotion remains unnamed, the habit endures, regardless of insight or willpower. Change often fails, not from lack of intention, but from insufficient emotional literacy. The goal is not to feel less; it is to feel more precisely.

This chapter reframes feeling as the map, not the obstacle. Emotional granularity—the capacity to differentiate between similar feelings—is crucial: knowing the difference between frustration and disappointment, shame and guilt. Research by Lisa Feldman Barrett and others links higher granularity to better regulation, lower inflammation, and improved decision-making. Precise feeling allows precise action; vague feeling leads to vagueness in response.

Consider someone who says they feel "bad" after overeating. That "bad" might conceal multiple signals: shame at breaking a promise, loneliness in eating alone, powerlessness at lack of control, anger at settling for less than desired. Each layer points to a different path toward repair. Naming these layers allows separation: we can hold feeling without being consumed by it, creating the micro-gap between stimulus and reaction—the hinge of emotional maturity. Viktor Frankl wrote, "Between stimulus and response there is a space. In that space lies our power to choose our response." Expanding that space demands reflective practice, not mere willpower. One asks, "What just happened inside me?"—not to critique, but to decode. This is the foundation of the emotional trigger chain: cue → emotion → belief → behaviour.

Imagine someone yelling at a partner over a minor remark. The cue: a dismissive tone. The emotion: hurt. The belief: "They don't take me seriously." The activated part: a protector that equates loudness with credibility. Deconstructing this chain shifts focus from blame to understanding. The aim is not rationalisation but reclaiming authorship.

This does not require transforming emotions into intellectual puzzles. The goal is real-time engagement. Somatic awareness is essential. The body often signals emotion before the mind can name it—a tight jaw, a sinking chest, a fluttering gut. These are not mere symptoms; they are alerts. Somatic psychology reminds us that the body is the first responder. Tracking emotion through physical sensation allows earlier intervention, before behaviour dominates. It restores dignity: emotional intelligence is noticing, not just naming.

Throughout the chapter, readers will learn to combine reflective inquiry with embodied awareness to move from reaction to response. They will practise slowing down—not to suppress, but to sense; name emotions with specificity; identify associated beliefs; and explore how context, history, and neurobiology shape feeling. Disruptive emotional episodes are reframed not as derailments, but as invitations. Evidence not of failure, but of being alive.

To feel deeply is not to regress; it is to become precise in our humanity. In a culture that prizes dissociation under the guise of functionality, emotional fluency is quiet rebellion. It allows us to engage meaningfully with life, so habits shift from escapes into conscious choices. Emotion, properly understood, is not the problem—it is the path.

Feelings Are Not Obstacles

Most people spend their lives trying to manage feelings as if they were threats. Sadness is treated like weakness, anger like failure, anxiety like malfunction. In boardrooms, classrooms, relationships, and even therapy sessions, emotions are framed as hurdles to clear before clarity can emerge. But this view is not only misleading—it's neurologically incoherent. *Emotions are not interruptions to intelligence; they are a form of it.*

Cognitive neuroscience has steadily dismantled the myth that reason and emotion occupy separate domains. The old dualistic map—logic over here, feeling over there—has no basis in the actual workings of the brain. In fact, the two are in constant, recursive conversation. Antonio Damasio's groundbreaking research on patients with damage to the ventromedial prefrontal cortex (where emotion and decision-making integrate) showed that when people cannot access feelings, they cannot make choices. They can describe options but cannot prioritise. *Emotion is the value signal that makes cognition actionable.*

When a person says they "can't think straight" under pressure, they're not being irrational. They're describing what happens when affective data overwhelms the system. But the answer is not to suppress emotion. The answer is to decode it. Emotions are not vague sentiments. They are specific, embodied signals—urgent updates about what matters, what's at stake, and what needs to be protected. In survival terms, emotion precedes thought. You feel the heat of the burner before you register "hot." You wince at a sharp tone before you conclude "hostility." You recoil at a lie before you articulate "betrayal." *Emotion is the body's first language for assessing reality.*

And yet, the cultural training most people receive tells them to override, distract, push through. Consider how early this conditioning begins: toddlers are told to "calm down" before they have language for what they're feeling; adolescents are told to "toughen up" before they're taught how to regulate disappointment or shame. Adults are told to "stay positive" or "keep a stiff upper lip" no matter the depth of the loss or injustice they face. The net effect is a pervasive emotional illiteracy—people feeling things intensely while distrusting the very mechanism that is trying to help them.

This distrust is compounded by the fact that emotions often arrive with a somatic charge. The chest tightens. The jaw clenches. The skin tingles or flushes. The pulse races. For those untrained in nervous system literacy, these signals can be misinterpreted as emergencies rather than information. Somatic psychology shifts this understanding. It teaches that these bodily responses are not dysfunctions—they are *data channels*. The body isn't betraying the person; it's alerting them. *The heat in the chest during anger is not proof of volatility—it's a call to boundary awareness. The ache of grief is not a defect—it's a sign of attachment, of value.*

To treat these sensations as mere symptoms to medicate or override is to miss the intelligence embedded in them. It's akin to pulling the battery from a smoke detector because the noise is annoying. The signal persists; we just become less able to hear it.

Reframing emotions as data rather than disruption changes everything. It means a panic attack isn't just a crisis—it might be an unprocessed accumulation of silenced alarm bells. It means envy doesn't make someone petty—it might point to suppressed desire or self-abandonment. It means emotional overwhelm isn't weakness—it's a bandwidth issue, not a character flaw. *When emotions are treated with curiosity rather than contempt, they become navigable.*

Emotional granularity—the ability to distinguish between specific emotional states—is one of the strongest predictors of psychological resilience. Research shows that people who can label their emotions precisely (e.g., distinguishing between irritation, frustration, and resentment) are less likely to engage in maladaptive coping behaviours such as bingeing, avoidance, or aggression. This is not because labelling eliminates the emotion, but because *naming reduces ambiguity*. And ambiguity is what makes feelings frightening.

A vague emotional state is difficult to work with because it floods the system without direction. But a named emotion provides a foothold. Once a person can say, "I feel dismissed," rather than just "I'm upset," they can begin to locate the context, the trigger, the belief underneath it. They move from being inside the feeling to *being in relationship with it*—a crucial shift.

This is where reflective capacity develops. Rather than obeying the emotion reflexively (e.g., yelling, shutting down, pleasing), a person can pause and consider: *What does this emotion want me to know?* This isn't navel-gazing. It's strategic self-regulation. The better someone becomes at interpreting their emotional cues, the earlier they can intervene in self-destructive loops. The person who yells during conflict isn't irrational—they're often someone whose anger has never been metabolised safely. Their nervous system leaps to volume because they associate intensity with credibility. But if they can feel anger in the chest and say, "I notice heat and constriction, I feel unacknowledged," then *the body no longer has to scream to be heard.*

This kind of body-emotion-mind integration is not merely therapeutic—it is foundational to leadership, communication, and change. In high-stakes environments—boardrooms, emergency rooms, courtrooms—the most effective individuals are not those who suppress feeling, but those who *leverage it accurately.* They know how to track the gut-level signal without collapsing into it. They trust that emotion is part of their perception, not its enemy.

However, this capacity doesn't emerge from positive thinking or grit. It emerges from practice—specifically, from learning to relate to emotion *in its native language*: sensation, image, impulse. For example, instead of saying "I feel sad," which can remain abstract, a more embodied approach might be, "There's a heaviness behind my eyes. My breath is shallow. I have an urge to curl inward." From there, the brain can build a more precise emotional map. *Sadness stops being a fog and becomes a landscape with landmarks.*

This level of emotional awareness also allows for distinguishing between primary emotions (what is authentically felt) and secondary emotions (what arises in response to what is felt). For instance, someone might feel anger as a secondary emotion, masking a primary grief or helplessness. The anger gets them attention or control, while the sadness remains unseen. If we only address the anger, we miss the deeper wound. Emotional fluency requires asking: *What's beneath this? What is this feeling protecting me from feeling more deeply?*

Practically speaking, this means shifting the way we narrate inner experiences. Instead of framing emotions as problems—"Why am I like this?"—we begin to ask more fruitful questions: *What is this feeling asking of me? What threat or need is it signalling? What part of me is activated, and what story is it carrying?*

This orientation fosters both responsibility and compassion. Responsibility, because we are choosing to decode rather than discharge the emotion. Compassion, because we understand that the feeling itself is not an enemy. It's a message. *And most destructive behaviours are not problems in isolation—they are failed attempts to process ignored messages.*

By treating emotion as an obstacle, we build resistance to it. And resistance breeds reactivity. But when we treat emotion as information—worthy of attention, not avoidance—it becomes a guide. It tells us where the wound is, what the longing is, what the value is. And from that understanding, action becomes not only more aligned but more sustainable. *We stop reacting from habit and start responding from clarity.*

To feel is not to fail. To feel is to receive data that cannot be accessed any other way. The goal is not to stop feeling, but to *listen more precisely*. This is not softness. It is skill. And like all forms of skill, it can be trained.

Emotion, when respected, becomes intelligence. Not in opposition to logic, but in partnership with it. Not beneath intellect, but *at the root of it.*

Tracking the Emotional Trigger Chain

Most breakdowns in behaviour aren't surprises—they are the final link in a chain of unnoticed emotional events. A person doesn't simply "lose it," "relapse," or "implode." They arrive there, step by step, through an internal progression that often starts hours or even days before the visible outcome. But because modern life trains people to focus on outcomes—weight regained, words spoken, money spent—they miss the essential prelude: the subtle cues, the micro-emotions, the internal beliefs that set everything in motion. *Without tracking that chain, intervention is delayed until it's too late.*

Understanding this sequence—the emotional trigger chain—is not just a therapeutic tool; it is a form of personal sovereignty. By learning to map the anatomy of relapse, not only do individuals gain a clearer picture of what went wrong, but they also start to see *how early it began*, and therefore how early it can be interrupted. *Emotional trigger chains don't happen to people; they unfold within them.*

Every reaction is preceded by a cue. But cues are rarely dramatic. They're subtle: a sigh from a colleague, an unanswered text, the way someone glances away mid-sentence. The nervous system notices before the mind does. From there, a cascade begins—first somatic (tightness, racing heart), then emotional (irritation, rejection), then cognitive ("They're annoyed with me," "I'm too much," "Here we go again"). Those thoughts feed the emotion. The emotion justifies the thoughts. Soon, the person is *not responding to the moment—they are responding to a loop inside their own physiology and history.*

Let's take an example: someone trying to quit late-night binge eating. The visible problem—the binge—usually gets all the attention. But the binge is the end of the sequence, not the start. Earlier in the day, perhaps they skipped lunch. Perhaps a colleague interrupted them repeatedly during a meeting, and they smiled through it. Later, their partner made a throwaway comment about how tired they looked. That night, the familiar cue: restlessness. The body, confused and underfed, sends a signal—*move, soothe, fix.* The person opens the fridge not out of gluttony, but out of self-regulation. The food becomes a portal to relief because it bypasses words, judgment, delay. By the time they are "failing," they are really just *coping with a dozen unmet needs and unacknowledged micro-triggers.*

The conventional model of discipline urges people to "resist temptation." But this misses the deeper issue: *what does the temptation represent?* What is the need beneath the compulsion? When a behaviour becomes a reliable strategy for emotional resolution, it is not a mistake—it is an *adaptation.* To change it, one must understand what it is resolving.

This is where the trigger chain becomes essential. The sequence tends to follow a recognisable arc, though its specific content will vary:

1. **Cue** – a stimulus perceived by the nervous system (tone of voice, facial expression, lack of response)
2. **Emotion** – a felt experience (shame, fear, boredom, insignificance)
3. **Interpretation** – a belief activated by the emotion ("I'm not safe," "I'm a burden," "I'm unlovable")
4. **Impulse** – a behavioural urge to resolve or suppress the emotion (drink, scroll, lash out, withdraw)
5. **Action** – the eventual external behaviour
6. **Aftermath** – temporary relief, followed by regret, fatigue, or renewed shame

Most interventions focus on Step 5—behaviour modification. But *if one waits until impulse becomes action, the opportunity window has already narrowed.* The real leverage lies earlier—in the interpretation and the emotion. *Change becomes possible not by fighting the action but by decoding the trigger.*

Consider the role of belief in this sequence. Beliefs are not neutral lenses; they are predictive filters. Once activated, they shape how data is received. If someone holds a belief like "People always leave me," then a delayed response from a friend isn't just a delay—it becomes confirmation. The emotional response is not just disappointment; it's the resurfacing of abandonment. The action that follows—silent treatment, over-apology, detachment—is not irrational. It is a response calibrated to the person's inner model of how the world works.

The same logic applies to more private behaviours. Someone procrastinates, then spirals into a shame loop. But procrastination didn't start in laziness. It may have begun in fear of not measuring up, of having one's competence questioned. If that person carries an old wound around worth being tied to achievement, then beginning a task becomes more than just work—it becomes exposure. So they delay, not because they are undisciplined, but because they are avoiding emotional risk.

When people begin to track their own trigger chains, they reclaim the ability to interrupt the pattern before it becomes a crisis.

Practically, this means developing the capacity to notice:
— *Where did I first feel something shift in me today?*
— *What was the first moment my shoulders tensed, my breath shortened, my thoughts narrowed?*
— *What belief was activated in that moment, and how old does it feel?*
— *Did I respond to what happened, or to what I feared it meant?*

This kind of inquiry is not self-indulgent. It is high-fidelity emotional intelligence. It transforms vague self-awareness into actionable insight.

But developing this awareness takes more than reflection—it requires *nervous system literacy*. The body knows before the story. The earlier a person can catch the physiological cue (tightness in the gut, clenching in the jaw), the more likely they are to make a conscious choice. Somatic awareness tools—such as body scanning, breath tracking, or interoceptive journalling—can act as early warning systems. *These are not soft skills. They are precision tools for behavioural change.*

Another key leverage point in the chain is the *interpretive leap*—the story the mind tells about the emotion. Most of the time, this story is unconscious. The cue happens, the feeling follows, and the brain races to fill in meaning. But if that moment can be slowed—if the person can say, "This discomfort doesn't require immediate meaning"—then the feeling has a chance to move *through* rather than being acted *from*. This creates the space between stimulus and response where actual agency resides.

What makes relapse so defeating is not just the behaviour itself but the internal narrative that follows: *"I knew better. I always do this. I'll never change."* But these stories compound the chain rather than breaking it. They deepen shame, which tightens the grip of the very behaviour being resisted. *Breaking the trigger chain is not about punishment—it's about precision and compassion. It's about being willing to become intimate with one's own patterns.*

Over time, the act of tracking becomes less analytical and more intuitive. The person doesn't need a worksheet to recognise, "Ah, I'm in that story again." They feel it in the texture of their thoughts, the urgency of their breath, the narrowing of their focus. And this felt recognition is what builds new neural pathways. Because neuroplasticity isn't about insight alone—it's about repetition. When someone repeatedly interrupts the chain, even gently, the system starts to expect *something else is possible.* The compulsion loses its inevitability.

To map a trigger chain is to honour the logic of one's own behaviour—not to excuse it, but to understand its function. And once that function is known, *the need can be met more honestly.* A person who overeats because they feel abandoned might not need a diet plan—they might need a script for asking for reassurance. A person who lashes out in conflict might not need anger management—they might need a way to articulate vulnerability without shame.

Ultimately, emotional trigger chains are not enemies to defeat. They are *blueprints*—showing, again and again, where the real work lies. And by tracking them with curiosity instead of condemnation, people can finally stop trying to conquer themselves and start *collaborating with their own inner systems.* The goal is not to be perfect. The goal is to become *pattern literate*—to know, in real-time, what's driving a choice, and whether it's one they actually want to make.

Naming Without Collapsing

There is a silent skill that governs whether a person becomes consumed by their emotions or gains mastery over them—*emotional granularity.* The ability to name feelings with precision is not just an exercise in vocabulary; it is a neurological act that influences regulation, cognition, and behaviour. Yet, in most cultures, emotional language is shockingly underdeveloped. People are taught to recognise broad, often unhelpful categories—mad, sad, happy, anxious—without learning the subtle distinctions that might actually de-escalate the emotional system. The result is a tragic irony: the more overwhelming a feeling becomes, the less articulate a person is about what they are actually experiencing. And this lack of clarity fuels reactive loops that often get misread as character flaws rather than communication breakdowns between body and mind.

To name something precisely is to *contain it.* This is not a metaphor; it is a fact borne out by neuroscience. When a person accurately labels an emotion—"guilt," not just "bad"; "irritated," not just "angry"—the amygdala reduces its firing, and the prefrontal cortex comes online. This shift moves someone from threat reactivity toward reflective capacity. In other words, *naming emotions doesn't just describe experience—it changes experience.*

But precision is not simply a matter of more words. It requires intimacy with one's internal landscape, and that kind of fluency doesn't emerge by accident. It must be practised. It begins with tolerating the discomfort of *being with* feelings long enough to sense their texture, tempo, and terrain. Most people, especially in high-functioning environments, are conditioned to move *away* from feelings: suppress, override, intellectualise, or outsource. Granularity demands the opposite—it calls for slowing down, noticing, and risking the vulnerability of accurate self-description. That accuracy, however, is what makes discernment possible. And discernment is what makes change sustainable.

Consider the difference between saying "I feel anxious" and saying "I feel exposed." One is general and familiar; the other is specific and revealing. Or take "I'm angry" versus "I feel dismissed." The former can lead to defensiveness or retaliation. The latter invites understanding and boundary-setting. *The more precisely a person can identify the emotion beneath the behaviour, the more access they have to choice.* This is not psychological indulgence; it is executive function in action.

A key obstacle to developing this skill is the fear of collapsing under emotion. Many people believe—often unconsciously—that if they truly let themselves feel what they're feeling, they'll be consumed. This belief isn't irrational; it is learned from early environments where emotions were either punished, ignored, or met with unpredictability. In such cases, the person may have survived by avoiding specificity. To say, "I feel sad," in a dismissive household might have triggered ridicule or shame. To say, "I'm lonely," might have opened a floodgate of unmet needs. Over time, a protective habit forms: numbness over nuance.

That same pattern carries into adulthood. In corporate environments, therapy sessions, or even intimate relationships, many individuals default to safe but vague terms: "I'm just off," "I feel weird," "It's too much." These expressions act as placeholders that prevent collapse but also prevent clarity. What's needed is a middle path—*naming without collapsing.* This involves building the muscle to stay present with a feeling long enough to ask: *What exactly is this? Where is it in my body? What other feelings are underneath?* Crucially, the goal isn't to solve the feeling, but to *see* it, in its fullness and complexity.

One of the most effective tools for building this capacity is developing a personalised emotional lexicon. While psychology offers dozens of models—Plutchik's wheel, the Geneva emotion list, etc.—what matters most is internal relevance. For example, a person might learn that what they usually call "stress" is actually a blend of pressure, resentment, and fear of failure. Another might learn that "tired" is a stand-in for depleted, disrespected, and emotionally overextended. *The act of disaggregating these clusters brings intelligence back into emotional experience.* It also builds internal trust: when emotions are seen accurately, the psyche no longer needs to scream for attention.

There is also a difference between naming a state and over-identifying with it. "I feel rejected" is different from "I am unlovable." The former acknowledges a transient emotional experience; the latter collapses the self into a fixed identity. Granularity protects against that collapse by maintaining a degree of observational distance. It says, *I am noticing this emotion, not becoming it.* This distinction is especially vital in high-intensity emotional states like shame or grief, where the pull to define oneself by the feeling can be dangerously strong.

Naming without collapsing also supports relationship repair. In conflict, people often speak from reactivity: "You're always criticising me," "You never listen." These statements escalate defensiveness. But if one can name the underlying emotion with granularity—"I feel dismissed," "I feel unimportant," "I feel overwhelmed and ashamed"—the tone shifts. Precision creates room for empathy because it reduces generalisation. And empathy, in turn, facilitates repair not just with others, but with oneself.

Critically, emotional granularity is not the same as rumination. Ruminating involves cycling through the same emotional content without movement or insight. Granularity involves *differentiation*—getting clearer, not just louder. This is why simply "venting" doesn't always help; without precise language, venting may reinforce the vagueness of distress. With practice, however, granularity interrupts emotional automaticity. It invites reflection before reaction, clarity before collapse.

It's also worth noting that granularity must be practiced across a wide spectrum of emotions—not just distress. Most people are far more articulate about what's wrong than what's right. Yet naming joy, pride, gratitude, or even satisfaction with the same care is equally important. It reinforces the message that *all emotions contain information*, and that information is worth accessing in high-definition.

In practical terms, developing this skill might look like journaling with attention to synonyms, using body-based check-ins to locate feelings, or pausing during conflict to say, "Give me a moment—I need to find the right words." It might mean refusing the first label that comes to mind and digging deeper. It might mean building an emotional vocabulary not for performance, but for inner accuracy. These are not soft practices. They are executive skills. In fact, recent research shows that people with higher emotional granularity experience fewer depressive symptoms, less impulsive behaviour, and better social functioning. The precision *matters*.

Ultimately, naming without collapsing is about reclaiming language as a tool of agency. It is the difference between feeling helpless in a storm of unnamed affect, and standing with clarity in the centre of it, naming the winds, and deciding—deliberately—whether to seek shelter, or to stay and listen. It is not about mastering emotion, but about relating to it with dignity, precision, and respect. *Because what you can name, you can navigate.* And navigation—not suppression, not collapse—is what grants a person their fullest autonomy.

From Reaction to Response

Between stimulus and response, there exists a fleeting space—a neurological pause so brief it can vanish before we realise it was ever there. Yet within that space lies the power to transform not only our behaviours but the entire trajectory of our emotional lives. That interval, often milliseconds in length, is the difference between a slammed door and a clarifying conversation, between emotional reactivity and mature regulation, between damage and dignity. The ability to locate, extend, and use that space is among the most valuable psychological capacities a person can cultivate—and yet it's one most people never learn to develop. Instead, they live as though emotions are switches: once flipped, the outcome is predetermined. But reaction is not destiny. *It is habit.* And habits, though persistent, are not immutable.

Neuroscience confirms what contemplative traditions have long intuited: the brain is not merely reactive—it is also predictive and adaptive. The amygdala, our emotional alarm system, often initiates responses before the conscious mind is aware. But the presence of that reflex does not mean we are bound to it. The prefrontal cortex, responsible for executive function, self-awareness, and inhibitory control, can override reflexes with reflection. What stands between these two systems is *practice.* Not willpower, not character strength, but deliberate, ongoing training in how to engage with internal states as information rather than commands.

To understand how to widen the space between emotion and action, we must first stop pathologising the presence of emotion itself. Emotions are not interruptions—they are signals. Reactivity, however, is what happens when we treat that signal as a verdict. "I feel humiliated" becomes "I must retaliate." "I feel anxious" becomes "I must escape." These are scripts, not facts. And most were written long before adulthood, embedded in procedural memory through repetition. Widening the space requires rewriting those scripts—not by erasing emotion, but by naming it, tolerating it, and ultimately deciding what meaning to assign to it.

One of the most effective ways to begin interrupting reactive loops is through the cultivation of *meta-awareness*: the ability to notice thoughts and emotions as they arise, without becoming fused with them. In practical terms, this looks like recognising the moment of activation before it hardens into action. It might sound like: "I'm noticing a tightening in my chest and a rush of heat in my face—I think I feel cornered." That moment of naming allows the observer self to step in. And once an observing self is present, choice becomes possible. *This is the entry point into response.*

Of course, this is easier said than done. In emotionally charged situations—conflict with a partner, public embarrassment, a triggering memory—the nervous system moves swiftly into mobilisation. The sympathetic branch of the autonomic nervous system initiates a fight, flight, or freeze cascade. Blood flow is redirected from the cortex to the limbs. Reasoning becomes impaired. And here is the crucial insight: *in a reactive state, the brain sacrifices nuance for survival.* It's not interested in your values or your growth—it's trying to preserve your sense of safety. Widening the space between emotion and action therefore begins not with logic, but with regulation. Until the body feels safe, the brain cannot choose wisely.

This is where reflective practices enter—not as meditative luxury, but as *strategic necessity*. Techniques like focused breathing, grounding through sensation, and orienting to the present moment aren't "wellness hacks"; they're neural interventions. They tell the amygdala that the threat has passed and bring the prefrontal cortex back online. For example, a person who feels triggered in a work meeting may excuse themselves briefly, not to escape, but to down-regulate their system. They might run cool water over their hands, track five colours in the room, or breathe in a 4-7-8 pattern. These are not avoidance strategies; they are *pause buttons*—ways of preserving the very space in which intelligent response can emerge.

Crucially, once that space is preserved, the next task is meaning-making. What do I believe this feeling means? Often, emotional reactivity is driven not by the emotion itself but by the story we attach to it. For instance, a person might feel sadness but interpret it as weakness, prompting defensive rage. Or they might feel shame but interpret it as proof of unworthiness, prompting avoidance or dissociation. Reflective practice invites a separation between *emotion* and *interpretation*. It asks: "What else could this mean?" or "What if this emotion is a messenger, not a threat?" These questions shift the orientation from survival to inquiry—and inquiry opens the door to adaptive choice.

Another tool in this shift from reaction to response is *time*. Most people make poor decisions when pressured to respond instantly. This is especially true in digital environments where urgency is manufactured—emails, texts, social media comments. The reflex to reply immediately often bypasses reflection altogether. What's lost is nuance, integrity, and often emotional accuracy. Response latency—the practice of delaying action until insight has emerged—is not a delay tactic. It's an emotional filtration system. It says: "I will respond when I can do so from my values, not my reactivity."

Values are, in fact, the cornerstone of responsive behaviour. A person anchored in clear internal values can use them as a guide in emotionally turbulent moments. For instance, a parent might feel the impulse to shame their child for misbehaving. But if their value is to raise a secure and emotionally intelligent human, they can use that as a compass to respond differently. "I'm really angry right now" becomes "I'm going to step outside for a minute so I can talk to you the way I want to." The child learns not only that emotions are okay, but that they don't have to dictate actions. This is how intergenerational reactivity begins to unravel—*not through repression, but through practice.*

Of course, there will be times when the space between emotion and action disappears altogether. A trigger will come too fast, a wound too deep. But the aim is not perfection; it is repair. In these moments, recovery becomes the site of growth. "I didn't respond the way I wanted to" becomes a moment of inquiry: *What happened in my system? What emotion was I protecting? What story did I believe? What might I do differently next time?* These post-event reflections are not self-indulgent—they are *repatterning in motion*. They turn a reactive event into a learning opportunity. Over time, this builds what psychologist Dan Siegel calls "response flexibility"—the ability to adaptively modulate behaviour in real time.

To move from reaction to response is to become the author of one's emotional life, rather than its hostage. It is not about emotional control in the rigid sense, but about emotional stewardship—guiding rather than suppressing, inquiring rather than assuming, choosing rather than collapsing. It asks not that we eliminate feeling, but that we cultivate *clarity* within it.

That clarity, however, is cumulative. It does not arrive all at once. It emerges through a thousand tiny interruptions: noticing breath before speaking, asking a question before making an assumption, allowing discomfort before reaching for escape. These micro-pauses are not passive—they are acts of agency. And over time, they become a life architecture defined not by compulsive patterns but by conscious, courageous presence.

The emotional system may be ancient, but it is not fixed. Reaction may be fast, but it is not final. Between stimulus and response, there is not only a space—there is *you*. And within that space lies the power to build a life aligned not with your impulses, but with your intentions. That is the architecture of emotional maturity. Not reaction, but response. Not reflex, but reflection. Not control, but authorship.

Chapter 9
The Identity Barrier

Change is rarely just about discipline, insight, or sheer willpower. Beneath most behavioural inertia lies a more subtle and potent force: identity. The question that quietly haunts attempts at transformation is not merely, *Can I do this?* but, *Who will I be if I do?* The struggle is not always with the habit itself, but with the self that has grown around it. For many, the fear of relinquishing that self outweighs the discomfort of remaining stuck. Even patterns that cause suffering serve a purpose—they provide a framework for who we believe we are.

When someone says they feel lost during change, they are often describing the sensation of stepping outside the emotional architecture that has defined them. This disorientation is not incidental; it is central. Even painful psychological patterns provide coherence. Consider a person consumed by perfectionism: chronic anxiety and burnout accompany their life, yet letting go of the inner critic feels impossible. Not because they enjoy the suffering, but because hyper-vigilance has been equated with safety, loveworthiness, or self-worth. *If I'm not the one who always gets it right, then who am I?* This is not mere rhetoric—it is an existential question.

It is easy to articulate what we want to stop doing—overeating, overthinking, overpleasing—yet far harder to envision what comes next. Much self-help guidance jumps straight to action plans, as if the problem were logistical. But behavioural patterns are rarely the root issue. They are identity strategies: long-standing ways of securing belonging, control, or meaning. To change them is to tamper with a deeply ingrained answer to *Who am I?* Without consciously addressing this, the nervous system often treats change as threat rather than opportunity.

Some psychologists describe this resistance as "egoic attachment," though that term can mislead. The ego is not the enemy—it is the mind's organising force. What it resists is incoherence. The psyche craves narrative continuity; blank pages feel like danger. Removing an entrenched behavioural identity—the anxious one, the caretaker, the rebel, the fixer—rarely brings relief at first. Instead, it generates anxiety. Not having a role can feel like not having a self. This is especially disorienting for those whose early environments required adaptive identities to secure acceptance—children who learned to suppress needs, pacify conflict, or overachieve to earn love. These strategies were survival tools, not flaws. Relinquishing them can feel like betrayal.

The concept of secondary gain illustrates this phenomenon: hidden benefits derived from symptoms or struggles. A person who identifies as "the helper" may unconsciously rely on that identity to feel needed or worthy. Removing the behaviour without replacing the underlying need creates a void—and the psyche abhors a vacuum. Without intentional repopulation, the space will likely be filled by old patterns or equally rigid identity masks.

This is why reinvention is often perceived as betrayal. In collectivist cultures, or tight-knit family systems, altering one's identity—especially in ways that challenge tradition—can be read as selfish or disloyal. The fear of outgrowing others, or of being accused of changing too much too quickly, is not superficial; it taps into a primal need for relational safety. For some, it is easier to remain misaligned than to risk becoming unrecognisable to loved ones.

Yet authentic growth demands departure from the familiar self. True change does not merely decorate the old personality; it dismantles and rewires it. Someone who has long defined themselves as emotionally stoic may find themselves crying in therapy and immediately feel shame—not because tears are wrong, but because they contradict a well-worn identity. A recovering perfectionist may struggle to enjoy rest, because it conflicts with the old narrative of *value through effort.* The discomfort arises not from the new behaviour, but from identity dissonance. Even selves we no longer wish to inhabit must be mourned.

Psychological grief does not require affection for the lost self—only recognition that it shaped your life. To grow is to honour the old self without submitting to it. "You were once necessary," one might say. "You got me through. But I no longer need you to run the show."

The ego rarely relinquishes its narratives quietly. When identity is threatened, the mind offers protective fictions: *That's just how I am, I've always been this way, I'm not the kind of person who could…* These stories preserve the familiarity of a limited self. They are not signs of failure, but markers of identity expansion. The moment such scripts arise is the moment to pause: *What am I protecting? What do I fear losing? And what might I gain by loosening my grip?*

This is the psychological heart of transformation: allowing identity to expand without forcing it to crystallise prematurely. The common mistake is rushing to replace one rigid self-concept with another. If I am no longer the overachiever, I must become the "zen minimalist." If I am no longer the people-pleaser, I must become fiercely independent. These are costume changes, not transformation. True growth tolerates uncertainty. It experiments with new modes of being like garments—not as uniforms, but as possibilities.

This requires discomfort tolerance. The in-between self is vulnerable to judgment, both internal and external. There is no clear role to play, no stable narrative to fall back on. And yet, there is freedom: the freedom to choose intentionally rather than compulsively. Reflective practices anchor this stage. Journaling prompts such as *What feels truer than the old story, even if unfamiliar?* or *What would I do today if I weren't trying to prove or preserve anything?* shift identity from historical coherence to present alignment.

Ultimately, identity is not a fixed structure—it is a living process, evolving through action, reflection, and relationship. The fear of losing the familiar self is real, but it is often the gatekeeper to a richer, more flexible selfhood: one no longer shackled to its patterns, but informed by them. One that honours its history without being governed by it.

The identity barrier is not a flaw in the growth process. It is the growth process. Moving through it does not require erasing who you have been, but meeting who you might become. Not all at once, not perfectly, but deliberately and with courage. The remainder of this chapter is devoted to that work: not merely what to change, but how to hold space for the changing self.

Who Am I Without This Pattern?

Real change is not simply about subtraction. It is not the removal of an unwanted habit, the silencing of an inner critic, or the discarding of a compulsive behaviour. It is the psychological equivalent of amputation followed by rebirth: the cutting away of what is familiar, functional, and formative—even if painful—and facing the open question of who remains. When people say they want to change, they are rarely prepared for the grief that often follows. What they mourn is not just the suffering that shaped them, but the identity built through enduring it. For many, the hardest part of transformation is not beginning—it's *becoming unrecognisable to themselves.*

This is not melodrama. The human psyche is not a neutral container of change. It is an architecture of coherence. We build selves from patterns—not just from what we love and admire, but from what we had to endure. The anxious planner, the relentless achiever, the self-deprecating peacemaker—these aren't quirks of personality. They are responses to early emotional environments, crafted with precision to minimise rejection, maximise predictability, and stabilise belonging. Over time, these responses become indistinguishable from identity. *Not doing them feels like not being oneself.*

Which is why, when change is proposed—whether through therapy, habit disruption, or personal insight—it is not uncommon for people to experience disorientation, resistance, or even despair. It's not because the new behaviour is objectively worse. It's because the old one was *familiar.* And familiarity has a regulating effect on the nervous system. Even self-destructive routines can offer a perverse form of safety—like returning to a toxic but predictable home. People don't stay stuck because they are irrational. They stay stuck because coherence is neurologically soothing.

To break from a pattern, then, is to confront a psychological and emotional void. The overfunctioning manager who decides to stop micro-managing suddenly loses their sense of importance. The chronic helper who stops overgiving starts to feel useless. The perfectionist who lets a task be "good enough" may feel like a fraud. This is not regression—it's a natural identity crisis. *Patterns are not just behaviours; they are scripts for being.* Remove the script, and you remove the structure.

Modern neuroscience affirms this tension. The brain, especially the default mode network responsible for constructing narrative continuity, is deeply invested in preserving self-consistency. When identity is challenged, this system flags it as an error—something to be corrected, not celebrated. In practical terms, this means that even positive changes can feel "wrong." Someone trying to be more assertive after years of accommodation might feel aggressive. Someone trying to rest after years of hyperproductivity might feel lazy. These distortions aren't failures of insight; they are *neurological echoes of the old self defending its territory.*

There is an emotional weight to this, one that is rarely addressed in mainstream behavioural advice. Much of what passes for self-improvement literature encourages rapid implementation: "Just stop overthinking," "Start the new habit," "Push through the discomfort." But it fails to acknowledge that for many people, discomfort is not a sign of effort—it's a signal of identity loss. When someone says, "I just don't feel like myself anymore," they're often describing the psychological price of change: *the severance from an internally consistent narrative.*

Consider the example of someone recovering from disordered eating. At the surface level, the behavioural shift might be eating without restriction, learning satiety, or unlearning food-related fear. But deeper down, the person may also be giving up the identity of being "disciplined," "in control," or "good." And in a culture that valorises restraint, this relinquishment can trigger not just anxiety but shame. The new behaviour feels like a moral failing—not because it is, but because the old pattern held moral meaning.

Similarly, take someone raised to be emotionally stoic. If they begin accessing grief or vulnerability, their emotional expansion may feel like weakness or exposure. Not because sadness is inherently unsafe, but because the absence of it was previously equated with strength. When the self has long equated numbness with maturity, *feeling can feel like regression.* In this way, even healing can feel like betrayal.

It's important, then, to make space for this internal tension without pathologising it. The fear of reinvention is not a sign of weakness. It is a natural psychological threshold. Identity, after all, is not just who we are—it's how we know ourselves. And when that scaffolding is removed or restructured, the entire cognitive and emotional system has to reorient. This process can be exhilarating or devastating, but it is rarely neutral. People do not simply wake up into a new self. They arrive there slowly, clumsily, and often reluctantly, through repeated acts of disidentification from the old.

What complicates this further is that identity is often relational. A person who has always been the "strong one" in a family system, for instance, may find that change destabilises others even more than themselves. As they begin to show vulnerability, those around them may resist—"You're not acting like yourself." This interpersonal feedback, though often unconscious, reinforces the very patterns the person is trying to release. It becomes a loop: any deviation from the expected role is interpreted as a threat, and the pressure to revert becomes intense. *It is not just who we think we are—it is who others expect us to be that binds us to old patterns.*

That is why the fear of reinvention is so frequently underestimated. It is not just internal uncertainty, but *external tension.* People are not afraid of growth in theory. They are afraid of being alienated by the cost of it. They are afraid of becoming too different to be loved in the ways they've always known. And sometimes, they're afraid that once the pattern is gone, there will be nothing left worth loving.

Which brings us to an essential point: *every meaningful behavioural pattern once solved a problem.* It offered safety, belonging, coherence, or control. Even the most seemingly irrational tendencies—self-sabotage, procrastination, overachievement—were at one point brilliant strategies for navigating emotional reality. If we do not recognise this, we risk approaching change with violence—trying to "break the habit" without understanding what it protects. But if we approach with reverence—acknowledging the intelligence of the original adaptation—we create space not just for change, but for integration.

To ask "Who am I without this pattern?" is to face both the grief of letting go and the creative challenge of becoming. It is not a question to rush through. It is a question to sit with. And in that pause, we begin to realise something quietly radical: *identity is not discovered—it is chosen.* It is revised. It is sculpted through attention, reflection, and choice. The past may explain who we've been, but it does not limit who we can become.

This reframing is not about discarding the past self, but about expanding it. It is about saying: "Yes, I was this. And I am also more." True reinvention does not require erasure. It requires *permission.* Permission to evolve. To be incoherent for a while. To contradict old labels. To not have a script. To write a new one. Not because the old one was wrong, but because it no longer fits.

The fear of that freedom is real. But so is the promise. And when we learn to tolerate the identity void—not fill it prematurely with another role, but explore it with curiosity—we become capable of something deeper than change. We become capable of *self-authorship.* A life not inherited, but created. A self not performed, but inhabited. And that is the real frontier of transformation. Not doing differently. *Being differently.*

The Safety of the Familiar Self

A person may spend years longing for change, voicing a deep frustration with the roles they inhabit or the labels they've internalised—"I'm tired of being the one who always says yes," "I wish I could stop sabotaging everything good," "Why do I always retreat when things get real?"—and yet, when offered real tools for transformation, they hesitate, stall, or even reject them outright. This isn't hypocrisy. It's protection. Beneath most stuckness lies not a lack of desire, intelligence, or discipline, but something more complex and often unconscious: *a quiet allegiance to the self they've always known.*

The paradox is that even painful identities offer coherence. Even when a person feels limited by their patterns—like the high achiever who never rests, the self-effacing empath who never speaks up, or the cynic who pushes everyone away—those patterns stabilise their internal world. They may constrict growth, but they protect the individual from fragmentation. When life has been unpredictable or emotionally unsafe, psychological coherence often takes priority over fulfilment. In this sense, *the problem is not that the old identity is working too little—but that it has worked too well.*

Consider someone who's spent decades believing they are "not enough." This belief may have begun in early environments marked by criticism, neglect, or inconsistency. Over time, that internal narrative doesn't just explain the world—it becomes *how they know who they are.* It shapes what they reach for, whom they trust, what risks they take. If that person suddenly adopts a belief in their inherent worth, they don't just experience an emotional shift—they destabilise an entire framework that once helped them navigate relational life. To change it is to *become unfamiliar to oneself.* And that unfamiliarity, even when positive, can feel threatening.

Neuroscience supports this. The brain's default mode network, which constructs a sense of identity and autobiographical memory, is less concerned with truth than it is with *continuity.* It prefers a coherent story over a happy one. This is why people often cling to outdated self-concepts, even when they cause suffering. The "I'm unlovable" story might lead to loneliness, but it also shields against the terror of hope. The "I can only trust myself" identity might fuel isolation, but it spares the person from the risk of disappointment. *The brain is not wired for liberation—it is wired for survival through familiarity.*

This is especially true in developmental terms. Children adapt to their environments not by forming an objective self-image, but by internalising the roles that maximise attachment. A child who learns that they receive approval when they excel, please, or disappear will shape their identity around those responses. These become not just behavioural strategies, but existential anchors. And even when those adaptations become maladaptive in adulthood, they are still emotionally charged with the memory of safety. To give them up feels like betrayal—not just of the old self, but of the original emotional contract.

This helps explain why identity-level change often evokes outsized emotional responses. Someone trying to step out of a martyr role might experience guilt that far exceeds the situation. Someone learning to receive care after years of self-reliance might feel exposed, childish, or ashamed. These reactions aren't signs of failure. They are echoes of an older logic: *If I change this part of myself, I will no longer belong.* And in human psychology, few threats are more potent than the threat of disconnection.

Moreover, we often organise our social worlds around our familiar identities. The sarcastic friend builds friendships on shared detachment. The always-helpful colleague becomes indispensable by never setting boundaries. The self-deprecating sibling is tolerated because they don't challenge the family hierarchy. In each of these cases, identity isn't just internal—it is *relational currency*. Change one part, and the whole social contract is renegotiated. This creates immense internal conflict: if I stop playing this role, *who will I be—and will anyone still choose me?*

Such conflict is rarely acknowledged in standard behavioural change models. They often assume that if people want to change and know how, they will. But in truth, change requires not just cognitive permission, but *identity mourning*. There is grief in letting go of who we've been. Even unwanted selves carry history, loyalty, and logic. They've helped us survive shame, loss, and trauma. Discarding them abruptly can provoke emotional vertigo—a sense of groundlessness that is terrifying, even if it opens the door to freedom.

That's why identity expansion must be approached with reverence, not speed. For someone whose familiar self is rooted in invisibility, taking up space may feel aggressive. For someone who's defined themselves by competence, being vulnerable may feel humiliating. These are not irrational responses—they are *identity dissonance*, the nervous system's alarm in the face of unfamiliar embodiment.

Psychologist Carl Rogers noted that "the curious paradox is that when I accept myself just as I am, then I can change." This is not just poetic insight—it is a neurological truth. Acceptance calms the nervous system. It creates safety. And only in safety can identity loosen its grip. When a person feels secure enough to stop defending their familiar roles, they gain the freedom to imagine new ones. This doesn't mean discarding the old self, but *differentiating from it*—recognising that it is a part of them, not the whole.

In this way, psychological growth is not about self-improvement, but *self-integration.* It means asking: which parts of me have been overdeveloped for survival, and which have been underdeveloped due to fear? It means recognising that the familiar self, while effective, may have been a mask worn too long. And it means approaching that mask not with shame or urgency, but with curiosity. Not "how do I get rid of this?" but "what did it protect, and what do I need now?"

Take, for example, a client who describes themselves as "just someone who avoids conflict." Rather than interrogating that pattern for dysfunction, a deeper question might be: *What did avoidance once protect you from? What belonging did it buy you? What chaos did it prevent?* By exploring the logic of the familiar self, the person can begin to see it not as a flaw, but as a function—one that made sense in context. And from that compassionate lens, they can begin to explore new capacities without disowning the old.

This is also why new behaviours often don't "stick" when they are implemented from a place of identity rejection. A person can try to be more assertive, but if they still believe they are fundamentally burdensome, their nervous system will resist. They may speak up once, but they'll feel shame for days. In contrast, when the new behaviour arises from a revised self-concept—"It's safe for me to be seen," or "My needs matter too"—the behaviour becomes sustainable. *Lasting change is identity-consistent change.*

But that identity must be built gradually, with room for regression, contradiction, and uncertainty. Just as the familiar self was built through repeated experiences of reinforcement, the emerging self must be developed through repeated experiences of *belonging in a new way.* That means surrounding oneself with people who recognise the new self, even when it's shaky. It means finding internal language that honours growth without pathologising fear. And it means tolerating the in-between: the moments when the old self no longer fits, and the new one hasn't fully formed.

This is the liminal space of real transformation. It is not glamorous. It is not immediate. But it is sacred. And in that space, something extraordinary happens. When the need for coherence no longer outweighs the desire for authenticity, the familiar self loses its grip. Not because it was wrong, but because it has been understood. And understanding, unlike rejection, *frees us to grow.*

The Ego's Last Stand

When a person stands on the threshold of meaningful change—armed with insight, tools, even a sense of readiness—it is not always laziness, ignorance, or fear that halts their progress. More often, it is the mind's deep and adaptive resistance, camouflaged as truth. *"I've just never been a consistent person." "That's not who I am." "I've tried before and failed." "I'm not someone who sticks with things."* These are not simply self-assessments. They are the ego's final lines of defence. In the face of transformation, the ego does not retreat—it reorganises. And it does so by offering up well-rehearsed truths that feel so embedded, so factual, that to challenge them would seem like self-denial. But what if these statements are not insights, but immunities? What if they are *the ego's last stand*—a final attempt to preserve psychological coherence in the face of destabilising growth?

The ego, in psychological terms, is not simply arrogance or vanity. It is the mental mechanism by which we maintain continuity of self. It helps us interpret experience, prioritise information, and predict outcomes based on our internal model of the world and of ourselves. But while the ego is useful—essential, even—for navigating complexity, it is *conservative by design.* It favours what is familiar over what is accurate. Its job is not to update the self-image, but to protect it. When that self-image is threatened—even by progress—the ego often becomes less flexible, not more.

This is why change so often feels like inner warfare. On one level, a person may sincerely want to alter a pattern, a belief, or a habit. But on another, deeper level, that same person may feel that doing so would compromise who they fundamentally are. In that moment, the ego steps in not with fear, but with certainty: "This just isn't me." The seductiveness of such statements lies in their authority. They don't sound like resistance; they sound like *clarity*. And that is precisely what makes them dangerous.

Take the example of someone who wants to develop a daily writing practice. They begin with enthusiasm but soon miss a few days. Rather than returning with flexibility, they tell themselves: *"I've never had discipline. I'm just not wired that way."* That statement does more than describe a behaviour—it justifies its continuation. It insulates the person from the emotional discomfort of trying and failing again. And in doing so, it maintains identity coherence at the expense of possibility. The ego would rather the person be consistently stuck than risk becoming inconsistent in growth.

This psychological phenomenon is not merely anecdotal—it is structurally encoded. Studies in cognitive dissonance theory have shown that humans experience significant stress when their behaviour contradicts their self-concept. To resolve this dissonance, we don't always change the behaviour. More often, we *adjust the narrative*. Instead of saying, "I haven't yet built the skill of consistency," which keeps change possible, the ego settles on a more final story: "I'm not someone who follows through." That story alleviates discomfort—but at the cost of transformation.

The ego's resistance often appears most powerfully when a person is *on the cusp* of change, not far from it. At a distance, change feels abstract and even romantic. But as it becomes embodied—when the person starts eating differently, speaking more honestly, or stepping into new relational roles—the stakes rise. Old identity structures begin to erode, and the ego senses a threat not just to function, but to *selfhood*. Its retaliation is not loud or reactive. It is strategic, quiet, and persuasive. It begins with phrases like:

"This just doesn't feel like me."

"I need to wait until I'm really ready."

"I'm being unrealistic about what I can change."

These statements often masquerade as wisdom. They are not shouted, but whispered, dressed in the language of prudence and self-knowledge. And that makes them harder to challenge.

Yet what they often conceal is emotional avoidance. The ego is not trying to sabotage; it is trying to protect. The self-image that it guards may have originated in pain: "I'm not loveable unless I perform," "If I'm not useful, I'll be abandoned," "If I stand out, I'll be attacked." These implicit beliefs were formed not through logic, but through lived relational experience. As such, they are not easily overwritten by cognitive insight alone. *To challenge the ego's 'truths' is to revisit the wounds that made them necessary.* That is no small task.

This is why many people feel an unexpected wave of grief, anxiety, or even rage when they attempt to move beyond their old limits. These emotions are not evidence that something is wrong. They are signs that the old ego scaffolding is being disassembled. What hurts is not just the difficulty of the new—it's the mourning of the known.

The solution is not to demonise the ego, but to dialogue with it. To say: "I understand why this belief protected me. I see how it made sense. But I am not obligated to carry it forever." This is not positive thinking. It is *honest reckoning.* It acknowledges the psychological function of the ego's resistance without granting it permanent authority.

One of the most powerful practices in such moments is to convert identity statements into skill-based language. Instead of "I'm not disciplined," one might say, "I haven't yet built the conditions for consistency." Instead of "I'm not a confident person," they can say, "I'm still practising expressing myself without defaulting to apology." This linguistic shift matters. It preserves the dignity of the past self while making space for future growth. It keeps the narrative open.

It is also essential to recognise that the ego's resistance often intensifies in environments of shame. When a person feels judged—for their stuckness, their perceived flaws, or their failed attempts—the ego retreats even further into defensive identity. It hardens into positions not because they are true, but because they feel *safe.* That's why environments that promote self-compassion, curiosity, and non-judgement are not luxuries in transformation work—they are *prerequisites.* Change cannot occur in the presence of psychological threat.

This insight aligns with Internal Family Systems (IFS) theory, which views the ego not as a singular self, but as a protector part. In IFS, what appears as stubbornness or rigidity is often a part that has been over-functioning for years, trying to prevent the reactivation of deeper pain. From this lens, the statement "I'm just not someone who can change" is not a conclusion—it's a shield. And the work is not to rip the shield away, but to meet the part behind it with enough patience and presence that it might lay the shield down itself.

Crucially, the ego's defences are not signs of failure—they are signs of proximity to growth. The more convincingly the mind insists, "This is just who I am," the more we might wonder, *what would have to be true for that statement to no longer serve me?* Often, the answer is sobering: I would have to feel safe enough to change. I would have to believe that my worth is not contingent on my consistency, perfection, or past. I would have to allow the story to end—not in disgrace, but in evolution.

And this is the final irony: the ego resists change in order to protect a stable self-image, yet it is only through change that the self can become more whole. Not by rejecting the ego's logic, but by *expanding* it. By seeing every identity statement not as a wall, but as a doorway. One that leads not to a fantasy self, but to a self that is finally allowed to outgrow the stories it was once forced to live inside.

The question, then, is not whether the ego will resist. It will. The real question is whether we can learn to hear its resistance not as a verdict, but as a signal. *The closer we get to transformation, the louder the ego yells. Not because we're going the wrong way—but because we're almost there.*

Allowing Identity Expansion

When change becomes more than theoretical—when it begins to interrupt the scripts, roles, and reactions that have scaffolded a person's sense of self—many will find themselves paralysed not by fear of failure, but by fear of incoherence. There is a particular vulnerability that emerges when we are no longer who we were, but not yet who we might become. It is here, in this suspended space, that identity expansion becomes less a metaphor and more a psychological threshold. The nervous system registers it not as evolution, but as threat. The mind scrambles to stabilise meaning. The body searches for orientation. And in the absence of familiar self-concepts, many retreat—not because they lack desire or discipline, but because they have never been taught how to *tolerate the in-between.*

Identity, for all its complexity, functions as a map. Even painful self-concepts—"I'm the anxious one," "I'm the overachiever," "I'm bad at relationships"—offer internal coherence. They help explain the past, anticipate reactions, and secure belonging through predictability. But when these identities no longer serve, when they begin to conflict with the life a person wants to build, letting them go can feel like a form of self-abandonment. Who are we without the patterns that shaped us? What happens to our social positioning, our relational contracts, our sense of consistency? The loss of identity is not merely cognitive; it is existential. *It feels like erasure.*

This is why expansion cannot be approached as replacement. If the old self is discarded too quickly, without respect for what it protected or accomplished, the psyche responds with rebellion. Rejection breeds regression. The task, then, is not to destroy the former identity, but to *decentre* it—to soften its dominance, to place it within a broader constellation of possibility. This requires a kind of psychological ambidexterity: holding on loosely enough to grow, yet firmly enough to stay oriented. It means developing the capacity to say: "This is one part of me. And there are others I'm just beginning to meet."

Reflective practice becomes essential here—not for the purpose of insight alone, but for *containment.* Expansion, paradoxically, needs boundaries. Just as a plant needs both soil and space, identity needs both structure and stretch. Without reflective anchoring, attempts at reinvention can become performative or erratic—chasing novelty rather than integration. The goal is not to become someone else. It is to make room for the selves we've historically disallowed.

One of the most effective practices for this is dialogical writing—not as catharsis, but as inquiry. A person might sit down and write from the voice of the "old self" that's losing ground, asking: *What did I protect you from? What were you afraid of happening if I had grown sooner?* Then, from the perspective of an emerging self: *What do you want that you haven't had space to express? What does 'freedom' actually mean to you?* This exercise is not about finding a final answer. It is about legitimising the *multiplicity* within.

Another practice involves "trying on" micro-embodiments of new identities in low-stakes contexts. For example, someone experimenting with confidence might attend a meeting and contribute one opinion without caveat or apology—not to become "a confident person," but to *observe how the body tolerates visibility.* These are not performative rehearsals. They are experiential inquiries: What happens when I act outside my known identity? What narratives activate? What physical sensations arise? By treating identity shifts as experiments rather than declarations, the nervous system is less likely to register threat, and more likely to open into curiosity.

This approach also protects against the common trap of overcorrection. Many who outgrow an old self rush to replace it with a new one—often just as rigid, only dressed in more appealing language. The former perfectionist becomes a "self-care guru." The chronic appeaser becomes "brutally honest." The overworker rebrands as an "entrepreneurial visionary." While these may seem like evolutions, they often function as identity swaps—*not expansions.* The psyche, still uncomfortable with liminality, demands a role to cling to. What is needed instead is the capacity to *occupy the transitional self*—to say, "I don't fully know who I'm becoming. And that is okay."

This willingness to remain undefined is what psychologist Dan McAdams calls a "narrative openness"—the ability to revise one's self-story without collapsing into chaos. It is also aligned with the concept of psychological flexibility, a trait strongly correlated with well-being and adaptive functioning. The most resilient people are not those who maintain the strongest sense of who they are, but those who can *reconstruct themselves meaningfully* in the face of change. This requires a mindset shift from identity as *certainty* to identity as *contextual coherence*. Who I am is not a singular truth—it is an evolving integration of experiences, values, and relationships, continuously reinterpreted.

Of course, identity expansion does not occur in a vacuum. It unfolds within families, cultures, workplaces, and communities—many of which may resist or reject the person's evolving self. This is why allowing expansion is not only an intrapersonal task, but also an interpersonal negotiation. As one's identity shifts, relational dynamics often recalibrate. The "quiet one" who begins speaking up may be perceived as aggressive. The "responsible one" who sets boundaries may be accused of selfishness. These reactions are not indicators of regression. They are evidence that the former identity served a systemic function. And systems, even unhealthy ones, resist disruption.

This is where the inner work becomes most tested: Can I continue expanding, even when the world prefers my smaller self? Can I honour my evolution, even when it disorients those around me? These questions require not only courage, but *compassionate clarity*. The task is not to sever all ties to the past, but to *renegotiate presence*. The old self does not need to disappear—it simply needs to stop running the show.

At its core, identity expansion is not about reinvention. It is about *integration without exile*. It is the refusal to reduce the self to a single story, even a more flattering one. It is the practice of making space—for ambiguity, for contradictions, for emergent truths. And it is, above all, a form of intimacy: with oneself, with one's past, and with the ever-unfolding mystery of what it means to become.

In this spirit, the reflective practices offered here are not tools for transformation as performance. They are invitations to inhabit one's inner life with greater honesty. To let go of false clarity. To resist the urge to label prematurely. And to allow, perhaps for the first time, an identity that is less about who one has always been, and more about *what becomes possible when one finally stops needing to be only one thing.*

Chapter 10
The Behaviour Beneath the Surface

Most discussions of change today fixate on the visible: a promotion, a milestone, a transformed body, a neatly edited résumé of self. Yet the most consequential psychological shifts rarely make the news—or an Instagram post—and seldom gratify society's hunger for stories of breakthrough and arrival. These are subtler alterations: a recalibration of impulse, a shift in inner weather, a quiet adjustment in how one relates to oneself. They may not yield measurable outcomes for weeks, months, or even years. To dismiss them as "not real change" is to confuse silence with stagnation. This chapter begins by dismantling that misconception.

True behavioural transformation is rarely linear, aesthetically pleasing, or publicly evident. A person who once raged but now pauses, hands clenched, before letting the anger pass—that is change. The binge eater who still eats the cake but no longer despises themselves afterward—that is change. The habitual overfunctioner who cancels a meeting to rest, even just once, is quietly rewriting contracts that took decades to form. Celebrating transformation only when it is pristine, public, and permanent risks overlooking the real work: the subtle, often invisible recalibrations that sustain growth.

This chapter challenges the tyranny of optics that shapes our understanding of progress. The pressure to be "recovered," "healed," or "fully transformed" often becomes another persona to uphold—another mask for the approval of the very systems that caused the original wounding. But psychological safety is not performative; it is cultivated through interruption of old patterns, emotional recalibration, and a redefined relationship to failure. Healing is not an appearance—it is a capacity.

At the heart of this approach lies the notion of depth progress: growth that may not be visible in what a person does, but in how they relate to what they do. Behavioural psychology teaches us that actions are merely the tip of a deeper iceberg, composed of cues, triggers, reinforcement loops, and identity scaffolds. To create lasting change, one must attune to shifts in repertoires, not merely routines. These subtle indicators—an increase in self-compassion, a reduction in catastrophic thinking, a new willingness to pause rather than react—are not finish lines; they are inflection points. For many, these microvictories demand more effort than a year of sobriety or a ten-kilogram weight loss.

Much of the difficulty arises from the widespread belief that change equates to eradication. If the behaviour still manifests, the reasoning goes, then nothing has changed. This misunderstanding obscures the learning inherent in relapse—or, more precisely, reactivation. Behavioural resurfacing often provides insight, new data, and leverage for future shifts. A person who slips into avoidance but notices it within an hour rather than a month is not regressing—they are developing the metacognitive awareness essential for long-term stability. Falling back is part of the learning loop, not its opposite.

This chapter also confronts one of the most seductive illusions in behaviour change culture: the myth of the quantum leap. While appealing in cinematic terms, it often paralyzes genuine momentum. It leads individuals to overlook microshifts—small, repeated deviations from old scripts that gradually forge new neurobiological and emotional pathways. A single decision not to send a reactive email, to resist a habitual critique, may seem inconsequential externally, but internally it represents significant rewiring. Change happens in the moments before habit, not merely in the outcomes.

Yet microshifts are often dismissed because they offer little external validation. They are quiet, internal, and unglamorous. They provide neither the dopamine rush of achievement nor the social kudos of visible transformation. And yet, they are the foundation of enduring behavioural sustainability. They turn change into lived experience rather than performative ideal.

The modern culture of self-optimisation compounds this challenge. Pressure to appear emotionally evolved, perpetually improving, or high-functioning can encourage performance over integration. One may speak eloquently about boundaries, yet struggle to enforce them. Post affirmations, yet remain hostile to personal vulnerability.

This is not hypocrisy—it is disconnection. When language outpaces embodiment, the gap between aspirational and actual self widens.

Hence, this chapter emphasises recognition over reinvention. Readers are invited to become students of their own microbehaviours—not to judge, but to decode. What do I do when fatigued? What do I reach for when feeling unseen? What precedes defensive humour, perfectionism, or withdrawal? Behaviour becomes a portal, not a verdict. Even relapses are reframed—not as moral failures, but as signals awaiting interpretation.

Equally, this chapter addresses the internalised shame that often accompanies behavioural lapses. Shame does not reduce compulsive or destructive patterns; it entrenches them. When one equates behaviour with identity, clarity is lost. Observation gives way to suppression and avoidance. To break this loop, behaviour must be understood as communication rather than definition. The guiding question shifts from *What is wrong with me?* to *What is this part of me trying to resolve, avoid, or restore?*

By cultivating emotional literacy over suppression, readers gain agency. They move from managing habits to understanding the conditions that generate them. Here, enduring change resides—not in perfection, but in intimate knowledge of patterns. Not in public triumphs, but in private recalibrations. Not in the disappearance of old behaviours, but in the emergence of new responses to familiar triggers.

The work, then, is less about doing differently and more about perceiving differently. It begins with trusting that meaningful transformation is occurring, even when invisible to others. Especially then. Because it is in the quiet hours—those micro-moments of choice, reflection, and recalibration—that a person ceases to perform change and begins to embody it.

This is depth work. This is the behavioural revolution that leaves no hashtags. And this chapter is dedicated to helping readers see, measure, and honour it—for themselves.

Not All Change Is Visible

Progress, in its most essential form, is not a spectacle. It is not something others can verify, applaud, or easily measure. It is not always visible, dramatic, or linear. Yet modern culture has cultivated a deeply skewed relationship with what "counts" as change. People are taught—explicitly and implicitly—to view transformation through the lens of outcomes: abstinence, weight loss, promotions, improved relationships, resolved symptoms. When change does not take on these concrete forms, it is often dismissed, both internally and externally, as insufficient or illegitimate. But this view reveals more about societal impatience and the fetishisation of control than it does about the nature of true growth. *Not all change is visible. Not all progress performs well in public. And not all transformation can—or should—be forced into narrative coherence.*

Consider the case of someone trying to unlearn a pattern of emotional avoidance. Outwardly, they may still withdraw in moments of tension, still fail to voice their discomfort in a conflict, still look composed when anxious. But what has shifted—what is in fact the signal of change—is that they *notice*. They know they are avoiding. They feel the dissonance between the act and the truth. They sit with the discomfort instead of numbing it entirely. This is *depth progress*—internal shifts in awareness, intention, and relational engagement that precede lasting behavioural transformation. It is not glamorous, but it is foundational. And because it doesn't present as "results," it is too often overlooked, under-recognised, and abandoned prematurely.

The emphasis on visible markers of success also distorts how relapse and reactivation are interpreted. A person may believe that the return of a behaviour—be it bingeing, withdrawing, procrastinating, or self-criticising—is proof that they have "gone backwards." But this assumption ignores the role of context, self-awareness, emotional literacy, and intention. Falling back into a pattern without awareness is very different from doing so *with* awareness, from *within* a new emotional schema. If the behaviour looks the same, but the relationship to it has changed, then the underlying psychology has shifted. And *this* is what matters most for long-term transformation.

In behavioural psychology, this principle is well-supported. Cognitive restructuring—changing the way one thinks about a behaviour—is often the first step toward lasting modification. The lag between cognitive shift and behavioural shift is normal, not pathological. Yet in most cultural narratives of change, this lag is seen as failure. People are rarely taught how to *recognise the value of becoming aware before becoming different*. But awareness is not passive. It is a neurocognitive achievement. It reflects an upgraded self-observing capacity, a breaking of automaticity, and an invitation to interrupt reactivity. *Depth progress* is the space between old behaviour and new awareness. It is the moment the story stops writing itself.

Take another example: someone in recovery from people-pleasing. They still say "yes" too often, still overextend, still feel unable to set boundaries. But unlike before, they now experience discomfort after they agree to things they don't want. They replay conversations with new insight. They begin to imagine alternatives. This kind of invisible progress—growing discomfort with self-abandonment—is a precondition for boundary work. It signals that the old pattern no longer fits, even if the new one isn't yet accessible. That is how identity change begins: not with new performance, but with old patterns losing their internal coherence.

This misunderstanding of what change looks like is also compounded by the culture of public healing. In an era where mental health language and recovery narratives are highly visible online, there's a pressure to *display* progress. People feel they must showcase their new habits, post their insights, or narrate their transformations to be seen as valid. But when change becomes performative, it becomes divorced from authenticity. The focus shifts from *embodiment* to *optics*. And when change is pursued for validation, it rarely penetrates beneath the surface. The person may say the right things but feel increasingly disconnected from their inner experience. The public self improves while the private self suffers in silence.

This kind of split creates an illusion of progress that is ultimately unsustainable. And worse, it teaches others to mimic the appearance of growth rather than engage with the reality of it. In this model, relapse becomes shameful. Ambivalence becomes failure. Depth work becomes irrelevant. The result is a behavioural culture obsessed with the quantifiable—calories, sobriety dates, hours meditated, tasks completed—rather than the *quality* of one's emotional relationship to the behaviour. *When the bar for success is external, the inner shifts that make change real are devalued, dismissed, or entirely missed.*

That's why it's vital to reorient progress around *internal data points*: moments of self-honesty, shifts in impulse, reductions in self-judgement, the ability to pause. These are the linchpins of transformation, even when nothing changes on the outside. In fact, these often have to occur *first*. You cannot maintain new behaviour from an old mindset. You cannot sustain a boundary if your nervous system is still fused with fear. You cannot stop self-sabotaging until you know what the sabotage is trying to protect. Seen this way, slow, internal change is not a detour. It is the work.

It is also important to recognise that some of the most profound behavioural shifts occur in response to subtle neurobiological recalibration. For instance, through regular somatic practices—such as breathwork, movement, or grounding techniques—a person's capacity to tolerate distress can increase without any visible behavioural upgrade. But that nervous system capacity is what eventually enables more functional behaviour. The problem is, because the early work doesn't "look" like progress, it's easy to discard it. Someone might say, "I've been meditating for weeks and still react the same way." What they don't realise is that they're building *internal margins*. They're installing the scaffolding for the behaviour to have somewhere to land.

This is where the concept of *depth progress* becomes indispensable. It challenges the impulse to measure success only in externalised terms. Instead, it teaches us to track emotional tone, not just output. To ask: Am I less fused with my fear? Do I pause before reacting? Can I recognise when I've left myself? Am I able to return more quickly? These are internal metrics. They don't show up on scales, spreadsheets, or sobriety trackers—but they represent a fundamental upgrade in one's self-regulatory system. And that is where sustainable change lives.

Culturally, we are just beginning to understand the cost of ignoring these internal metrics. Therapists see it when clients self-flagellate for "not making progress," even as they grow more fluent in their own emotional life. Coaches see it when clients abandon practices that were working—just not fast enough. Friends see it when loved ones relapse and think the whole journey was pointless. All of this stems from a narrow, punishing model of what change should look like. And it keeps people stuck not because they can't change, but because they don't recognise that they *already are.*

One of the most radical acts of transformation is to affirm change before it has fully bloomed. To trust the small signals: that extra breath, that moment of reflection, that flicker of regret that wasn't there before. These are signs of life. And in the context of behaviour change, they are signs of a new psychological ecosystem forming beneath the surface. The work, then, is to attune to this subterranean growth. To validate it. To build on it. And to resist the urge to demand proof before recognising value.

Ultimately, when we widen our definition of change, we create more space for people to *stay* in the process. We reduce shame. We expand hope. We dismantle the myth that if nothing has changed outwardly, nothing has changed at all. And in doing so, we begin to practise the kind of behavioural compassion that makes real growth possible—not only for ourselves, but for others as well.

Progress is not what it looks like. *It's what it shifts inside you.*

Microshifts Over Masterplans

The assumption that change must be grand to be meaningful is one of the most persistent and misguided ideas in modern psychology and personal development. This bias towards spectacle—that real transformation requires sweeping plans, visible outcomes, and dramatic reinventions—has deeply compromised how people perceive and pursue emotional growth. In truth, *the most enduring forms of change do not begin with large gestures but with small, repeated interruptions to old emotional patterns.* These microshifts—fleeting moments of pause, brief flashes of awareness, subtle reductions in self-judgement—are not detours on the path to change. They *are* the change.

The human brain is not built for masterplans. It is built for pattern recognition. From early development, the nervous system wires itself according to predictable feedback loops—rewards, threats, needs met or unmet. By the time one reaches adulthood, many emotional reactions are deeply encoded not because they are rational, but because they are familiar. To alter this embedded circuitry, what's needed is not a wholesale personality transplant, but *a series of consistent emotional micro-adjustments* that gradually rewrite the nervous system's expectations about safety, identity, and belonging.

Imagine someone working to unlearn a lifelong pattern of reactivity in conflict. They've read the books. They know what they're *supposed* to do—pause, breathe, respond thoughtfully. But in the moment, their body floods. They snap. They regret it. If success is measured solely by whether they *stop snapping*, then every failure is total. But what if success were measured differently? What if noticing the rise in emotion—even a few seconds earlier than before—*counts*? What if the moment they say, "That didn't feel right," five minutes after the argument *is* a gain in self-awareness? What if microshifts in the internal environment—*a softened tone, a slower breath, a reduced need to defend*—are understood as signs that something foundational is changing?

This is not romantic optimism. It is rooted in the science of neuroplasticity. The brain rewires not through epiphanies, but through repetition. *New pathways are strengthened through use, not insight alone.* Insight opens the door, but microshifts walk us through it. Repeatedly. Quietly. Without applause.

The problem is that these changes are easily dismissed. They don't announce themselves. They don't look impressive. No one else may notice. Which is why many people abandon the process just as it begins to work. They're waiting for a feeling of transformation that never comes, because they've been taught to equate progress with intensity. But *intensity is not the metric of truth.* In fact, the more deeply wired a habit is, the less dramatic its unwinding is likely to be. A strong inner critic won't disappear overnight, but a person might *begin* to hear it and choose not to obey. That choice—a slight redirection of emotional loyalty—is a microshift. And it is enormously consequential.

A useful way to track microshifts is to shift the measurement frame from outcomes to patterns. Instead of asking, "Did I succeed today?" ask, "Did I relate to my difficulty differently?" Instead of, "Did I avoid the behaviour?" ask, "Did I pause before doing it?" This doesn't mean abandoning standards. It means deepening them. *The more refined the lens, the more evidence of change becomes visible.* And this visibility sustains motivation over time.

Much of the allure of the "masterplan" model stems from its promise of control. It is neat, trackable, binary: success or failure, plan or deviation. Microshifts are messier. They require trust in processes that don't yield immediate proof. They demand that people find meaning in *subtler territory*—a sigh of self-compassion where there used to be silence; a second thought before the self-sabotage; a more curious question posed to a part of oneself previously avoided. These may not satisfy the craving for measurable milestones, but they point to something far more enduring: a change in how the self relates to its own vulnerability.

A person recovering from chronic self-abandonment may still defer to others out of habit. But in microshift terms, progress might look like a *fleeting* awareness that they had a choice. Or a quiet resentment that they didn't speak. These signals are often uncomfortable—but that's because they represent *emergent self-respect.* Emotional discomfort is not always a step backwards; it can be evidence that something dormant is waking up. And it is precisely these moments that signal the start of new internal alignment.

One of the most overlooked benefits of focusing on microshifts is that it cultivates emotional patience. People stop demanding that every effort deliver immediate returns. They learn to tolerate ambiguity, to rest in tension, to become students of their own process rather than enforcers of an idealised version of themselves. This *emotional decentralisation*—the ability to observe without rushing to correct—is what makes sustainable change possible. It is also what makes self-trust grow. When someone learns to honour small wins, they are more likely to stay engaged during long, uncertain seasons of change.

Microshifts also shift the narrative from heroism to honesty. Instead of waiting for a reinvention arc, the person learns to live within their contradictions. The perfectionist doesn't have to become unbothered. They just need to notice when they're bracing, and soften. The person with avoidance tendencies doesn't need to become relentlessly expressive. They just need to tolerate one more second of discomfort before retreating. *Each small act of emotional integrity weakens the grip of the old narrative.* And over time, a new one emerges—not proclaimed, but lived.

This orientation also protects against one of the most pervasive saboteurs of growth: shame. When progress is defined by large behavioural shifts, any deviation is seen as failure. But in a microshift framework, difficulty becomes data. If someone returns to a familiar behaviour, they are trained to ask: *What part of me needed that? What moment did I miss? What do I know now that I didn't before?* This fosters inquiry rather than self-recrimination, which is *crucial* because shame itself is a regressive force. It doesn't just halt progress—it often reverses it by collapsing the very self-trust on which growth depends.

To value microshifts is to practise *compassionate precision.* Not the vague kindness of "everything's fine," but the focused attention that sees subtle change and respects its trajectory. It requires attunement, presence, and a commitment to witnessing the unfolding without rushing to reframe or repackage it for others' understanding. *It is a private revolution—quiet but seismic.*

And it requires abandoning the myth of mastery. Masterplans are comforting because they provide a fantasy of arrival. But real change has no finish line. It is recursive, seasonal, and often anticlimactic. What replaces the grandiosity of reinvention is something sturdier: *emotional fidelity to one's evolving self.* The point is not to become someone else. It's to become *more available* to who you already are—beneath defence, beneath habit, beneath survival.

The more people are trained to notice their own microshifts, the less likely they are to outsource authority over their progress. They stop needing external markers to validate their growth. They stop needing others to recognise what they're doing right. They begin to build an internal lexicon of self-trust, anchored in the knowledge that *small shifts become new norms when repeated under pressure.*

What begins as a whisper—"I don't want to keep doing this"—can, over time, become a new voice entirely. But it does not arrive through overhaul. It arrives through thousands of tiny departures from what used to be automatic. These microshifts may never be praised, documented, or externally confirmed. But they are *real.* And they are *enough.*

When Falling Back Isn't Failing

Relapse is not proof of failure. It is proof that change is occurring in the real world, not just in the abstract. No behavioural transformation—whether in addiction recovery, emotional regulation, relationship dynamics, or self-talk—unfolds as a straight line. Yet many people measure their progress against the fantasy of uninterrupted success, and when they inevitably slip, they treat the return of old behaviours as an indictment of character rather than an invitation to investigate what needs more support. *This rigid framing doesn't just distort the change process—it disrupts it entirely.*

Relapse, in behavioural psychology, is not a moral regression. It is a moment when old neural pathways regain temporary dominance, often under stress, fatigue, or emotional overwhelm. That isn't surprising; it's predictable. The brain is a pattern-preserving machine. It defaults to what it knows, especially under pressure. And if a person has spent years—often decades—relying on a particular coping mechanism, the occasional reappearance of that behaviour should not be read as a betrayal of progress, but as a reflection of the mind's conservative architecture. *The brain does not erase; it reroutes. And rerouting takes time.*

The cultural expectation that growth must be linear is both cognitively untrue and emotionally damaging. It suggests that any deviation from the desired behaviour undoes the work that preceded it, which is demonstrably false. A person who has paused mid-impulse ten times before acting is not the same as one who has never paused. A person who regrets a slip, examines it, and returns to their path with greater clarity is *not* back at zero. They are evolving.

One of the most corrosive narratives surrounding relapse is that it reveals the "real" self—as if the part that stumbled is more authentic than the part that was trying. But *behaviour is context-dependent.* The self that coped destructively did so under specific internal and external conditions. To view it as more "true" than the self that chooses restraint, reflection, or re-engagement is to flatten the complexity of human motivation. It's not that one is real and one is fake—it's that *both selves are part of a larger system, responding to different inputs.* Integrating them, not ranking them, is the work.

Reframing relapse starts by recontextualising it. Instead of asking, "Why did I fail?" ask, "What changed in my environment, emotions, or state that made this behaviour feel necessary again?" Often, what's discovered is that the relapse was not random. It was preceded by a cue—an argument, a disruption in routine, a spike in shame, a drop in self-attunement. This is where cognitive-behavioural and somatic frameworks converge: relapse is rarely about the behaviour itself. *It is a downstream event—a signal that something earlier in the chain was missed, ignored, or underestimated.*

The concept of *relapse as feedback* is not a euphemism for indulgence. It is a strategic reframing that allows for greater diagnostic clarity. When someone stumbles, the question becomes, *What was this behaviour trying to manage? What felt intolerable in that moment? What skill, support, or insight was missing?* This shift in inquiry helps remove moral weight from the event and replaces it with curiosity—a much more sustainable position for long-term change.

From a behavioural reinforcement standpoint, slips do not undo gains unless they are interpreted as permission to abandon the process. What matters is not the occurrence of the behaviour, but the story told about it. Shame-induced narratives ("I'm back to square one," "I always do this," "Nothing has changed") recruit the very emotional states that *precede* relapse: hopelessness, guilt, helplessness. In contrast, a self-respecting frame ("That was a data point," "Something in me was overwhelmed," "Let's track the pattern") engages the executive brain. It reintroduces choice, strategy, and nuance.

It is important to acknowledge that not all relapses are benign. Some carry consequences—financial, relational, or psychological. But even in these cases, the pathway forward is not through punitive self-rejection. It is through *increased granularity of awareness*. If someone returns to an old behaviour, they are not "proving" they haven't changed. They are demonstrating that change has *limits* under current conditions. The work then becomes identifying those limits—not with condemnation, but with skill.

Consider the person recovering from a pattern of emotional eating. They've gone weeks making more conscious choices, eating when hungry, responding with awareness. Then they hit a difficult week—grief resurfaces, deadlines compress, sleep is poor—and the urge returns. They binge. Shame sets in. In the traditional narrative, this is regression. But in a reframed lens, it is a flare—a signal that *something in the system is under-resourced.* Instead of focusing on the act of eating, the person is encouraged to investigate the context: What felt like too much to hold? Where did their inner resourcing begin to thin? Which earlier cues—tension, fatigue, loss of joy—were overridden?

Behavioural psychology offers a concept called *extinction burst*—the idea that just before a conditioned response disappears, it may intensify. A child who stops getting candy when whining might whine louder before giving up. The same is true of internal habits. Just before a behavioural loop dissolves, it may reassert itself forcefully. *That escalation is not failure—it's a final flare of an old pattern losing ground.* Recognising this helps people stay the course without mistaking noise for truth.

This applies equally to mental habits. A person trying to disarm a harsh inner critic may notice that, just as they begin to cultivate self-compassion, the critic grows louder. Not because they are failing, but because *the system is adjusting.* These internal surges often represent *resistance to integration*—a psychological immune response to the unfamiliar. The key is to view these spikes as part of the process, not proof that the process is broken.

There is also the matter of *identity resilience*. People who frame themselves as "always falling back" develop identities organised around struggle. But this is where the importance of narrative agency comes in. Change requires not only new habits, but new self-permissions. It asks a person to say: "I am someone who is learning, not someone who is failing." "I am someone who notices, not someone who collapses." These rephrasings are not self-help platitudes—they are *cognitive scaffolds*. They hold up new patterns while they take root.

In systems thinking, relapse is a reversion to a prior equilibrium. It signals that the organism is under strain, trying to return to familiar ground. If the conditions around the system change—support increases, stressors lessen, self-awareness deepens—the equilibrium shifts. Relapse becomes less frequent, less intense, and eventually less compelling. But the path there is not marked by binary success or failure. It is marked by *adaptive responsiveness*—the capacity to revise, recalibrate, and recommit without internal collapse.

This shift in frame changes everything. It moves the goalpost from perfection to *resilience under tension*. It invites the person to ask: When I slipped, did I return faster? Did I learn more? Did I soften instead of shatter? These are not consolation questions—they are precision tools for tracking *emotional recovery*, which often precedes behavioural stability.

Ultimately, relapse is not a detour from the path. It *is* the path. It reveals where the old wiring still holds sway, where tenderness is still needed, where the illusion of control gives way to the real work of relationship—with the self, with the body, with the unresolved. And when that relationship is governed not by shame but by integrity, change becomes something deeper than achievement. It becomes *a practice of returning*—not perfectly, but persistently.

The Danger of Performing Change

There is a particular kind of self-sabotage that masquerades as transformation. It is not immediately obvious because, on the surface, it resembles genuine growth: new routines, public affirmations, well-framed insights, and declarations of newfound boundaries. But beneath the curated progress lies an old compulsion, repackaged—*the need to be seen as evolving rather than the slow, private work of actually changing.* This is the danger of performing change: it can seduce the ego into cosplaying healing while avoiding its core discomforts. When the process of inner work is co-opted by the desire for external validation, the transformation becomes brittle—hollowed out by its dependence on being witnessed.

Psychologically, performance is not inherently malicious. Human beings are social creatures, wired for mirroring, approval, and group inclusion. But when the motivation to appear changed becomes dominant, it warps the healing process into a spectacle. The metric shifts from *"Am I learning something true about myself?"* to *'Do others think I'm doing well?"* And because performance can be rehearsed, rehearsed healing can become a strategy for avoiding the very vulnerability that authentic change demands.

Consider the individual recovering from chronic people-pleasing, who begins posting about setting boundaries while still anxiously over-accommodating in private. Or the high-achieving executive attending mindfulness workshops, not to sit with discomfort, but to prove their emotional intelligence to peers. These are not cases of hypocrisy, but of fragmentation. The outer expression and inner state are misaligned. The person is not being false—they are *protecting.* And in most cases, they're doing so unconsciously.

This dynamic is especially common in environments where self-optimisation is a social currency. In therapy culture, wellness spaces, and even corporate leadership programmes, there is often unspoken pressure to *signal growth.* But the signalling itself can create performance anxiety: if people believe they must demonstrate perpetual progress, they will conceal their regressions. What emerges is a culture of silent comparison, where everyone is quietly wondering if they're doing "change" correctly while feeling privately off-track.

The psychological impact of this pressure is significant. Performing change demands coherence before it has arrived. It forces premature integration—a façade of stability that short-circuits the messiness required for real inner rewiring. In practice, this might look like someone saying they've "let go" of a destructive pattern while still feeling emotionally entangled with it. Or someone claiming to have "forgiven" a parent while unconsciously reenacting their relational wounds in intimate partnerships. The performance becomes a defence mechanism—a shield against shame, uncertainty, or the fear of still being broken.

In this sense, the danger is not just personal—it is systemic. When healing is judged by its optics, people learn to manage perception instead of root-level drivers. They learn to say the right things before they feel them, to adopt language of healing without embodiment, and to bypass the necessary disorientation of real psychological unravelling. *Healing that performs too soon often petrifies into persona.* And the persona, no matter how refined, is not the self.

This is not an argument against sharing one's growth or inviting community into the process. Social reinforcement can be a powerful motivator, and visibility can dissolve shame. But the *why* matters. When the sharing stems from authenticity and shared humanity, it opens dialogue. When it stems from fear of inadequacy, it becomes another mask—albeit one dressed in therapeutic vocabulary.

To understand why people perform change, we have to examine the reward systems of identity. Many behavioural patterns—perfectionism, avoidance, self-sacrifice—are not just habits. They are identities built to survive early environments. To dismantle them means to face not just discomfort, but *disorientation.* Who am I if I am not the fixer? Who am I if I no longer achieve to feel worthy? Who am I without this struggle to narrate? This identity crisis is normal, but rarely celebrated. So instead of sitting in the in-between, many rush to reconstruct a new self—one that *looks* evolved, even if it hasn't yet metabolised the change.

The problem with this rush is that it recreates the exact relational dynamic that many people are trying to heal: conditional belonging. The core wound of many is not that they were never loved, but that they were loved only *when* they performed. They were appreciated for being helpful, calm, independent, successful, or low-maintenance. And so, even in change, the old template persists—*I must appear a certain way to remain safe.* Healing then becomes another role to play, another metric to chase.

This is why premature performance is not a harmless detour. It can delay actual healing by reinforcing the very neurobiological defences one seeks to dissolve. It keeps people in performance zones of the brain—executive functioning, image management—rather than allowing them to enter the somatic, relational, and emotional spaces where change actually imprints.

The solution is not to avoid being seen but to prioritise *inner congruence over outer coherence.* True transformation often begins quietly—*not with declarations, but with micro-decisions that nobody sees.* A pause before reacting. A refusal to betray oneself. An honest admission of regression. A conversation that reveals rather than conceals. These are the invisible revolutions of healing. They rarely get applause. But they matter more than performative benchmarks.

This calls for a shift in how we narrate change, both to ourselves and others. Instead of saying "I'm good now," we might say "I'm working through it." Instead of broadcasting victory, we might share confusion. Instead of showcasing control, we might allow moments of contradiction. Because healing is not a rebrand. It is a deconstruction. It requires spaciousness to not-know, to experiment, to contradict ourselves, to drop polished scripts in favour of emergent honesty.

That level of vulnerability is not performable in the conventional sense because it is not audience-oriented. It does not ask, "Do you approve of this version of me?" but "Can I live with what is true right now?" That is the axis of change that endures. Not one that seeks applause, but one that seeks integrity.

Of course, social dynamics complicate this. In therapeutic spaces, online platforms, and self-improvement groups, performative healing is often incentivised. The person who articulates their growth best is seen as the most advanced. But language is not transformation. Awareness is not integration. And the most articulate person in the room may be the one least in contact with their unprocessed grief.

This doesn't mean silence is superior. It means discernment is essential. Can we tell when we are performing versus expressing? Can we feel the difference between rehearsed reflection and emergent truth? Can we allow ourselves to be in-process rather than postured?

One simple but profound practice is to ask before sharing: *Am I saying this to be seen, or to be honest? Am I sharing what is real, or what is aspirational? Is there a part of me that feels pressured to appear okay before I am?* These questions are not accusations—they are invitations. They help dislodge performance from its throne and return healing to its rightful domain: the quiet, messy, nonlinear work of change.

When healing stops being a performance, it becomes something far more interesting—an inquiry rather than a campaign, a conversation with the self rather than a show for the world. And in that quieter theatre, something remarkable happens. Growth becomes less about proving, and more about belonging. Not to an audience, but to one's own unfolding self.

Chapter 11
Designing New Emotional Ecosystems

Lasting behavioural change rarely arises from sheer willpower alone; it takes root in environments—both internal and external—that make healthier choices feel safe, coherent, and attainable. A common misstep in attempts at transformation is the assumption that motivation and information suffice. Humans are not purely rational machines; we are emotional organisms, constantly seeking regulation, predictability, and meaning. When change initiatives disregard this emotional architecture, they collapse beneath the weight of their abstraction. Transformation, then, is not merely the eradication of maladaptive behaviours—it is the replacement of the emotional functions those behaviours serve with responses that are adaptive, sustainable, and humane.

To appreciate this, we must start with a simple but often overlooked premise: behaviours—especially those labelled 'bad'—are solutions before they become problems. The nightly binge, the outburst of rage, the endless scrolling, the retreat into isolation—all were attempts to self-soothe, gain control, or signal distress when no better mechanism was available. Remove the behaviour without addressing the emotional utility it provides, and a vacuum is left. Human nature, like nature itself, abhors a vacuum; the old pattern returns, often more entrenched than before.

This chapter examines the imperative of designing for emotional safety before performance, and how to create conditions that anticipate vulnerability rather than demand perfection. For many—particularly trauma survivors or those who experienced emotional neglect—change cannot be built on scaffolds of pressure or deprivation. It must be anchored in felt safety. And here, "safety" is not merely physical or intellectual; it is neurobiological. The nervous system must believe it is secure before the body can release coping strategies, even those that have become corrosive over time.

We exist in cultures obsessed with outcomes. Productivity is treated as a virtue, and struggle is only tolerated when it produces visible success. This distorts feedback loops: behaviours are judged by the performance they signal rather than the regulation they provide. Yet true healing often appears unremarkable. It may look like resting, saying no, sleeping more, or prioritising boundaries over visibility. Sometimes it is about reducing intensity, because safety has become more important than stimulation. Durable change is the gradual stabilisation of one's internal ecosystem—not the rapid optimisation of external appearance.

Part of this ecosystem design is recognising that the self does not function in isolation. Habits do not exist in a vacuum; they are embedded in cues, relationships, spaces, scripts, sensory stimuli, and symbolic rituals. Sustainable change requires shifting the emotional meanings that surround our behaviours. What does alcohol signify for the person who drinks to manage social anxiety? What does busyness signal for the individual who fears irrelevance? What does dieting mean for someone whose body image was their primary source of approval? Until these meanings are understood, change remains an intellectual abstraction rather than a lived reality.

This is where emotional scaffolding becomes indispensable. Rather than relying on grit or shame to enforce compliance, scaffolding provides a more intelligent structure. It surrounds the emerging self with supports, holding people in transition instead of leaving them adrift between the old and the new. These supports may take many forms: intentional morning rituals, post-relapse scripts, accountability partners, regulated social media exposure, or grounding objects in physical space. The crucial point is that they offer containment—a sense that the self will not collapse when experimenting with the unfamiliar.

This chapter does not offer a rigid formula. It provides a conceptual reframing: if we stop trying to "fix" behaviour and start listening to it as encrypted emotional data, we can ask smarter questions. Not "How do I stop doing this?" but "What need is this behaviour meeting, and how else might I fulfil it?" Not "Why do I keep failing?" but "Have I designed my environment to support this change, or am I relying on vague intentions and internal monologues?" These questions are not gentler—they are more intelligent.

They are also more honest. Many people are committed to change yet operate within psychological environments that make it harder than necessary. They attempt to rise earlier without reasons compelling enough to awaken. They try to quit doomscrolling without addressing the loneliness that renders silence unbearable. They seek to stop snapping at their partner without building systems for daily decompression. Change fails not due to laziness or resistance, but because the conditions necessary for transformation have not been aligned with emotional realities.

Designing new emotional ecosystems is therefore not optional; it is foundational. It demands humility to acknowledge that insight alone is insufficient, courage to reconceptualise discipline not as self-denial but as compassionate architecture, and skill to notice not just behaviours, but the emotions they regulate, the beliefs they express, and the unmet needs they reveal. Seen through this lens, human behaviour becomes intelligible rather than adversarial.

This chapter offers a new compass: one that points not toward faster fixes or shinier outcomes, but toward emotional congruence. A compass that asks: Does this behaviour feel coherent with who I am becoming? Does it leave me more whole or more fragmented? Does it facilitate access to safety, or reintroduce threat disguised as discipline?

Readers will explore the hidden logic of their behavioural loops and discover tools to replace, not suppress, old patterns. The emphasis is on function over form: meeting needs through healthier channels, designing for safety rather than spectacle, and scaffolding emerging selves without demanding immediate identity transformations. Compulsive patterns, avoidance behaviours, or emotional numbing are not to be conquered; the self is to be nurtured and supported.

If behaviour is a survival code, then change must be treated as a new dialect—not imposed by force, but co-created through insight, gentleness, and intelligent design. Once we learn to speak that language, the compulsion to "force" behaviour fades, replaced by rhythms that feel less like tasks and more like lived truths—from the inside out.

Replace the Need, Not Just the Habit

Behaviour change that overlooks emotional utility is unsustainable. This is not a philosophical statement—it's a neurobiological fact. A behaviour, especially one repeated compulsively, endures not because it's rational or moral or healthy, but because it *works*, at least in the narrow sense of serving a felt need. To assume that a harmful pattern can be broken without addressing the psychological function it performs is to ask someone to cut the brakes off a car without installing a new stopping system. Something will take over. The question is whether that *something* is deliberate, adaptive, and internally coherent—or simply another reflex in disguise.

Consider the man who drinks nightly to "unwind" after work. The drink, on the surface, is the habit he wishes to change. But the real dependency is not on alcohol—it's on the *state* the alcohol provides: decompression, lowered vigilance, a temporary break from self-surveillance. Remove the drink without replacing that regulatory mechanism and the brain will look for substitutes—binging, scrolling, snapping at loved ones, or disassociating. To create sustainable change, we must ask: *What does this behaviour achieve emotionally, and how else could I offer myself that experience without self-destruction?*

This is the paradigm shift at the heart of meaningful transformation: *behaviours are proxies for unmet needs, and only by replacing the need can we reliably replace the habit.*

Modern behavioural science increasingly supports this reframing. In addiction psychology, for example, research on reward substitution shows that interventions focused on abstinence alone often result in high relapse rates—unless the emotional and relational terrain around the habit is addressed. Similarly, in trauma-informed care, practitioners recognise that many "maladaptive" behaviours function as survival adaptations. They are not miscalculations; they are calculated efforts to maintain emotional balance with the tools available at the time.

This reframing also reveals why certain behaviours persist despite high levels of self-awareness. Insight alone does not rewire behaviour. A person can know precisely why they binge, self-sabotage, or lash out—and still do it—because *knowing is not the same as having an alternative.* Emotional regulation requires practice, not just perspective.

The challenge, then, is not just to eliminate but to *translate.* What looks like addiction might actually be a need for reliable ritual. What looks like control might actually be a need for safety. What looks like laziness might actually be a need for decompression. And once the emotional function is identified, the work becomes designing a behaviour that meets that function in a way that is both humane and regenerative.

Take, for instance, the client who constantly procrastinates on creative projects. On the surface, the goal might be to eliminate procrastination. But closer examination reveals that the delay is not driven by laziness or distraction—it's driven by a deep association between output and judgement. This person doesn't just fear failure; they fear exposure. Creating becomes a threat to identity. The underlying need, then, is not to 'just start'—it is to feel *safe while being seen.* A new behaviour must address that first. Perhaps it begins with private creation only, rituals of self-containment, or working in emotionally neutral environments. Until that safety is established, "productivity strategies" will only ever scratch the surface.

Another example: the person who repeatedly chooses emotionally unavailable partners. The behavioural pattern is evident, but the underlying need is often unspoken—*the desire to remain emotionally close without vulnerability.* An avoidant partner allows one to simulate intimacy without risking full exposure. To change this pattern, it's not enough to *decide* to pick differently. The emotional need for connection without overwhelm must first be met in safer, more tolerable ways—through slow intimacy, platonic depth, or therapeutic alliance—before the nervous system will register secure connection as viable.

This work demands emotional granularity. We must become fluent in *what we are actually reaching for* beneath the action. Is the habit seeking comfort, power, relief, recognition, stillness, or stimulation? Is it about escaping sensation or enhancing it? Is it protective, expressive, punitive, or relational? Many behaviours serve multiple roles at once—and the deeper we examine them, the more precise our substitutions can become.

Too often, people attempt to change habits by layering punishment or performance over them. They try to out-discipline the behaviour, rather than understanding its emotional roots. This approach may create short-term suppression but rarely results in integration. *When a new behaviour feels emotionally incoherent, the nervous system will eventually reject it*—no matter how logically beneficial it may seem.

The more sustainable approach is to design replacements that feel *true.* This means honouring the original impulse without being enslaved by its current form. It means asking, *What is the best version of what this habit is trying to do?* If binge eating is a way to reclaim a sense of indulgence, can that indulgence be offered through nourishing sensory experiences—warm baths, favourite music, rich food eaten slowly and with permission? If lashing out is a cry for boundaries, can that energy be redirected into structured assertion, clear 'no's, or self-advocacy that doesn't destroy connection in the process?

These replacements must be emotionally satisfying—not just intellectually acceptable. A common failure point in behaviour change is selecting a substitute that is too bland, too distant, or too mismatched in tone. For example, replacing a compulsive shopping habit with an abstract budgeting app often fails not because the app is ineffective, but because it doesn't meet the same need for *self-celebration or visible reward.* A more emotionally aligned substitution might involve creating a personal ritual where achievements are marked with symbolic celebration—journaling accomplishments, curating meaningful tokens, or crafting beauty in less material forms.

This shift also requires a shift in self-narrative. Many people carry an internalised shame script: that they are broken because they cannot "just stop." But when we begin to see behaviour through the lens of emotional necessity, that shame can be transmuted into responsibility. Not in the punitive sense, but in the empowering sense—*I am responsible for learning how to meet my needs better now that I know what they are.*

In therapeutic contexts, this process is often framed as needs-based design. Instead of framing behaviour in terms of willpower or morality, it's reframed in terms of *emotional engineering*. What conditions need to be in place—internally and externally—for the nervous system to prefer the new behaviour? This might include environmental cues, emotionally congruent rituals, or social accountability rooted in empathy rather than evaluation.

A final note: replacing the need does not mean dismissing the habit. It means *honouring its logic*, then updating its strategy. Even the most destructive pattern began as an attempt to feel more alive, more safe, more known, more in control. That intention was never wrong. But with new tools and new awareness, we have the opportunity to evolve the execution.

The invitation is clear: *Don't just strip away what doesn't work—build what does.* Build it deliberately. Build it emotionally. And build it in a way that feels like self-recognition, not self-betrayal.

When behaviour becomes a form of need-meeting instead of need-escaping, change is no longer a punishment. It becomes a kindness. A homecoming. A better way of doing what you were always trying to do—survive, soothe, express, and belong. But now, with more choice, more congruence, and more care.

Safety First, Not Success First

Few myths are as deeply embedded in personal development culture as the idea that behaviour change begins with willpower. Grit, discipline, routines—these are often framed as the cornerstones of transformation. But for anyone whose habits are shaped by trauma, stress, or emotional fragmentation, this narrative is not only insufficient; it's harmful. *Lasting change cannot take root in a system that feels unsafe.* The nervous system will always prioritise survival over success. Until it believes that a new behaviour won't endanger the individual—physically, psychologically, or relationally—it will resist that behaviour, no matter how logically beneficial it may appear.

This is the crucial insight that trauma-informed frameworks offer: change doesn't begin with action; it begins with safety. Without a felt sense of safety—internal coherence, emotional predictability, relational trust—the very act of change can feel like a threat. And the more someone's early environment was defined by instability, the more their default behavioural responses will be organised around self-protection, not self-improvement. The goal, then, is not to enforce new behaviours through pressure but to *build conditions in which new behaviours become possible.*

To understand why safety must come first, we must look beyond behavioural theory and into neurobiology. The autonomic nervous system—particularly the vagus nerve—regulates whether we are in a state of mobilisation (fight/flight), immobilisation (freeze/shutdown), or social engagement (connection and openness). When the system perceives threat, it shuts down non-essential functions, including complex decision-making, impulse control, and curiosity. That means no matter how many cognitive tools someone possesses, they will not access them in a moment of perceived danger. For trauma-impacted individuals, that danger may not be logical—it may be encoded in the body as a learned association: *success equals exposure*, *relaxation equals vulnerability*, *assertiveness equals punishment.*

In this light, seemingly irrational self-sabotage often becomes understandable. The person who abandons a fitness plan just as it starts working may not fear failure but *success*, because success invites visibility, responsibility, or disruption of identity. The individual who avoids connection may not lack social skill but associate intimacy with betrayal. These reactions are not laziness or resistance—they are intelligent survival strategies adapted to past environments.

For behaviour to shift, the nervous system must learn—through repeated, embodied experience—that it is *now* safe enough to try a different approach. This is why trauma-informed change prioritises regulation before expectation. It asks: *What would make this behaviour feel safer in my body? What would help my system feel less threatened by this choice?*

In practice, this means designing for emotional tolerance, not just behavioural performance. A client struggling with compulsive overeating might be encouraged not to 'stop cold turkey' but to create a ritual around eating that feels emotionally nurturing rather than secretive. The goal is not immediate restraint but a gradual increase in felt safety—turning the act from a dissociative escape into a self-attuned experience. Over time, this builds the internal trust needed to make deeper changes possible.

Similarly, in therapeutic contexts, survivors of relational trauma often resist boundary-setting—not because they don't know how, but because *asserting needs has historically been punished.* For them, the work is not about learning boundary scripts but about *restoring nervous system capacity to tolerate the relational consequences of saying no.* That might involve visualisation, co-regulated practice with a therapist, or small, low-risk exposures to controlled conflict. The behaviour—the boundary—is only as strong as the system that can contain it.

This is also where mainstream productivity culture often fails. Many self-help protocols assume a baseline of emotional safety: that the individual trusts their environment, their relationships, their capacity to repair rupture. But for many, these assumptions are false. A new behaviour may require not just a shift in schedule but a *rebuild of inner trust.* And until that inner scaffolding is present, behaviour change efforts often collapse under the weight of unprocessed threat.

Safety must also be distinguished from comfort. It is not about avoidance or indulgence—it's about internal coherence. It's the difference between numbing out and soothing, between detaching and grounding. Safety means that the body is not bracing against itself. It means that the mind is not being hijacked by unintegrated loops. Only then does change stop feeling like self-abandonment and begin to feel like self-alignment.

Importantly, the perception of safety is not universal—it's deeply personal. One person may feel safest when highly structured; another when things are flexible. One may need solitude; another needs support. Trauma-informed change respects this subjectivity. It invites people to ask not *what's the right routine?* but *what rhythms allow me to stay connected to myself while trying something new?*

Safety also demands relational reconfiguration. People heal in context. If the environment continues to reinforce patterns of threat—criticism, inconsistency, shame—then internal work will be limited. A person can practice grounding all they want, but if their closest relationships are chronically dysregulating, their nervous system will remain primed for defence. In many cases, the first behavioural shift isn't diet, fitness, or productivity—it's reducing contact with unsafe people. Until this shift occurs, efforts to change habits are often sabotaged by the emotional turbulence of toxic proximity.

Behavioural science, when properly integrated with nervous system research, shows that people are not resisting change because they are weak or unmotivated. They are resisting because their system still perceives the new behaviour as more dangerous than the old one. This reframing is profoundly liberating. It removes the moral charge from behaviour. It restores compassion to the process of change. And it shifts the metric of success from 'how fast can I change?' to 'how safely can I expand?'

Consider the person who has spent years in high achievement mode, fuelled by anxiety. To them, resting might feel unbearable. Slowing down triggers a collapse into shame or panic. They do not need more discipline—they need more safety in stillness. That safety cannot be downloaded from a podcast. It must be built—through relational repair, somatic practice, and small experiences of rest that *don't* result in failure. Eventually, the body learns that rest does not equal collapse. And from there, a new behaviour—true rest—becomes available.

Trauma-informed models like Internal Family Systems, Polyvagal Theory, and Sensorimotor Psychotherapy all echo this wisdom. They teach that healing is not linear and that behaviour follows safety, not the other way around. Progress is often non-visible at first: a smaller fight with a partner, a shorter shame spiral, a single breath before a meltdown. But each of these is evidence that safety is increasing—and that, in turn, makes greater change possible.

Safety is not the reward for behaviour change. *It is the requirement.* Until a person feels safe enough to choose differently, they will continue to default to what is familiar. Not because they want to stay stuck, but because stuckness was once the only way to survive.

The work, then, is to reverse the usual order. Instead of demanding success to feel safe, we must *cultivate safety in order to succeed.* Safety of self-regard. Safety of emotional permission. Safety of trial and error. Safety of not knowing yet.

Once that foundation is in place, change doesn't need to be forced. It emerges—like a body finally unbracing, like a pattern finally no longer necessary. Because when safety returns, so does choice. And where there is choice, there can be transformation.

Designing for Emotional Containment

Emotional chaos is not always loud. It does not always look like crisis or collapse. More often, it manifests as background noise—disorganised mornings, spiralling decisions, overreactions to minor events, or a creeping sense of fragility beneath a high-functioning surface. For many, this lack of emotional containment is the invisible barrier that undermines sustained change. *Without containment, even the best habits unravel under stress; with containment, even the hardest work becomes endurable.* The challenge is that containment is rarely taught. It is assumed to be innate or outsourced to external systems like workplace structures, intimate relationships, or routines imposed by others. But real emotional containment must be *designed deliberately*—through rituals, environments, and relational cues that hold the self steady when inner weather turns volatile.

At its core, containment is about stability—internal predictability that does not suppress feeling, but gives it form. A person who lacks emotional containment often vacillates between numbness and overwhelm, between dissociation and reactivity. They may swing between hyper-independence and desperate co-dependence, trying to anchor themselves in people or patterns that ultimately intensify instability. Containment provides the emotional scaffolding needed to *feel without flooding, to reflect without collapsing, and to act without fracturing.* It is not control—it is capacity.

This capacity is not primarily cognitive. It resides in the body and the environment. Emotional containment emerges not just from insight, but from *systems* that communicate consistency to the nervous system. A consistent wake-up routine, a designated space for reflection, a sensory cue that signals transition—these are not trivial. They are carriers of safety, enabling the mind to return to itself when dysregulation threatens to derail the day.

Ritual is a foundational tool for emotional containment because it communicates temporal stability. It says, *this is what we do when we wake, when we're overwhelmed, when we end the day.* Rituals need not be elaborate or spiritual. They only need to be repeatable and embodied. Lighting a candle before journaling. Stretching while the kettle boils. A short breathing cue before answering a difficult message. These small acts create *predictable islands* in the emotional ocean. Over time, they form a rhythm the nervous system can trust. And trust is the precursor to resilience.

Environment is another overlooked dimension of containment. Many emotional patterns are *context-dependent,* meaning they are reinforced by particular sensory, spatial, and relational cues. For someone prone to procrastination, a cluttered workspace is not just inefficient—it's activating. For someone healing from relational trauma, a room without visual privacy may unconsciously replicate feelings of exposure or violation. Emotional containment often begins with *making the external space less chaotic,* so the internal space can begin to stabilise.

This is why minimalism resonates with trauma survivors—not because they are naturally orderly, but because less visual input reduces cognitive and sensory overwhelm. A simplified environment demands less from an already overstimulated system. It becomes an ally, rather than another variable to manage. This is containment by subtraction—not as aesthetic aspiration, but as a psychological intervention.

Relational design is equally essential. Emotional containment is not a solo project. While internal resourcing matters, co-regulation—the ability to return to calm in the presence of another—is a core function of the social nervous system. But not all relationships support containment. Some destabilise, even if they appear close. The friend who reacts with intensity to every disclosure. The partner who avoids hard conversations. The colleague who rewards burnout but shames slowness. These dynamics may be familiar, but they erode the emotional boundary conditions necessary for growth.

To design for containment, relational boundaries must be *curated, not just enforced.* It's not only about saying no—it's about intentionally investing in dynamics where containment is mutual. Where emotional weather is allowed, but not magnified. Where regulation is supported, not sabotaged. This might mean replacing dramatic conversations with reflective ones. It might mean telling someone, "I'd like to share, but I'm not looking for solutions today." The goal is not emotional censorship, but *emotional alignment*—building patterns of contact that restore, rather than destabilise.

Containment also requires internal leadership—the ability to *track inner states without becoming them.* For clients using Internal Family Systems or parts work, this often involves cultivating a Self that can hold conflicting internal parts in compassionate tension. The part that wants to isolate and the part that longs for connection. The part that resents structure and the part that fears collapse without it. Emotional containment means none of these parts get exiled or allowed to run the system unchecked. They are heard. But the leadership stays centralised.

One practical technique here is "naming the room"—a brief daily practice in which individuals list the dominant inner parts or emotional currents they're noticing that day. "The Planner is anxious about time. The Critic is watching my food. The Exile is missing someone." This practice externalises emotional content without judgment. It acknowledges the chaos without becoming it. Over time, this naming becomes its own form of containment—*language that gives shape to states that once felt formless.*

Another design principle for containment is *micro-transitions.* Many people move from one emotional or contextual state to another without signalling the shift to their nervous system. They go from an intense meeting to parenting duties, from an argument to sleep, from scrolling into deep work. These unmarked transitions contribute to dysregulation. To counter this, small rituals can be inserted between emotional zones—a quick breath with the door shut before going home, a five-minute journal between work and socialising, a symbolic act like changing clothes or turning on a lamp. These rituals cue the body that a new state is beginning. They offer containment through *narrative continuity.*

In high-performance environments, containment is often confused with repression. But true containment enhances performance, because it preserves emotional energy. It reduces volatility and decision fatigue. Leaders who build emotionally contained environments—not through emotional suppression, but through relational trust and clarity—often see better results, because their teams feel less threatened by ambiguity. The same applies to individuals: *a contained system is a more creative, more sustainable, more intelligent one.*

It's also important to acknowledge that some people unconsciously resist containment because chaos was their earliest form of belonging. If one grew up in households where unpredictability equalled intimacy—where crises were the only time affection appeared—then calm may feel like abandonment. In these cases, containment must be titrated. Too much order, too soon, can provoke panic. The body reads the stillness as dangerous. For these individuals, designing for containment begins with *gentle structure that honours their nervous system's history.* One small container at a time. One boundary. One ritual. One room made slightly more manageable.

Ultimately, containment is not the opposite of emotionality. It is the condition that allows emotional truth to emerge without destruction. It does not dull life—it deepens it. Because when feelings are held rather than leaked, they become intelligible. When environments are stabilised, they stop scripting our reactions. And when relationships are designed with care, they become containers themselves—vessels for presence, not projection.

To design for emotional containment, then, is not to reduce our range. It is to *create the capacity to hold it.* To move from reactivity to authorship. From chaos to coherence. Not all at once, but with intention. Not through force, but through form. And in a world that moves fast and fractures easily, such containment is not just a skill—it is a kind of wisdom. A way to stay whole in the middle of everything.

Beyond Discipline: Building Emotional Scaffolding

Discipline has long been romanticised as the gold standard of personal change—the force that carries us through adversity, keeps us accountable, and sharpens our will. But beneath the motivational slogans and morning routines lies a less glamorous truth: *discipline without emotional scaffolding eventually collapses under stress.* It isn't a lack of grit that derails most people—it's the absence of an infrastructure that supports consistent choice-making when emotions run high. The belief that we must wrestle our way into better habits has created a performance model of change, one that privileges control over coherence, suppression over support. The alternative is not laziness or leniency. The alternative is emotional design—building systems that *make it easier to do what's good for us, especially when we don't feel like it.*

At its essence, emotional scaffolding refers to the psychological and environmental structures that reduce internal friction. Just as scaffolding supports a building during its most fragile construction phases, emotional scaffolding supports the psyche when it is learning new patterns, healing old wounds, or enduring unfamiliar territory. This is not indulgence—it's intelligent design. Healthy behaviour becomes sustainable not when it is imposed through effort alone, but when the emotional context around it makes it feel natural, supported, and congruent with the self.

Consider the example of someone trying to reduce compulsive eating. The conventional model says: exert more willpower. Plan better. Distract yourself. But these interventions often fail not because the person is weak, but because the behaviour is compensating for unmet emotional needs—comfort, reward, dissociation, regulation. Grit addresses the action; scaffolding addresses the *need behind the action.* Emotional scaffolding might mean having a cue-based check-in ritual when urges rise. It might involve a curated environment with fewer triggers, a supportive text chain with a friend, or a post-urge recovery practice that brings the nervous system down gently instead of shaming it into compliance. Over time, these systems help shift the behaviour not by fighting it, but by rendering it obsolete.

This is the critical distinction: emotional scaffolding doesn't just enforce better choices—it *restructures the conditions under which choices are made.* It is architecture, not alarm. This distinction matters, especially for trauma-informed readers, who often find that "discipline" feels less like empowerment and more like a replay of coercive dynamics. If early life taught someone that success required self-abandonment, pushing harder only compounds the wound. Scaffolding, on the other hand, centres safety. It says: you don't have to be at war with yourself to grow.

One of the most practical tools of emotional scaffolding is **cues**—signals that prompt supportive action without requiring internal debate. A cue might be visual (a post-it on your mirror), sensory (a scent associated with calm), spatial (a chair designated for journaling), or temporal (an alarm that prompts a breathing practice). These cues operate as externalised memory—reminders that bypass the need for motivation. Especially during emotionally dysregulated moments, cues act as anchors. They allow the self to shift gears without relying on executive function, which is often compromised during distress.

But cues alone aren't enough. They must be paired with **affirmations**—not the pop-psychology platitudes that provoke eye rolls, but precision statements that *calibrate the nervous system toward grounded effort.* A strong affirmation is not aspirational—it is regulatory. "I can't do this" becomes "It's hard to feel capable right now, and I can still move one step forward." "I'm so behind" becomes "My pace is valid for what I've lived through." These are not tricks of language—they are *scripts for safety*, linguistic scaffolds that hold the inner dialogue steady when emotion distorts perception.

Boundaries are the third, and often most neglected, pillar of emotional scaffolding. Not just interpersonal boundaries—though those matter—but internal ones. The boundary between a thought and an identity. Between urgency and importance. Between an emotional impulse and an irreversible action. Emotional scaffolding means having *invisible walls that keep temporary states from defining the whole system.* When someone says, "I always sabotage myself," they are describing a collapse of boundary. They are mistaking a pattern for a truth. Scaffolding reintroduces containment: "This is a familiar pattern, not a fixed identity. I can interrupt it." These boundaries don't shrink the self; they *protect its expansion.*

Scaffolding also includes **designing rituals that prepare the psyche for effort**. Instead of relying on brute will to begin a difficult task, a person might develop a short pre-task ritual—a cup of tea, a walk around the block, a single page of reflective writing. These rituals signal safety, reduce anticipatory anxiety, and prime the nervous system for engagement. In behavioural psychology, this is known as *shaping*: altering the conditions before a behaviour to increase its likelihood. In emotional terms, it is about *pacing change to the body's readiness.* No one lifts a heavy weight without first positioning their stance. The same logic applies to emotional effort.

Importantly, emotional scaffolding recognises the role of *context fatigue.* People do not fail because they lack desire to change—they fail because the demands of modern life erode the bandwidth required to sustain change. Decision fatigue, relational stress, sensory overload, and digital fragmentation all drain the cognitive and emotional fuel needed to stay aligned with intentions. Scaffolding compensates for this by *removing unnecessary decision points* and *streamlining supportive defaults.* A structured calendar. A digital detox container. A pre-decided meal routine. These are not signs of rigidity—they are acts of mercy. They allow more energy to be spent on growth, less on micro-negotiation.

There is also a crucial psychological shift embedded in scaffolding: it transitions the self from *combat mode to collaboration mode.* Rather than treating the mind and body as things to overcome, scaffolding treats them as *partners in co-regulation.* It respects the nervous system's wisdom without letting it dominate. For instance, someone who freezes in conflict might scaffold a difficult conversation by scripting it in advance, naming their fear aloud, and giving themselves permission to pause and return. This is not avoidance. It is *designing conditions where the nervous system can stay present enough to participate in change.*

It is worth naming that many people resist scaffolding because they associate ease with weakness. There is a deeply embedded cultural script—especially in high-achieving environments—that says struggle is a sign of virtue. But struggle is not strategy. Nor is it necessary. Some of the most transformative progress happens not when people push harder, but when they finally *permit themselves to build smarter.* When they realise that enduring doesn't prove worth—thriving does.

Still, emotional scaffolding requires patience. It is not a quick fix. The systems must be tested, adjusted, and tuned to the individual. What calms one person overstimulates another. What feels grounding today may feel restrictive tomorrow. Scaffolding must be *adaptive and alive*, not another rigid framework to perform. The goal is not to automate behaviour at the cost of self-awareness. The goal is to *create enough support that self-awareness can flourish without panic.*

In the end, discipline has its place—but it cannot carry the whole structure. Emotional scaffolding makes the work of becoming not just possible, but sustainable. It replaces grit with grace. Control with design. Resistance with resonance. It honours the complexity of human emotion by crafting systems that support it, not silence it. And for anyone serious about change—not just performative, not just temporary, but integrated, embodied, and enduring—scaffolding is not optional. It is the architecture of transformation. A quiet form of intelligence. A structure that makes space for the self to rise.

Chapter 12
Choosing Change Without Shame

Most approaches to personal transformation carry an unspoken hostility: the notion that a flawed version of oneself must be disciplined, eradicated, or defeated. That the 'better self' emerges only through opposition to the 'worse self'. Yet, genuine change rarely grows from internal warfare. It arises from understanding—grasping why our most frustrating habits once served us, and learning to choose differently without shaming the self that once relied on them.

The urge to shame our past selves often masquerades as discipline. It sounds like accountability. It can even appear as progress. But beneath this surface, it perpetuates the same pattern that created the behaviour in the first place: a self relating to itself through fear, rejection, or exile. Phrases such as "I hate who I used to be" or "That wasn't the real me" are attempts to distance oneself from pain, yet in doing so, they often cement the very identity they hope to shed. Real growth does not come from disowning the past; it comes from metabolising it. Recognising what our "worst" behaviours were attempting—regulation, belonging, survival—is not self-pity. It is precision. It is the clarity that stops repetition at its source.

This chapter confronts the illusion that shame motivates. Evidence from behavioural science, and lived experience alike, shows that shame narrows perception, distorts clarity, and binds the self to the very patterns it seeks to escape. Rather than catalysing change, shame entrenches old coping mechanisms. It creates an internal climate of punishment where creativity, nuance, and emotional risk are stifled. And since meaningful change often requires exactly those qualities—experimentation, flexibility, vulnerability—shame becomes a structural barrier. This is a functional, not a moral, argument.

What replaces shame is not indulgence. It is compassion wielded with precision. Self-compassion is not a soft excuse, nor a lowering of standards. It is the willingness to observe the internal system without distortion, to name with accuracy the functions of different behaviours, and to relate to oneself in a tone that invites transformation rather than enforces it. Compassion does not imply anything goes. It implies that all actions make sense when placed in context. Even those aspects of ourselves we might want to discard can become fertile ground for learning.

Integration—relating to past behaviours with understanding rather than contempt—requires emotional maturity. Not everyone chooses it; many prefer the language of blame, which creates distance from pain and signals to the world, and to oneself, that change has occurred. But blame does not complete the emotional process. It leaves an invisible fracture between past and present, draining energy and clarity until confrontation becomes unavoidable. Integration, by contrast, is the act of saying: "That was me too. And I can meet the one who didn't know better with care, even as I act differently now." It is not erasure; it is reunion.

Too many self-improvement models obsess over replacement—discarding the old self entirely, constructing a new identity atop a foundation of shame. This might appear empowering, yet it creates fragility. Any regression or lapse threatens the entire edifice. Performance replaces embodiment. Language is curated. Ambivalence hidden. Evolution becomes editing, and editing becomes its own prison.

Choosing change without shame demands letting go of performance. It asks us to stop using growth as a measure of legitimacy. We stop trying to be a person who deserves a better life, and instead become the kind of person who trusts themselves enough to live it. This shift is subtle but radical. It is the difference between changing to be lovable and changing because you already are; between obedience and authorship.

A powerful tool in this transition is narrative reconstruction: rewriting the story we tell about our past without casting ourselves as villain or victim. This does not deny harm, but recognises that our worst moments were shaped by unmet needs, inherited patterns, and limited tools—not by any essential defect. We were adaptive, not broken. And the person we are today exists not despite those experiences, but in part because of them. They revealed systemic gaps. They taught us what required repair.

This chapter invites the crafting of an internal story grounded not in heroism or redemption, but in continuity. Reinvention is unnecessary; deep understanding suffices to make change the natural next step. When behaviour aligns with values—not to prove something, but because it flows from authentic alignment—the compulsion to relapse softens. The need to justify or punish diminishes. Choices are made from congruence, not coercion.

That shift—from coercion to coherence—is the essence of true healing. It is quiet, subtle, often invisible, yet it creates profound internal stability. Even difficult decisions feel lighter. We are no longer dragging a reluctant self forward; we are moving with clarity, consent, and care.

There is no final arrival. There is, instead, integration. A slow, quiet transformation that occurs when we meet the past without flinching and inhabit the present without apology. When we act from the knowledge that we were always permitted to move forward, real freedom begins.

Ending the War Within

The popular imagination tends to frame personal transformation as a kind of internal conquest. The flawed self must be confronted, corrected, and ultimately overpowered. In self-help culture, this is often dressed in the language of "discipline," "tough love," or "becoming your best self." But beneath these motivational slogans lies an unspoken assumption: that parts of you are inherently wrong, and that growth depends on keeping them under constant surveillance or suppression. This is not growth. It is internal hostility dressed up as self-improvement. And the cost is high—not only in emotional exhaustion, but in the chronic fragmentation of the self. *Lasting change does not come from defeating your worst self. It comes from understanding why that self came into being in the first place, and learning to relate to it with clarity instead of contempt.*

This insight is not merely philosophical; it is empirically grounded in decades of research across trauma therapy, behavioural psychology, and neurobiology. The so-called "worst self"—the one who binges, lies, dissociates, explodes, avoids—is rarely acting from malice or defect. It is acting from necessity. It formed in response to specific conditions: environments where needs went unmet, emotions were invalidated, or survival required contortion. The coping strategies that frustrate us most today often *began as solutions.* They kept the system operational when nothing else would. They are not the enemy. They are *outdated strategies* doing their best with incomplete data.

To declare war on these parts is to misunderstand their function. You cannot punish a survival strategy into extinction without provoking resistance, rebound, or replacement. This is why so many people who try to "crack down" on a behaviour—whether it's emotional eating, procrastination, perfectionism, or people-pleasing—find themselves locked in a cycle of relapse and shame. They believe they are too weak, too undisciplined, or too broken to change. But what they are actually up against is *a self-protective adaptation doing its job.* Until that adaptation is understood and gently reoriented, no amount of discipline will make it disappear.

Understanding, however, is often mischaracterised as indulgence. There is a widespread cultural suspicion that if we are too compassionate toward ourselves, we will lose our edge. That being "soft" on our inner saboteur will invite chaos or mediocrity. But this misunderstands the nature of precision. *True understanding is not vague sympathy—it is strategic empathy.* It asks: What role is this behaviour playing in the system? What need is it meeting, however inelegantly? What story does it believe, and how old is that belief? These questions are not a detour from change. They are the fastest route to sustainable transformation, because they respect the functional intelligence behind every pattern—even the painful ones.

Consider the example of someone who constantly sabotages their own success. On the surface, this looks like laziness or fear. But when explored with curiosity, it often reveals an internal part that equates visibility with danger. Perhaps in childhood, being exceptional provoked envy or punishment. Perhaps standing out once led to being abandoned or exploited. So success is not simply a goal; it is a perceived *threat to safety*. Unless that association is updated—not overridden, but gently revised—the system will continue to pull back the moment progress becomes tangible. No amount of "pushing through" will override a nervous system that still perceives progress as peril.

Ending the war within requires an internal posture shift: from dominance to dialogue. It means replacing the punitive inner voice with one that asks questions instead of issuing commands. This does not mean you let every part run the show. It means *every part gets a seat at the table*. You don't hand over the wheel to the bingeing part—but you do ask why it keeps grabbing for control at 2am. You don't pretend the inner critic is a truth-teller—but you do examine what it's trying to prevent, and why it believes shame is a safer strategy than vulnerability. Each part becomes a messenger, not a menace. And from this place of contact, change becomes collaborative rather than combative.

This approach echoes insights from Internal Family Systems (IFS), a therapeutic framework that treats the psyche as an internal ecosystem of distinct parts, each with its own voice, history, and intention. While IFS is just one model, its core premise resonates across disciplines: *wholeness is not achieved by exiling parts of the self, but by integrating them*. When we move from judgement to curiosity, from silencing to listening, the system begins to relax. The internal threat level drops. And in that lowered arousal state, choice becomes available in a way it never was under duress.

It is in this gap—between reaction and reflection—that real change becomes possible. Not because the "bad self" has been vanquished, but because it has been *heard, honoured, and recalibrated*. Often, the most stubborn behaviours dissolve not through force, but through accurate understanding of their role and a meaningful alternative being offered. The bingeing part is more willing to step back once it knows there's another way to soothe. The explosive part softens when it trusts that boundaries can be enforced without violence. *Safety—not shame—is what creates flexibility*. And flexibility is the foundation of change.

There is also a critical identity shift that takes place when we stop framing ourselves as being at war with our own mind. We begin to see ourselves not as defective or broken, but as intelligent systems responding to complex conditions. We develop a stance of internal leadership—one that neither indulges nor suppresses, but listens, learns, and leads. And from this position, the past no longer becomes a weight to drag, but a map to consult. Every pattern contains information. Every reaction points to an old belief. And every time we choose to respond with presence rather than punishment, we teach the system something new.

That "worst self" you've been trying to defeat may, in fact, be the most loyal part of you. It has stood guard through chaos, rejection, abandonment, trauma. It has taken on burdens too heavy for the age it was formed in. And now, it is simply tired. It wants rest, not exile. It wants to be understood—not applauded or shamed, just seen for what it was: *a makeshift guardian, doing its best under threat.* And when that part feels safe enough to put down its weapons, something extraordinary happens: the system reorganises. You no longer need to brace against yourself. You can move forward with all parts on board—not silenced, but integrated.

This is the end of the war within. Not a surrender, and not a victory in the traditional sense. But a reconciliation. A return to internal coherence. From that place, change is no longer a battle to be won. It becomes an act of alignment—one chosen not from fear or force, but from clarity and care. And that is a form of power that doesn't fracture the self. It heals it.

Compassion as Precision, Not Permission

For those steeped in high-performance culture or steeped in early environments where love was conditional, the concept of self-compassion often lands as a threat. It feels suspiciously soft, dangerously permissive, or simply ineffective. If you give yourself too much leeway, won't you become complacent? Undisciplined? Excusing the inexcusable? This belief is not only common—it's a major obstacle to sustainable change. Because without real self-compassion, most change efforts default to coercion. And coercion, however well-dressed in grit or ambition, breeds internal rebellion rather than resilience. *Compassion, when correctly understood, is not a loophole—it is a lever. Not softness, but strategy. Not indulgence, but intelligent design.*

The misunderstanding begins with a caricature. In popular discourse, self-compassion is often equated with leniency, self-pity, or motivational bypassing—"I was stressed, so it's okay I ghosted that meeting," or "I deserve the entire cake, I've had a rough week." These narratives are not compassion; they are rationalisation masquerading as care. True self-compassion does not obscure consequences. It does not enable the ego's evasions. What it *does* is interrupt the automaticity of shame, which is perhaps the least useful response when trying to change deeply ingrained patterns. Shame floods the system, narrows cognitive scope, increases rigidity, and reinforces the very behaviours it condemns. *Compassion, in contrast, creates a container for clarity.*

To understand compassion as precision, we need to reconsider its purpose. At its core, compassion is not an emotion—it is a skill. It is the capacity to witness pain without being overwhelmed by it, to sit with complexity without collapsing into confusion or judgement. In trauma-informed neuroscience, this is known as "dual awareness": the ability to hold distressing material *and* maintain presence. From this vantage point, you can evaluate behaviour not simply as failure or flaw, but as meaningful data. You can ask: What part of me did that? What were they trying to accomplish? What belief were they operating from? And—most critically—what safer, wiser alternative could be offered *without shaming the old strategy into silence?*

This is not theoretical. It is testable in moments of rupture. Imagine, for example, you lash out at someone you love. The immediate reflex might be either self-reproach or defensive justification. But neither of those reactions leads to repair. Compassion, instead, steps in and says: "Yes, you hurt them. That matters. And we need to understand what got activated so that it doesn't repeat." Now you are not bypassing accountability—you are *deepening* it. Because now, the accountability is precise. It's not "I'm a terrible person," which is paralysing. It's "Part of me felt cornered and reacted from an old script. What does that part need to feel safer next time?" That's adaptive leadership, not excuse-making.

Critically, this approach also preserves your internal bandwidth. Because while shame may feel like a moral stance, it is actually an energy drain. Neuroscientific studies show that high self-criticism activates the brain's threat-detection network—specifically the amygdala and dorsal anterior cingulate cortex—resulting in cortisol surges, increased anxiety, and decreased cognitive flexibility. Compassion-based interventions, in contrast, have been shown to increase vagal tone, reduce inflammation, and improve prefrontal regulation. In other words, *compassion is not just emotionally intelligent; it is biologically efficient.* It optimises the nervous system for learning, not just survival.

One of the most overlooked aspects of this precision-based compassion is how well it aligns with behavioural change models. Consider the core principle of motivational interviewing: resistance arises not from lack of information, but from ambivalence. The goal is not to confront, but to *collaborate with the part that resists.* This requires respect for internal conflict, and an approach that treats avoidance not as weakness, but as wisdom from a part that is scared, tired, or unconvinced. Compassion here is a stance of curiosity, not capitulation. "What's the concern here?" becomes more powerful than "Why aren't you trying harder?"

The strategic role of compassion becomes even clearer when examined through the lens of habit formation. James Clear, in his work on atomic habits, notes that environment design, identity reinforcement, and friction reduction are more effective than raw willpower. But none of these strategies work if the underlying emotional resistance is ignored or shamed into submission. A person who wants to stop drinking may succeed at avoiding alcohol for days—but if the emotional driver behind the behaviour is loneliness, and they shame themselves for even *having* that need, the desire will return with doubled intensity. Compassion says: "Let's acknowledge the loneliness. Let's name it without collapsing into it. And let's design alternatives that respect that need, rather than pretending it shouldn't exist."

This reframing also reveals compassion's function in identity development. As people change, they inevitably encounter friction between the new behaviours they want to adopt and the self-concepts they've long internalised. "I'm not someone who finishes things." "I've never been consistent." "I always let people down." These are not mere descriptions—they are *psychological anchors*, often formed in adolescence or trauma contexts, reinforced by years of internal repetition and social feedback. Compassion, here, is not simply saying "It's okay." It is saying, "That belief made sense based on what you went through. But it is no longer precise. Let's update it." In this way, compassion becomes an editor—not a flatterer, but a clarifier of what is still true and what is no longer useful.

Of course, precision requires restraint. Not every urge to comfort should be followed. Not every impulse deserves immediate soothing. And this is where the nuance of compassion matters most. *Compassion without boundaries becomes enabling; compassion with clarity becomes transformative.* You can hold space for your exhaustion while still choosing to honour your values. You can validate your fear without letting it decide your next move. And you can acknowledge past harm without making it the architecture of your future choices. In each of these cases, compassion offers containment, not collapse.

Perhaps the most radical aspect of compassion-as-precision is how it subverts the punitive logic of self-betterment. It rejects the idea that suffering is the price of virtue, or that only the harshest internal critic can motivate change. Instead, it asserts that *respect leads to responsibility*. That the more you treat your internal system as something worth stewarding—not policing—the more likely it is to cooperate with growth. And that when each part of you knows it will be met not with punishment but with perspective, it becomes less reactive, less avoidant, and more aligned.

To be clear: this is not always fast. Precision-based compassion requires sustained attention, emotional honesty, and a willingness to slow down long enough to hear what the old behaviours were trying to communicate. But it is durable. It builds a foundation where growth is not something forced from the top down, but invited from the inside out. And in a culture addicted to the spectacle of the breakthrough—where healing is judged by its performance value—

this kind of quiet, consistent compassion is not only subversive. It is revolutionary.

The future of self-development will not be led by those who shout the loudest about their routines, their hacks, their morning cold plunges. It will be led by those who can sit with discomfort, ask precise questions, and act from wholeness rather than warfare. *Compassion is not a detour from excellence. It is the path to precision.* And that precision is what turns fleeting change into embodied wisdom.

Integrating, Not Erasing, the Past

Change that is genuine and sustainable does not require disowning who you once were. In fact, it demands the opposite. If transformation is to last, it must include—not amputate—the versions of the self that made it necessary. Yet in modern discourse around growth, there is a dangerous allure to dissociation. Former selves are cast as enemies, habits are demonised as betrayals, and the desire to "reinvent" often masks an unexamined urge to escape. This creates an internal split: one part of you moves forward, another remains locked in a past it was never allowed to explain. *The unintegrated self becomes the unfinished business of every breakthrough.*

It is far easier to rewrite a narrative than to reconcile it. Motivational culture celebrates the phoenix story: dramatic change that severs all ties to the before. "I used to be that kind of person—but not anymore." The statement carries conviction, but often lacks depth. What happens to the pain that version of you carried? What happens to the needs it was trying to meet, however clumsily? When former selves are banished rather than befriended, they do not vanish—they resurface. Usually not in words, but in impulses, projections, emotional overreactions, and unfinished grief. What seems like sabotage in the present is often the past asking to be included.

To understand this, consider the nervous system's core function: to protect. Every adaptation you formed—whether it was overworking, people-pleasing, withdrawing, controlling—originated as a response to a perceived threat. In childhood, that threat may have been disapproval, neglect, chaos, or unpredictability. In adulthood, it may have been betrayal, burnout, or shame. Either way, your body and brain did not fail you—they adapted. What now feels maladaptive was, at one point, your best attempt at safety or coherence. *To reject those strategies without acknowledging their origin is to insult your own intelligence.* Integration begins when you recognise not just that you changed, but why those old versions existed in the first place.

This is not an abstract psychological exercise—it has clear consequences. Clients who rush to define a "new self" without integrating the old often find themselves stuck in repetition loops. They relapse, not because they're weak, but because the part of them that relied on the previous behaviour was never heard. One client, for example, left behind a binge-eating pattern through sheer discipline—only to find it replaced by obsessive over-exercising and food perfectionism. Her body had changed, but the need for control and emotional regulation had simply migrated. Until she could meet the original version of herself with understanding, not judgment, the adaptation remained incomplete.

Integration demands maturity. It requires the humility to say: *There are parts of me I would not choose again, but they chose me for a reason. I will not glorify them, but I will honour them.* This stance does not dilute accountability; it refines it. You are not excusing what you did—you are contextualising it. You are acknowledging that the person who made those choices had different resources, different fears, and often, fewer options than the person you are now. Compassion without context becomes enabling. But accountability without compassion becomes cruelty.

Neuroscience reinforces this view. Memory reconsolidation research shows that it is not the past itself that changes healing trajectories, but how that past is revisited. When we revisit old memories with new emotional framing—through presence, safety, and coherent language—the brain updates them. The amygdala no longer flags them as unprocessed threat; the hippocampus begins to store them as resolved narrative. This is not symbolic—it is structural. *The past can be metabolised, but only if it is allowed to speak first.*

Therapeutic models across disciplines agree: Internal Family Systems (IFS) speaks of "unburdening" exiled parts, not exiling them further.

Somatic Experiencing talks about completing thwarted defensive responses, not overriding them. Jungian depth psychology frames integration as the union of opposites—light and shadow, strength and vulnerability. All of these approaches share one insight: wholeness is not perfection. It is coherence. And coherence means nothing is discarded simply because it is difficult to explain to others.

There is also a cultural dimension to this. In a digital age that rewards rebranding and linear success arcs, the temptation to curate one's identity is constant. But self-concepts built on image management are brittle. If your new self is sustained only by what others see—or what you refuse to revisit—it will collapse under the weight of unacknowledged grief, shame, or dissonance. Integration offers another path. Not broadcasting the past, not confessing it for applause, but *privately integrating it so that it no longer leaks into every decision you make.*

This might mean acknowledging that the version of you who stayed too long in a toxic relationship wasn't "dumb," but hopeful—and terrified of abandonment. It might mean sitting with the choices made during a depressive fog, not to justify them, but to understand what inner logic was driving your numbness. It might mean grieving a former life that you have outgrown but secretly miss, not because it was good, but because it was *known.* In each case, the goal is not narrative control but narrative truth: the kind that sets you free not because it's flattering, but because it is *fully yours.*

There are, of course, psychological challenges to this work. Integration requires the ability to tolerate contradiction: to admit that you were both victim and participant, both trying and avoiding, both vulnerable and complicit. Binary thinking—where you were either entirely wrong or entirely justified—must give way to nuanced self-honesty. This is difficult, especially for trauma survivors, whose early experiences often trained them to choose between self-blame and self-idealisation as the only two survival strategies. But complexity is not the enemy. *It is the gateway to emotional sovereignty.*

Practically, integration involves rituals of closure. This could mean journalling to a former version of yourself with the explicit aim of thanking, grieving, or forgiving. It could mean voice-dialogue work:

allowing different internal parts to speak, not to be judged, but to be heard. It could mean sharing your story with a trusted other—not for validation, but for reflection and containment. It might even mean creating a symbolic "retirement" for a particular identity or defence mechanism: a quiet acknowledgment that it once served you, and now no longer needs to.

Integration also changes how you relate to others. When you stop disowning your past, you become less reactive to it in others. You see defence not as defiance, but as history. You no longer need to "fix" people to feel safe, because you are no longer afraid of being reminded of what you used to be. This makes space for actual compassion—not performative tolerance, but *real empathy rooted in understanding your own complexity.*

Ultimately, integration is the difference between change that performs and change that endures. When the past is integrated, it loses its grip. When it is rejected, it grows louder—through patterns, triggers, and the insatiable need to prove something. Real peace comes not from replacing the old self, but from including them in the story of who you've become. Not as a scar to hide or a shadow to outrun, but as a character whose arc had meaning. *You don't need to erase your past to evolve—you need to bring it with you, consciously, into a future it helped prepare you for.*

The New Story You Can Live

Every person walks around with a self-concept—a silent script that dictates what they expect from themselves, what they believe is possible, and how they interpret their failures and triumphs. But few realise how outdated this script often is. Most self-concepts are not consciously chosen; they are accumulated. Shaped by early feedback, emotional wounds, cultural codes, and repetitive patterns, they become default narratives: "I'm not good with change." "I always mess things up in the end." "I'm the kind of person who sabotages when things get too good." These aren't character insights—they are inherited conclusions. And unless examined, they solidify into constraints.

The premise of psychological growth is not simply behavioural change, but narrative revision. If you continue to interpret your choices through the lens of shame, sabotage, or irredeemable defectiveness, you will unconsciously re-enact those identities—no matter how many habits you upgrade. *Real transformation requires a rewrite.* Not a sentimental rebranding, but a rigorous, earned shift in how you understand your past, your patterns, and your potential.

This shift is not cosmetic. It's structural. A self-concept built on shame cannot house sustainable change. Shame is not a motivator—it is a paralytic. It may spark short-term hypervigilance or self-punishment, but it does not support curiosity, resilience, or emotional regulation. When your inner narrator is punitive, every slip becomes evidence of unworthiness, every pause a prelude to collapse. You don't grow under that gaze; you shrink. *To rewrite your self-concept, you must dismantle the authority of that voice.*

But this dismantling must be strategic. It is not about swinging to blind affirmation ("I'm amazing and unstoppable!") but cultivating a new kind of internal accuracy—one that accounts for complexity, adaptation, and capacity for change. It requires you to track not only what went wrong, but also *why it made sense at the time.* It asks: what was the logic behind that behaviour? What did it protect you from? What resource were you missing then that you now have access to? These are not excuses. They are context. And context is what allows new narratives to be both honest and humane.

Rewriting your story begins with recognising that your former interpretations were just that—interpretations. They were not facts. "I'm a failure" is not a fact. "I'm undisciplined" is not a fact. "I ruin good things" is not a fact. These are narrative overlays placed upon a set of events. Events that, if revisited with more sophisticated frameworks—attachment theory, trauma science, emotional development—begin to look very different. Behaviour once labelled as lazy might be re-understood as shutdown. Conflict avoidance might be reframed as a strategy learned in a volatile home. Overachievement might be revealed as a compulsive strategy to avoid rejection. *Every maladaptive behaviour was adaptive at some point in time. That realisation changes the story.*

To live a new story, you must also practice *evidencing* it. The brain resists new narratives unless they are grounded in experience. This means collecting proof of change—even when the changes are small. Did you pause before reacting in a conflict? Did you name an emotion you previously disowned? Did you resist the urge to perform healing for external validation? These are not trivial wins. They are narrative disruptors. By recording them—literally or metaphorically—you start to build an archive that supports the emerging identity. You are no longer just aspiring to a new self; you are *documenting* it.

This process also demands language upgrades. Language is how identity gets coded. A person who always says "I'm a mess" will behave in accordance with that label. It's not semantics—it's psychology. The nervous system hears that identity and prepares accordingly: with reactivity, collapse, or impulsivity. Contrast that with language like: "I'm someone who's learning to manage intense emotion." Or, "I have old patterns that are becoming more optional than automatic." These aren't slogans. They are accurate descriptors of an evolving process. *Precision in language fosters precision in identity.*

Still, many resist narrative change because they confuse it with denial. They believe: if I stop calling myself a saboteur, I might lose accountability. If I stop defining myself by past mistakes, I might forget them. This is a false binary. You do not need shame to maintain accountability. You need clarity, compassion, and memory—held in balance. Remembering your past behaviour does not require *identifying* with it. You can say, "That's what I did" without adding, "And therefore that's who I am."

There is also a cultural reckoning to be had here. Many high-achievers, especially those raised in performance-oriented environments, mistake self-loathing for self-discipline. They believe the internal drill sergeant is responsible for their successes. But in reality, shame is a short-term motivator with long-term costs. It narrows the field of vision. It suppresses risk-taking. It chokes innovation. When identity is rooted in fear of regression, every setback feels fatal. A better framework is one built on adaptive evolution: "I don't need to fear the worst version of myself. I need to understand it, so I can evolve beyond it—intelligently, incrementally, and sustainably."

Psychological flexibility is the cornerstone of this evolution. Rather than clinging to a rigid self-definition—"I'm this kind of person"—the emerging self-concept becomes fluid but grounded. You begin to hold identities as provisional rather than permanent. "I've been someone who coped through avoidance. I'm learning how to face discomfort more directly." Or, "I used to disappear in relationships. I'm now experimenting with visibility, even when it's uncomfortable." These are statements of identity-in-progress—honest, compassionate, and dynamically accurate.

Living a new story also requires discerning which narratives are *yours* and which were inherited. Much of what people internalise as truth—"You're too sensitive," "You're never satisfied," "You always need attention"—originated in someone else's discomfort with their emotions. Unconscious family scripts become personal mantras unless consciously examined. Part of self-authorship is returning inherited beliefs to their original source: "That was never mine. I just carried it long enough that it started to sound like my voice."

From here, narrative architecture can begin. It is not built overnight, and it cannot be outsourced. No therapist, mentor, or coach can write your story for you. But they can serve as witnesses, mirrors, and editors. They can challenge distortions, affirm complexity, and remind you that *a self-concept is a living document.* You don't need to erase the past to write a new page. You only need to stop letting the old chapters define what comes next.

Ultimately, the new story you can live is not a fiction—it's a reclamation. It does not require pretending the past didn't happen. It requires placing it in context, integrating what was learned, and clarifying what no longer applies. It invites you to become a more accurate narrator: one who acknowledges the full arc of the character, not just the lowest point in their development. And it challenges you to update the story as you go—not to seek perfection, but to reflect movement.

You are not a static personality. You are an evolving system of responses, insights, and intentions. The most powerful story you can live is one where your past is integrated, your present is accurate, and your future is open—not to fantasy, but to intelligent adaptation. That's not indulgence. That's psychological integrity. And it is what makes sustainable change not only possible, but inevitable.

About the Author

Mira Ellison writes with the precision of a thinker and the compassion of someone who's walked through the struggle herself. Her work blends emotional honesty with psychological insight, helping readers navigate the hidden patterns that shape their lives. Drawing from a lifelong curiosity about the mind's inner workings and a deep respect for behavioural science, she crafts books that challenge, comfort, and clarify. Mira believes that lasting change doesn't begin with discipline—it begins with understanding. Her writing invites readers to stop fighting their flaws and instead learn what those flaws are trying to say. When she's not writing, she's usually walking in quiet places, reading about how humans heal, or asking better questions.

www.ingramcontent.com/pod-product-compliance
Lightning Source LLC
Chambersburg PA
CBHW031342230926
51848CB00002B/348
9789371771603